ODDBALL OHIO

ODDBALL OHIO

A Guide to Some Really
STRANGE PLACES

JEROME POHLEN

CHICAGO
REVIEW
PRESS

The author has made every effort to secure permissions for all the material in this book. If any acknowledgment has inadvertently been omitted, please contact the author.

All photographs courtesy of Jerome Pohlen unless otherwise noted.
Cover and interior design: Mel Kupfer

© 2004 by Jerome Pohlen
All rights reserved
First Edition
Published by Chicago Review Press, Incorporated
814 North Franklin Street
Chicago, Illinois 60610
ISBN 1-55652-523-0
Printed in the United States of America
5 4 3 2 1

CONTENTS

INTRODUCTION

*O*hio is odd.

Do you need evidence? Look no further than its flag . . . excuse me . . . *burgee.* Not content with a traditional, boring, rectangular flag, the Ohio legislature adopted a two-pointed pennant—a burgee—as its state banner. That same outside-of-the-box thinking resurfaced years later when a bill to abolish January and February from state calendars was introduced in the capitol. The missing days were to be reassigned to June, July, and August, with the goal of reducing Buckeye voters' winter heating bills. Asinine? Or ingenious?

If you picked ingenious, *Oddball Ohio* is the travel guide for you. Why look at the world the way everyone else does? Have you ever wondered if the earth is hollow, or whether George Washington is *really* the father of our country? Would you like to know if Chef Boyardee was a real person? Do you want to see Jamie Farr's buns? The answers to your strange questions, and more, are right here in the state that's round on the ends and high in the middle.

You will discover that Ohio is weirder than you ever imagined. It is the only state where Jerry Springer has been elected the mayor of a major city, where a brick outhouse is on the National Register of Historic Places, where Buster the Dog voted for president, and where Mary Hartman worried about waxy yellow buildup. It is the birthplace of bar codes, Airstream trailers, televangelism, Paul Lynde, Alcoholics Anonymous, and the banana split, and it is where Pretty Boy Floyd, Balto the Wonder Dog, Eugene the Mummy, Annie Oakley, and Martha, the world's last surviving passenger pigeon, drew their final breaths.

Now correct me if I'm wrong, but you don't get enough vacation time, do you? Use it wisely! Why spend hours in lines at Cedar Point when you can be the day's only visitor at Goodyear's World of Rubber? Why flush away rolls of quarters at a floating casino slot machine when a single quarter will allow you to see the World's Largest Cuckoo Clock? And isn't your energy better spent knocking back brews at the World's Longest Bar than wasted on a bike ride through the Hocking Hills?

OK, I've made my point. If you're a weirdo, read on.

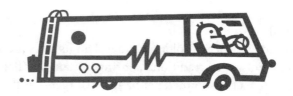

While I've tried to give clear directions from major streets and landmarks, you could still make a wrong turn. When driving the backroads of Ohio, the quaint small towns all start to look alike. Here are a few Oddball travel tips to help you reach your destination:

➡ **Stop and ask!** For a lot of communities, their Oddball attraction might be their only claim to fame. Locals are often thrilled that you'd drive to their sleepy little burg to marvel at their underappreciated shrine. But choose your guides wisely; old cranks at the town café are good for information; teenage clerks at the 7-Eleven are not.

➡ **Call ahead.** Few Oddball sites keep truly regular hours. Many Ohio attractions are seasonal, or can close up at a moment's notice, particularly if there's an approaching tornado. Always call. And if there's a tornado, you shouldn't be looking for the World's Largest Cockroach, you should be looking for a ditch to hide in.

➡ **Don't give up.** Think of the folks at the Orrville Toy and Hobby Museum; they could have stopped collecting pencils when they reached 2,000 or 5,000, but they kept at it. So should you.

➡ **Don't trespass!** Don't become a Terrible Tourist. The reason the Manolio family makes their Egg Shell Land mosaics large enough to be seen from the street is because they want you to view it *from the street.* Don't go knocking on their door. If an attraction is not open to the public, stay off the property.

➡ **Obey the law.** Ohio has a couple of travel-related laws you should be aware of. First, you may not stick your feet out a car window to feel the wind. But more important, if you want to travel by mule, you may not force it to carry you more than 10 miles at a time, nor light a fire beneath it to persuade it to move more quickly.

Do you have an Oddball site of your own? Have I missed anything? Do you know of a location that should be included in a later edition? Please write and let me know: c/o Chicago Review Press, 814 N. Franklin Street, Chicago, IL 60610.

THE NORTHWEST

*H*ard as it is to believe today, Ohio almost went to war
with Michigan in 1835 . . . over *Toledo*. Yep, because of a
misdrawn map used when Ohio was admitted to the Union in
1803, a six-mile-wide strip of land stretching from Lake Erie
at Toledo to the present-day Indiana border was in dispute.
Michiganders pointed to the boundary laid out by the Northwest Ordinance of 1787, which clearly gave them Toledo.
Soldiers from both future states were headed for Toledo to do
battle when President Andrew Jackson stepped in. He forced
Michigan to relinquish its rightful claim to the land, and in
exchange Michigan received the Upper Peninsula and statehood
in 1837. If Ohioans consider the case closed, some Michigan
residents do not. As recently as 1972, the U.S. Supreme Court
heard 170-year-old arguments as to which state owned the
land. The justices sided with Ohio.

Whichever state you sympathize with, one thing seems clear: a
lot of outsiders still want a piece of northwest Ohio. And why
shouldn't they? It's home to the first man to walk on the moon,
the bathtub from the USS *Maine*, a couple of dead presidents,
and the first outhouse to be placed on the National Register of
Historic Places . . . and that's just for starters!

Jealous, Michigan?

Archbold
Bathroom Museum

First things first: did you remember to visit the Bathroom Museum? Because we're not going to stop once we get on the road. . . .

Actually, the Voight Collection of antique bathroom fixtures at Sauder Village isn't so much a museum as a display within a museum, but it's got a lot more on historic plumbing than you're likely to see anywhere else in Ohio. There are 954 artifacts in the collection, including sinks, tubs, faucets, piping, sitz baths, toilets, and more. It's kind of like going to Home Depot, but a century ago.

There's more to Sauder Village than the toilets. This working historic community is filled with costumed guides who will show you how to weave a broom out of broomcorn, churn butter by hand, shoe a horse, and make a dress out of a flour sack—skills that will come in handy if the economy keeps going the way it has recently.

Sauder Village, 22611 Rte. 2, Archbold, OH 43502

(800) 590-9755 or (419) 446-2541

E-mail: info@saudervillage.org

Hours: May–October, Monday–Saturday 10 A.M.–5 P.M., Sunday 1–5 P.M.

Cost: Adults $11.50, Kids (6–16) $5.50

www.saudervillage.org

Directions: Head north out of town on Rte. 66/2, then east on Wauseon-Perkins Rd. (the continuation of Rte. 2) for one mile.

BELLEFONTAINE
Bellefontaine's Campbell Hill, at 1,519 feet above sea level, is the highest point in Ohio.

BOWLING GREEN
The Popular Culture Library at Bowling Green State University (in the Jerome Library on campus) contains the Marie Wakefield *Star Trek* Memorabilia Collection, as well as extensive holdings of greeting cards, comic books, pulp novels, and travel brochures. The collections are used for research only, not general browsing.

Where's Wonders?

Bellefontaine
America's First Concrete Streets

Automobile drivers across the nation owe a bunch of Ohio clean-freaks a debt of gratitude. In order to decrease the amount of mud tracked into the county courthouse, elected officials in this town decided to have all four adjacent streets covered in eight inches of concrete—they called it "artificial stone"—in 1891. First, an eight-foot strip was tested next to the downtown's hitching post. The test went well, but George Bartholomew of the Buckeye Portland Cement Company still had to post a $5,000 bond to land the job, as a guarantee the concrete would last at least five years.

It was a safe bet. In addition to its mud-repelling qualities, the roadbed was so durable that it has yet to receive its first pothole more than 110 years later, though there has been some wear. Bartholomew gets most of the credit for this innovation today, but equal praise should be afforded James Wonders, the Logan County engineer who oversaw the construction and suggested much of the methodology. Sadly, Bartholomew is the only one honored on the town square; a statue of him was erected in 1991 on the streets' centennial.

Incidentally, part of the road was pulled up and taken to the 1893 Columbian Exposition in Chicago, where Bartholomew won first place for Engineering Technology Advancement in Paving Materials. *There's an award that isn't handed out to just anybody....*

Columbus Ave., Main St., Opera St., and Court Ave., Bellefontaine, OH 43311
No phone
Hours: Always visible
Cost: Free
www.ci.bellefontaine.oh.us
Directions: Along Rte. 68 (Main St.), surrounding the courthouse.

COLDWATER
Joseph Oppenheim of Coldwater invented the manure spreader in 1899.

Site of the one-car traffic jam.

World's Shortest Street

Don't you just hate being on a traffic-clogged road? This happens all the time on McKinley Street, a thoroughfare west of downtown Belle-fontaine. In fact, every time somebody drives down it there's a jam from one end to the other. Why? Because at only 15 feet long, a single vehicle stretches its entire length.

Some dismiss McKinley as a glorified turn lane from southbound Garfield Avenue onto westbound Columbus Avenue, but it actually has both north- and southbound lanes. Because it runs parallel to the rail-road tracks, if eastbound cars on Columbus are stopped by a train, they can turn north onto McKinley and connect to Garfield without having to turn around. Yet another visionary street in this small Ohio town. All hail, Bellefontaine!

McKinley St., Bellefontaine, OH 43311

No phone

Hours: Always visible

Cost: Free

Directions: Five blocks west of Main St. (Rte. 68) on Columbus Ave. at Garfield Ave., two blocks south of Sandusky Ave. (Rte. 47).

Bowling Green
Mary Bach's Fingers

If you think a display of three severed, pickled human fingers sounds disturbing, wait until you hear the rest of the story. Back in early October 1881, farmer Carl Bach went a little "teched in the head" and took a corn knife to his wife Mary. Apparently she hadn't completed her chores. A few days later Carl turned himself in to the local sheriff and told him to go look in the couple's barn. Authorities found the woman's dismembered body and, needing evidence to convict Carl, took three of Mary's fingers and placed them in a jar filled with formaldehyde.

It was an open-and-shut case, and Carl Bach eventually went to the gallows . . . which were erected for him on the front steps of the Wood County Courthouse. Officials didn't want to turn the execution into a public spectacle that unsuspecting citizens might just happen upon. Instead, they sold tickets. The hanging was scheduled for October 13, 1883, to coincide with the final day of the county fair. By all accounts, both were well attended.

Bach's execution was the last the county ever held in public. Still, local leaders didn't want to surrender the positive educational benefit of a good old-fashioned hanging, so they put up a display case inside the courthouse. It featured the knife used to hack up the victim, the noose her husband wore for a few brief moments, a ticket to the execution, and a jar containing Mary Bach's fingers.

The entire display was eventually moved to the local historical society where you can still see it today. The museum also features a pheasant shot by actor Clark Gable (but stuffed by somebody else). There are also historic outbuildings from the old Wood County Infirmary, including a slaughterhouse, chicken coop, pest house (for men with communicable diseases), and lunatic house (don't ask).

Wood County Historical Center, 13660 County Home Rd., Bowling Green, OH 43402
(419) 352-0967
E-mail: wchisctr@wcnet.org
Hours: Monday–Friday 9:30 A.M.–4:30 P.M., Saturday–Sunday 1–4 P.M.
Cost: Free
www.woodcountyhistory.org
Directions: Exit I-75 at Rte. 6, heading east, and make the first right on County Home Rd.

Bryan
Birthplace of Etch A Sketch

In 1959, Arthur Granjean introduced the world to the L'Ecran Magique at the Nuremberg Toy Fair. The inventor had created a plastic window, coated from below with aluminum dust, which could be drawn on using a two-knob mechanical device. Unfortunately, Granjean had neither an American manufacturer nor a distributor, let alone a catchy name. L'Ecran Magique. Who'd want *that*?

Enter the Ohio Art Company. They licensed the toy from Granjean under the new name: Etch A Sketch. (OK, so Bryan is technically the birthplace of the *name*, not the device itself.) The first prototypes hit the U.S. market on July 12, 1960. Millions of Etch A Sketches later, the Ohio Art Company is still going strong. The Etch A Sketch continues to be distributed out of this small burg. And while the facility is not open to drop-ins, they will gladly give a plant tour if you prearrange it.

Ohio Art Company, 711 E. High St., PO Box 111, Bryan, OH 43506

(440) 636-3141

Hours: By appointment

Cost: Free

www.world-of-toys.com

Directions: Seven blocks east of Rte. 127 (Main St.) on Rte. 2 (High St.).

DEFIANCE

A werewolf was spotted in and around Defiance from July to August 1972. It was seven to nine feet tall and had fangs. It was ornery, too—it struck a railroad employee with a big stick.

Defiance claims to be the City of Industry, Agriculture, Education, Patriotism, Scenic Beauty, and Civic Pride. What, not Modesty, too?

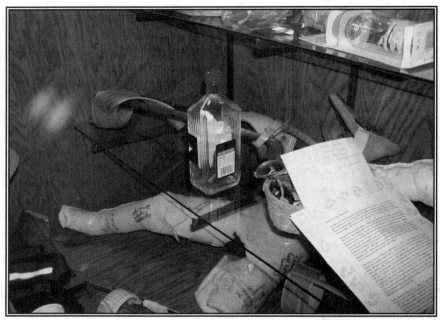

Who needs a doctor?
Photo by author, courtesy of Basilica and National Shrine of Our Lady of Consolation

Carey
Heal!

Are you feeling under the weather? Got a touch of lumbago? Is your foot a tad gimpy? Then drop on by Our Lady of Consolation for a tune-up! The miraculous healing statue in this minor basilica is a replica of a Luxembourgian statue of Mary, Consoler of the Afflicted, who was said to ward off the bubonic plague in the 17th century. Apparently it worked, because she drew quite a following. Two centuries later, in 1875, one of Mary's devotees, Father Joseph Gloden, established a mission in Carey. That year the statue was brought from nearby Frenchtown, and though the procession of followers marched through a torrential thunderstorm, *nobody got wet*. It was a miracle!

On April 28, 1878, Pope Leo XIII gave the go-ahead to build a church on the spot. The original chapel is now part of a larger religious megaplex. Upstairs, to the right of the main altar, you'll see Our Lady behind her own altar, way up high, behind Plexiglas. In the basement—

just follow your nose, the votive candles are overpowering—you'll find crutches, braces, whiskey bottles, and canes, a testament to the healing power of this shrine.

Of course, none of this works if you don't *believe* it works, and the fact that you're reading this book puts you in very suspect company. Also downstairs is a collection of more than 500 relics from every saint imaginable, and more than 200 ornate, miniature vestments sewn by pilgrims for the holy statue upstairs; Barbie would be jealous, but remember, jealousy is a sin. Outside, on the right side of the building, you will find a half-dozen spigots that dispense free holy water. Bring a jug.

Basilica and National Shrine of Our Lady of Consolation, 315 Clay St., Carey, OH 43316

(419) 396-7107 or (419) 396-3355; Gift Shop (419) 396-6080

Hours: Always open; Gift shop, Monday–Friday 10 A.M.–4:30 P.M., Saturday 10 A.M.– 5 P.M., Sunday 10 A.M.–2:30 P.M. and 3:15–5 P.M.

Cost: Free

www.olcshrine.com

Directions: Two blocks south of Rte. 568 (Findlay St.), two blocks west of Rte. 23 (Glenn Ave.).

Clyde
Winesburg, Ohio

When Sherwood Anderson first wrote a collection of short stories called *Winesburg, Ohio* in 1919, the folks in Clyde were not amused. The book was an honest, scathing indictment of small-town America, and since Anderson had grown up in Clyde, the town folk took it personally. It didn't help that many of the book's characters and settings in Winesburg bore more than a passing resemblance to the citizens and businesses in Clyde. So while critics were hailing Anderson as the Dostoyevsky of the Corn Belt, it was quite clear that he was no longer welcome in his boyhood home. (It didn't help, either, that he'd earlier walked out on his wife and fled to Chicago.)

Time seems to have healed most of the wounds, and now Clyde bills itself as America's Famous Small Town. There's a collection of Anderson family artifacts at the local museum. A free map is available at the museum, in the library, or on-line for folks who want to take a walking tour of the town. It includes Anderson's boyhood home (129 Spring Avenue) where he lived from 1888 to 1895.

Clyde Museum, 124 W. Buckeye St., Clyde, OH 43410

(419) 547-7946

Hours: Thursdays 1–4 P.M., or by appointment

Cost: Free

www.clydeohio.org

Directions: One block west of Main St. (Rte. 101) on Buckeye St.

Clyde Public Library, 222 W. Buckeye St., Clyde, OH 43410

(419) 547-7174

Hours: Monday–Thursday 9 A.M.–8:30 P.M., Friday 9 A.M.–5 P.M., Saturday 9 A.M.–4 P.M.

Cost: Free

Directions: Two blocks west of Main St. (Rte. 101) on Buckeye St.

Elmore
Wear Your Helmet . . . and Your Head!

Getting dumped isn't fun, but it's nothing to lose your head over. Just ask the doughboy who returned home to his fiancée in Elmore at the end of World War I, riding on his brand-spankin'-new motorcycle, only to find she'd up and married somebody else—a traveling salesman, no less! She was apparently unimpressed with the bike he'd purchased with his discharge money, so the GI hopped back on and took off down the road.

He didn't get too far. The kaiser may not have had his number, but the gravel shoulder sure did. Still within eyesight of his ex's farmhouse, the bike spun out of control and flew off into the ditch near the Portage River bridge. Police found his mangled body, but they never found his head.

Why should you care? Local legend says that every March 21, on the anniversary of the tragic event, the headless ghost of the jilted biker speeds away from his former lover's farm, roars off down the road, and disappears halfway across this bridge.

Rte. 590, Elmore, OH 43416

No phone

Hours: March 21 only, after dark

Cost: Your head!

Directions: East of town, where Rte. 590 connects South Rd. to Rte. 105 over the Portage River.

HEADLESS IN OHIO

What is it about Ohio ghosts? They can't be just the run-of-the-mill spooks, they've got to run around like spirits with their heads cut off... literally! In addition to the headless Elmore biker, there are a few more Buckeye ghosts who have shed this mortal coil but are still looking for their noggins.

Route 40 near **Cambridge** has no less than *two* skull-less specters. The first, a paver who was robbed and murdered by another employee and buried beneath the roadbed, appears to drivers along the deep cut east of town, on the road to Old Washington. Rotting and angry, he's said to be quite a bit scarier than the woman who rides a white horse on Route 40's Lady Bend Hill. She was beheaded by her husband during an argument in the 1890s, but she refuses to cross over until she finds a suitable skull—preferably hers—to rest atop her shoulders.

Poor James Buckley. Authorities *did* find this Englishman's head after intruders decapitated him in a cabin along **Bellbrook**'s Little Sugar Creek sometime in the 1880s. The noggin was found sitting in the middle of a road. Though it was buried with him, the undertaker didn't think to reattach it before burial. Buckley's ghost has been spotted along the creek for years, still searching for it. Hey, buddy— look in the coffin!

Another headless murder victim, a stagecoach driver, has taken up residence at the Wickerham Inn on Route 41, between **Peebles** and **Locust Grove**. He was killed in the early 1800s while spending a night at the inn—his room was splattered with blood in the morning, but his body was never discovered . . . or at least not until 1922 when workers were digging in the basement. They unearthed a skeleton, sans skull, which might explain why this ghost is never seen with anything above its shoulders.

There was no doubt that the mill worker at **Doylestown**'s Chidester Wool Mill was dead—his coworkers watched helplessly as he was crushed beneath the waterwheel. His head fared the worst, so when he reappears today, he doesn't bring it with him.

If that squished mill worker wants to make an especially frightening entrance, he might try appearing with Doylestown's other headless ghost, the Phantom Horse of Rogues' Hollow. This creepy creature haunts the road just south of town, along Clinton Street. It lost its head in a freak galloping-horse-meets-oak-branch-and-horse-loses-head accident.

Findlay
"Down by the Old Mill Stream"

Back in 1908, onetime shoe salesman Tell Taylor went down to the banks of the Blanchard River near Findlay to do some fishing, but he found he wasn't getting so much as a nibble. To pass the time he wrote a song, "Down by the Old Mill Stream." The mill he described in the song was actually the old Misamore Mill that once stood near his family's farm, five miles east of town (about seven miles upstream, southwest of Vanlue).

Taylor didn't publish the song until 1910, but when he did it was a big hit. It sold more than a million copies, and its popularity lasted well into the 1920s. When his career as a composer and vaudeville performer started to dwindle, Taylor returned to Findlay. Then, in 1937, Hollywood decided to make a musical based on the song, and a producer summoned Taylor to California. On his way west he stopped in Chicago, collapsed from a heart attack, and died on November 23. Talk about your bum luck. . . . (He was buried in Van Horn Cemetery, east of Vanlue.)

The site where Taylor wrote the song has not been forgotten, at least not in Findlay. Three engraved boulders mark the spot where he reposed, writing the ditty that would be on his lips at death.

Tell Taylor Memorial, Riverbend Recreational Park, 231 McManness Ave., Findlay,
   OH 45840
(419) 424-7176
Hours: Always visible
Cost: Free
www.findlay.lib.oh.us/telltaylor.html
Directions: Between Main Cross St. and Tiffin Ave. (Rte. 224) on McManness Ave., east of downtown.

FINDLAY
On October 2, 1889, furniture in the Findlay home of Samuel Miller began bursting into flames for no apparent reason; first a bed, then a chest of drawers, then another bed. Nothing in the vicinity of the burning furniture was harmed.

USS Maine's Bathtub

Do you remember the *Maine*? You would if you were 120 years old . . . assuming you could remember anything at all. Yet for those living a century ago, it was their generation's Pearl Harbor. *Nobody* forgot the *Maine*. When the ship exploded and sank in Havana Harbor on February 15, 1898, it claimed 266 lives. Newspaper kingpin William Randolph Hearst used the event to drum up support for what became the Spanish-American War, best known for the battle cry, "Remember the *Maine*!"

When the *Maine* was raised from its watery grave in 1911, long after the war was over, everyone wanted a piece of the ship, particularly in the Buckeye State. After all, Ohio was the birthplace of William McKinley, the U.S. president during the drummed-up conflict. (After the pieces were removed, the ship was scuttled at sea with honors.) Ohio Congressman Frank B. Willis ended up with Captain Charles Sigsbee's galvanized steel bathtub, a sorry artifact at best. Willis later donated the rusty tub to the town of Urbana, which passed it along to Findlay after receiving a 10-inch shell instead.

The tub was used as the coal bin at Findlay City Hall until the local VFW post got wind of the disgrace. It was put on display in the courthouse until most of the older veterans passed away. The city then donated it to Findlay College Museum, which later gave it to the Hancock Historical Museum where you can still see it—too famous to throw away, too junky to keep in any one place for too long.

By the way, recent analysis of the *Maine* wreckage strongly indicates that a massive structural failure within the ship itself caused the disaster, not foul play. In other words, the war had been launched on flimsy evidence, the American public being goaded on by a cheerleading press. Good thing *that* doesn't happen anymore!

Hancock Historical Museum, 422 W. Sandusky St., Findlay, OH 45840

(419) 423-4433

E-mail: stucker@hancockhistoricalmuseum.org

Hours: Monday–Friday 9 A.M.–5 P.M.

Cost: Adults $3, Seniors $2, Kids Free

www.hancockhistoricalmuseum.org

Directions: Two blocks south of Main Cross St., three blocks west of Main St. (Rte. 37).

Remember the *Maine*'s conning tower!

REMEMBER THE MAINE'S PIECES!

Findlay isn't the only Ohio town with remnants of the Maine on display. The base of the **ship's conning tower** sits in Canton's Starke County Veterans Memorial (13th Street and I-77), and a **hollow metal lifesaver**, donated by Vice Admiral H. H. Christy, can be found in Ashville's Small Town Museum (see page 186).

Fostoria Jesus on an Oil Tank

What's next?

Whether Jesus Christ bestowed his blessing on low-cholesterol soybean oil, or whether it was a non-affiliated miracle, we may never know, but this much is certain: the Messiah (or somebody who looked very much like him) *did* appear in the rusty stains on the side of an ADM oil storage tank in the summer of 1986. The Son of God was first spotted by drapery installer Rita Ratchen while she was driving home from work one evening. Ratchen observed, "I see it as a natural phenomenon.... It is caused by the lights and the rust ... but I believe the Lord permitted it to happen." The image revealed Jesus up to his old tricks, walking on water and holding the hand of a child.

Word got around and soon believers were lining up along Route 12 to see for themselves. Because it only appeared at night, the cars on the shoulder created a traffic hazard. That September, a local drunk tossed balloons filled with paint at the rusty tank. The incident convinced the folks at ADM that enough was enough, so they painted over it. Pilgrims were forced to look elsewhere. Like on tortillas.

End of story? Maybe not. The tank has begun to rust again. Lord only knows what will show up next time.

Archer Daniels Midland Company, Rte. 12, Fostoria, OH 44830

No phone

Hours: Always visible

Cost: Free

Directions: One mile west of Fostoria on Rte. 12; it's the last tank in the line.

Fremont
Old Whiteys

Look near the fence surrounding the burial grounds at Spiegel Grove and you'll find the grave of Old Whitey. No, not President Rutherford B. Hayes, the estate's former owner, but Old Whitey, the horse he rode into 19 battles during the Civil War. One of Hayes's other horses, Old Ned, is also interred here, as is Hayes's wife, old teetotaling "Lemonade Lucy," and Hayes himself, who died here in Fremont on January 17, 1893.

Of course, most folks don't come to see the dead horses; they come to visit the home and presidential library (the nation's first!) of His Fraudulency. Hayes earned that unwelcome nickname after he took office following the disputed 1876 election, which was thrown into serious doubt after questionable returns from—you guessed it— Florida. Hayes served only one term in the old Whitey House, then returned to Ohio.

Rutherford B. Hayes wasn't just buried in the Buckeye State—he started out here. On October 4, 1822, Hayes was born in Delaware (E. William and Sandusky Streets, torn down) to the newly widowed Sophia Birchard Hayes, and was supported by his bachelor uncle, Sardis Birchard. Spiegel Grove was built and named by Birchard (*Spiegel* is German for "mirror"), who later signed it over to his nephew. Spiegel Grove was still in the family in 1921 when Webb Hayes, Rutherford's oldest son, picked up four of the Whitey House's old gates at an old whitey elephant sale. These famous gates had guarded the nation's executive residence since 1871, but were removed in 1921 to allow the new wider horseless carriages in.

1337 Hayes Ave., Fremont, OH 43420

(800) 998-PRES or (419) 332-2081

E-mail: hayeslib@rbhayes.org

Hours: Monday–Saturday 9 A.M.–5 P.M. (Home and Research Center), Sunday Noon–
   5 P.M. (Home only)

Cost: Home or Museum, Adults $6, Seniors $5, Kids (6–12) $2; Both, Adults $10.50,
   Seniors $9.50, Kids (6–12) $4

www.rbhayes.org

Directions: At Buckland Ave. (Rte. 602), southwest of downtown.

Very nice Little Building. Now does anyone know where a person can take a dump in this town?

Genoa
Pretty Privy

The oldest building in Genoa was erected about 150 years ago, and the reason it is still standing today is because it was built like a brick shithouse. Actually, it *is* a brick shithouse.

Really.

No kidding.

Of course, few people call it that. Locals have named the twelve-seater (six for boys and six for girls) behind the old high school the "Little Building." That's also what they told the folks doling out historic preservation grants leading up to the nation's bicentennial. Genoa used the funds to fill in the pits, tear out the seats, and make it into a storage shed for the town. It now has the unique distinction of being the only former pit toilet on the National Register of Historic Places.

Big wup. If you ask me, it seems a little disingenuous to use these types of funds to convert a historic structure for something that was not its original function. Then again, maybe I'm just cranky. I sure was when I visited Genoa—I couldn't find a public toilet to save my life!

Camper Elementary School, 4th and Main Sts., Genoa, OH 43430

No phone

Hours: Always visible

Cost: Free

Directions: Just west of Woodville-Genoa-Clay Rd. (Main St.) on Rte. 163 (4th St.).

Jackson Center
Airstream Birthing Center

Anyone who loves to travel and has the slightest shred of style needs to come to Jackson Center to pay homage. Why? This factory, sometimes called the Silver Palace, manufactures every Airstream trailer and motor home on the market today—and it's open for tours! The company was founded in the 1930s by Wally Byam, and moved to this facility in 1952. Everyone recognizes Airstream's signature aluminum-shelled vehicles from the outside; here is your chance to look at them from the inside . . . while they're being built. From the welding of the initial steel chassis to the water test of the shell's seams, this tour explains it all.

Airstream has a variety of models, starting with their smallest trailer, the Bambi. Their Web site offers cool virtual tours of all their models, including the Classic, the Safari, the International, the Land Yacht, and the new 39-foot behemoth, the Skydeck Diesel. This baby has an oak grand staircase leading up to the roof, which is lined with comfortable seating and a retractable canopy, just in case it rains. It's the perfect vehicle for those who want to get away from it all but take most of their possessions with them.

Airstream, Inc., 419 W. Pike St., Jackson Center, OH 45335

(937) 596-6111

Hours: Tours, Monday–Friday 2 P.M.

Cost: Free

www.airstream.com

Directions: One block west of Rte. 65 (Main St.) on Rte. 274 (Pike St.).

Kelleys Island
Groovy

Etched into a rock outcropping on the northern shore of Kelleys Island is a fantastic reminder why you shouldn't drag the furniture across your hardwood floors. About 18,000 years ago, give or take a few centuries, a mile-thick Canadian glacier scraped across a limestone formation and left 400-foot-long, 10- to 15-foot-deep gouges in its surface. Mother Nature is still trying to sand it out.

She got a little help from a nearby quarry in the 1870s. The digging obliterated some of the larger grooves, but left enough for tourists to see today. The giant grooves are now protected from further human destruction, but if the earth enters another Ice Age, another mile-tall glacier could come barreling south at an inch a day, scratching up the earth once again.

Glacial Grooves, Division St., Kelleys Islands, OH 43438

(419) 746-2546

Hours: Always visible

Cost: Free

www.dnr.state.oh.us/parks/parks/lakeerie.htm

Directions: On the north side of the island, adjacent to the Kelleys Island State Park
campground, just past Ward Rd.

FREMONT
Fremont is the Cutlery Center of America.

LIBERTY CENTER
When the town of Liberty Center voted in 18-year-old Craig Myers in 1976, it elected the youngest mayor in our nation's history.

You'll let me out if you know what's good fer ya, copper!

Photo by author, courtesy of Allen County Museum

Lima
Dillinger Breaks Out

John Dillinger might not have become a well-known gangster were it not for his uncanny ability to escape from police custody. Yet he never broke out without plenty of help from his hoodlum friends. His 1933 escape from the Allen County Jail was no exception.

Dillinger had been taken into custody in a Dayton raid on September 25, 1933. At the time he was staying at the apartment of Mary Jenkins Longnacre, the sister of one of his old jailhouse buddies. He was charged in the robbery of the Citizens National Bank in Bluffton, a small town in northeast Allen County. It had been robbed of $6,000 earlier that year.

Dillinger was held at the Allen County Jail in Lima (just west of the courthouse), the county seat. There, on October 12, Harry Pierpont led a cavalry of five thugs to his rescue. The gang brandished their weapons at

Sheriff Jesse Sarber. When the sheriff reached for his gun, Pierpont shot him at point-blank range. Keys in hand, they sprung Dillinger and locked deputy Wilbur Sharp and Sarber's wife in the cell. The criminals fled to a hideout in Hamilton, Ohio.

Most of the gang was eventually apprehended in Tucson, Arizona, on January 25, 1934. Pierpont was extradited to Ohio and ended up back in the same jail where he committed the murder. Meanwhile, Dillinger broke out of the Crown Point Jail in Indiana (he'd also been nabbed in Tucson), and Lima residents prepared for another bold raid on their town. The National Guard was called out and machine gun nests were set up around the jail.

But Dillinger never arrived. Pierpont was convicted of first-degree murder and sentenced to the electric chair. He spent his last days in the Ohio Penitentiary (see page 212) where he tried unsuccessfully to escape on September 22, 1934. He was shot in the head and back during the attempt, but did not die. He was executed in the electric chair on October 17.

The Allen County Jail was converted into a larger jail years ago. Still later it was turned into a storage facility for the county. Its most famous cell has been moved to the Allen County Museum (see next listing), along with other mementos from the Sarber murder, including the sheriff's chair.

Allen County Museum, 620 W. Market St., Lima, OH 45801

(419) 222-9426

E-mail: acmuseum@bright.net

Hours: Tuesday–Sunday 1–5 P.M.

Cost: Free; suggested $5 donation

www.allencountymuseum.org

Directions: Two blocks south of Rte. 81 (North St.), three blocks west of Rte. 65 (West St.).

LIMA

By law, you cannot own a map in Lima that does not have Lima on it.

Phyllis Diller was born as Phyllis Driver in Lima on July 17, 1917.

Ready for the rain.

Photo by author, courtesy of Allen County Museum

Noah's Ark, Albino Critters, and Swallowed Things

If you're passing through Lima and have a few hours to spare, schedule a visit to the local history museum. There are cities in the United States, BIG cities, whose history museums couldn't hold a candle to the Allen County Museum. The collections go on and on and on, from one floor to the next, and though many of the exhibits are typical of small-town museums, there are a few one-of-a-kind displays, like the jail cell and sheriff's office from the Dillinger breakout (see previous listing).

Another popular exhibit is the Noah's Ark mechanical theater. Built between 1899 and 1901 by local undertaker and tinkerer James Grosjean, the seven-foot-high cabinet contains a mechanized performance of the Great Flood from the book of Genesis. For several years it toured the United States, wowing audiences at the 1901 Pan-American Exposition in Buffalo, New York, and shoppers at Macy's and Marshall Field's. Turn it on and carved wooden animals walk two-by-two up the gangway into the ark. Lightning flashes while rain falls. And when the sun comes out, a tiny dove flies out of the ark, circles the devastation, and returns with an olive branch. What a show!

In the same room as Noah's Ark you'll see a fabulous collection of albino animals, including a pink-eyed sparrow posed atop a nest it has built inside a human skull that has been hinged open like a jewelry box. The same taxidermist stuffed dozens of rare birds and mounted them in a giant Ferris wheel, also behind glass in its own portable case.

Medical buffs will appreciate the museum's collection from Estey Yingling and his son Walter. If you think kids will put anything in their mouths, you're right—and so will a few adults. The Yinglings were both local doctors and, for whatever reason, they kept every last item they ever fished out of the lungs or esophagi of their patients: buttons, pins, chains, screws, jewelry, rubber hoses, dentures, coins, toys, you name it. All of the objects are carefully labeled and neatly displayed in individual cases. What does this have to do with local history? Does it matter? It's *cool!*

Allen County Museum, 620 W. Market St., Lima, OH 45801

(419) 222-9426

E-mail: acmuseum@bright.net

Hours: Tuesday–Sunday 1–5 P.M.

Cost: Free; suggested $5 donation

www.allencountymuseum.org

Directions: Two blocks south of Rte. 81 (North St.), three blocks west of Rte. 65 (West St.).

LIMA

Lima is named for Lima, Peru. The town's early setters used quinine from the South American city to treat their malaria.

Eat, dinosaur, eat! You're practically extinct!

Marblehead
Prehistoric Forest and Mystery Hill

Are you ready to step back in time? No, not all the way to the Jurassic Period, but to the 1950s when roadside dinosaur parks were as plentiful as a T. rex's teeth. Prehistoric Forest was built in the 1950s by James Q. Sidwell, a former dinosaur designer at Chicago's Field Museum of Natural History. As originally conceived, the park pitted humans against these great fake beasts. Visitors were each issued a toy M-16 before boarding a tram that was pulled through the forest by a jeep. Guests were encouraged to shoot first and ask questions later, firing at will at the animated prehistoric critters popping up all around them. If these dinosaurs hadn't already been extinct, they probably would be by now.

Sadly, the attraction has toned down the gunplay, which is not to say that it isn't worth visiting. There are still plenty of dinosaurs along the trail, some of which still move and squirt water at you. That's right, you're alone and on foot, unarmed and unable to defend yourself—just the kind of situation Charlton Heston warned us about. Damn you stinkin' lizards! Damn you all to hell!!

Attached to the park (and included in your admission fee) is Mystery Hill. Your teenage guide suggests that its strange powers were created when a meteorite fell nearby, warping the gravitational field of the earth, or some explanation that seems just as implausible. Water and golf balls run uphill. High-back chairs cling to the walls in the wacky shack. And folks seem to change height just by changing positions relative to one another. Mystery or optical illusion? They'll never tell.

8232 E. Harbor Rd., PO Box 477, Marblehead, OH 43440

(419) 798-5230

Hours: June–August, daily 10 A.M.–7 P.M.; May and September, Saturday–Sunday
   10 A.M.–7 P.M.

Cost: Adults $6.95, Seniors $4.95, Kids $4.95

www.mysteryhill.com

Directions: On Rte. 163 (Harbor Rd.), between Hartshorn Rd. and Englebeck Rd.

Train-O-Rama

Roadside attractions often are the result of somebody's hobby that got out of hand. That's exactly the case with Train-O-Rama. It started when Max Timmons built his first layout in his basement back in the 1940s. Assisted by sons Robert and Terry, Timmons built tracks that grew to fill three different levels within the basement itself. Max would have made it even larger had his wife Naomi not forbidden him from demolishing her laundry room to expand.

Then, in 1969, during a massive thunderstorm, the basement flooded. The writing was on the soaked walls: Timmons had to move the trains upstairs, which meant moving them out. Friends and family suggested he open his own attraction, and in 1972 he did. Train-O-Rama has gone through several locations since then, each time moving to a larger venue.

The current Train-O-Rama has dozens of track routes through alpine snowscapes and Jurassic jungles. It's even got a monorail, an amusement park, and a miniature train wreck that curators assure you was a *real* wreck. If you find yourself catching the train-building bug, there are plenty of Lionel products for sale in the gift shop.

6734 E. Harbor Rd., Marblehead, OH 43440

(419) 734-5856

Hours: June–August, Monday–Saturday 8 A.M.–5 P.M., Sunday 1–5 P.M.;

September–May, Monday–Saturday 11 A.M.–5 P.M., Sunday 1–5 P.M.

Cost: Adults $5, Seniors $4, Kids (3–7) $3

www.trainorama.com

Directions: On Rte. 163 (Harbor Rd.), west of Rte. 218 (Hartshorn Rd.).

Maria Stein
Saintly Stuff

Let's face it, it's not particularly difficult to find a Catholic church with holy relics. But so often the relics come from saints with names you've never heard of and can hardly pronounce—St. Maerobus, St. Polycarp, St. Rogatus, St. Notker, St. Dymphna, St. Gemma Galgoni. But the National Marian Shrine of Holy Relics is an exception. Not only does it have bone chips, wood splinters, and whatnot from the little-known saints, it's also got four relics of the Blessed Virgin Mary and a *dozen* from Jesus himself!

Mary's relics include a piece of her veil, her cincture (belt), her sepulchre (tomb), and a chunk of the House of Loretto. Jesus's relics are even more comprehensive, from birth to death to rebirth. They may be small, but they're important, and include pieces from his crib, his purple mantle (cloak), his less glamorous tunic, the Last Supper table, the *scala sancta* ("holy stairs"), the Pillar of Scourging (whipping post), Veronica's veil (on which Jesus left a facial imprint on the way to Calvary), a thorn from the crown of thorns, a nail used on the cross, a splinter of the "True Cross," his burial cloth, and his sepulchre.

This impressive collection was donated by Father J. M. Gartner when the Marian Shrine was established in 1875. The 1,000+ relics (the second largest collection in the United States) are maintained by the Sisters of the Precious Blood, a religious order organized by St. Gaspar del Bufalo. If you want to learn more about the sisters, the shrine also has a display case filled with dolls that illustrates the evolution of their habits.

National Marian Shrine of Holy Relics, 2291 St. Johns Rd., Maria Stein, OH 45860

(419) 925-4532

E-mail: mariasteinctr@hotmail.com

Hours: Tuesday–Sunday 9:30 A.M.–4:30 P.M.

Cost: Free; donations accepted

www.phonyexpress.com/mariasteincntr/index.html

Directions: Head east on Rte. 119, then north on St. Johns Rd.

Marion
Harding Home and Memorial

He was a popular Republican president, installed in office by the party's Old Boy Network. He rolled back taxes for the wealthy, appointed heads of industry to regulatory agencies overseeing their business partners, and opened federal land to dubious oil drilling. No, no, no, not George W. Bush—Warren Gamaliel Harding!

Harding entered the world on November 2, 1865, the first of eight children born to George and Phoebe Harding near Blooming Grove (Route 97, east of Route 288). In 1872 the family moved to a home in Caledonia (northeast corner of South and Main Streets, now a private residence).

Before he was even 20 years old, Harding purchased the *Marion Star*, which he kept until he left for Washington in 1921 as the president-elect. During his Marion years he met Florence Kling DeWolfe, and married her in 1891. In 1900 he was elected to the Ohio Senate, became the lieutenant governor in 1904, went to the U.S. Senate in 1914, and was chosen as the GOP's presidential candidate in a smoke-filled room at the 1920 national convention in Chicago. He won that race, even though he conducted most of the campaign from the porch of his Marion home. The Old Boys must have known they picked a winner.

Harding Home, 380 Mt. Vernon Ave., Marion, OH 43302

(800) 600-6894 or (740) 387-9630

E-mail: hardinghome@marion.net

Hours: June–August, Wednesday–Saturday 9:30 A.M.–5 P.M., Sunday Noon–5 P.M.; September–October, Saturday 9:30 A.M.–5 P.M., Sunday Noon–5 P.M.; November–May, Monday–Friday by appointment

Cost: Adults $3, Seniors $2, Kids (6–12) $1.25

www.ohiohistory.com/places/harding

Directions: One block south of Church St. (Rte. 95), four blocks east of State St. (Rte. 423).

In office, Warren G. Harding set the bar high for governmental corruption; his secretary of the interior, Albert Fall, was the first cabinet member in U.S. history to go to prison (for his involvement in the Teapot Dome scandal). Harding set the bar pretty low for his own personal conduct. Tales of his philandering make Bill Clinton look like a choirboy.

Almost. Though married, he maintained an active "social life" until the day he died. His most famous mistress, Nan Britton (a woman 30 years his junior, also from Marion) conceived a daughter out of wedlock, and is best known for her trysts with the prez in the Oval Office's coat closet. Florence was aware of her husband's diddling, and she was not happy about it. But was she angry enough to kill him?

In 1923, Harding fell ill on a trip to Alaska. By the time he reached San Francisco, heading home, he was doing even worse. There, at the Palace Hotel on August 2, with Florence by his side, he expired.

Old men in high-stress jobs croak all the time, but something in this case seems suspicious. First off, at the very moment Harding died in California, Florence's astrologer and palm reader, Madame Marsha, announced to a reporter in a Washington townhouse, "The president is dead." She was right, of course, but the death hadn't even been reported yet. Hmmmmmm. . . . Also, at the time of his death, Harding was under the care of one of Florence's old Marion friends, a quack named Dr. Charles Sawyer. Though Harding likely had a heart attack in Alaska, Doc Sawyer blamed his medical disposition on tainted crabmeat. To flush out the dreaded food, the doctor prescribed stimulants and purgatives. The combination might have led to Harding's death, but nobody will ever know since Florence forbade an autopsy. And why do you suppose she did that?

Delaware Ave. and Vernon Heights Blvd., Marion, OH 43302

(740) 387-9630

Hours: Daily 9 A.M.–5 P.M.

Cost: Free

www.ohiohistory.com/places/hardtomb

Directions: On the southeast corner of Rte. 423 (Delaware Ave.) and Vernon Heights Blvd.

MARION

Marion is the Shovel City of the World.

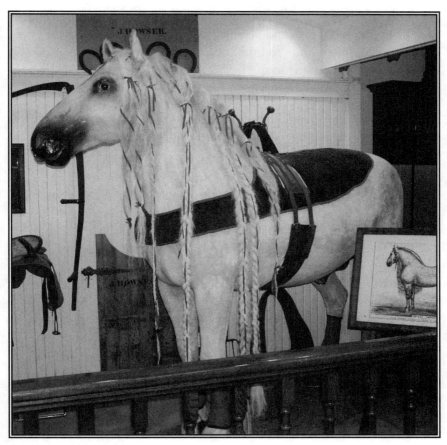

Cher on a bad hair day.
Photo by author, courtesy of Heritage Hall

Popcorn and Napoleon's Horse

Most towns would be lucky to have even one museum worth visiting. Marion has two, and they're both in the same building! Heritage Hall is home to both the Marion County Historical Society and the Wyandot Popcorn Museum.

Though Pilgrims ate popcorn at the first Thanksgiving dinner, it wasn't until Charlie Cretors built the first commercial popcorn popper in 1889 that the fluffy stuff became a staple of the American snack-food diet. Do you know that the average American eats 56 *quarts* of popcorn each year? Now you know.

This informative museum brags that it has the world's largest collection of popcorn poppers and peanut roasters. Virtually all of them have been cleaned up and fully restored, and nobody would think of gunking them up with butter anymore. They've got a 1899 Cretors No. 1 Popper, a 1911 R. O. Stutsman Ideal, a 1908 Improved Model 16 Bartholomew Nickel Mint Popper, and a Dunbar 1911 Model 950 Concession Wagon used in 1984 by Paul Newman to launch his Newman's Own popcorn line in New York's Central Park. (You probably thought all poppers were alike, eh?)

Each September on the weekend after Labor Day the town throws a Popcorn Festival (www.popcornfestival.com, (740) 387-FEST), complete with a kickoff parade; a popcorn-eating contest; the crowning of Miss Popcorn, Miss Tiny Pop, and the Wee Pop; and a Saturday night concert that has featured such acts as Huey Lewis, REO Speedwagon, and Myron Floren from *The Lawrence Welk Show*.

The Marion County Historical Society's collection of local artifacts is also housed in Heritage Hall. Prince Imperial is the star of the museum, a Percheron that toured the states for 20 years as Napoleon's horse. Its owner, Marion farmer Jacob Howser, purchased him in France in 1868. Howser charged folks 10¢ at county fairs to see the famous steed until it died in 1890. Not wanting to lose a lucrative source of income, Howser stuffed Prince Imperial and carted him around as if nothing had happened.

Visitors often ask about the creature's long, braided mane and tail. Did Napoleon groom all of his horses the same way? Nope; that was Howser's idea. For the record, while Prince Imperial had been owned by Napoleon III for the first three years of its life, it wasn't as if the emperor ever rode him into battle. He had *hundreds* of horses.

Heritage Hall, 169 E. Church St., Marion, OH 43302

(740) 387-HALL

E-mail: mchs@historymarion.org and georgek@wyandotpopcornmus.com

Hours: May–October, Wednesday–Sunday 1–4 P.M.; November–April, Saturday–Sunday 1–4 P.M.

Cost: Free

www.historymarion.org and www.wyandotpopcornmus.com

Directions: One block east of Rte. 423 (Main St.) on Rte. 95 (Church St.).

You figure it out.

The Revolving Ball

When Charles Merchant commissioned a granite marker to be placed at the family plot at the Marion Cemetery, he didn't know that he was buying a Perpetual Motion Monument. Then again, neither did the folks who built it.

Nobody noticed anything unusual about the marker—a 5,200-pound black granite orb atop a pedestal at the center of a circular arrangement of basketball-size headstones—when it was erected in 1896. But in 1898 it was obvious that the top had moved; an unpolished patch of granite on the ball, originally located where the sphere met the pedestal, had somehow rotated up, ever so slowly, to become visible on the side. Probably just a bunch of rowdy kids causing trouble, caretakers thought. Maintenance crews rotated the ball back to its original position and reinforced it with lead solder. It turned again. They glued it again. It rotated once more—nothing could keep that big-ass ball from moving around.

Scientists were called in, and they came up with several seemingly plausible theories. One stated that the rotation was a result of uneven heating by the sun on the ball throughout the day. Another theory blamed the base; it was the piece being heated by the sun. And still another theory posited that ice formed and expanded between the sphere and pedestal, then melted unevenly, thereby rocking the ball ever so slightly. None of these theories addresses one simple fact: the ball continues to rotate at the same rate, about an inch a month, whether it's summer or winter. It doesn't seem to make a difference how much sun it gets. And nobody has yet explained why the polished surface never gets scratched as it rubs along the base.

Marion Cemetery, 620 Delaware Ave., Marion, OH 43302

(740) 387-7050

Hours: Daylight hours

Cost: Free

www.mariononline.com/02entertain/monuments.shtml

Directions: On Rte. 423 (Delaware Ave.), just north of Vernon Heights Blvd., in the northeast corner of the cemetery.

Ostrander
Art in the Woods

Mac Worthington is an accomplished sculptor. His work can be found in hundred of locales across the nation, but nowhere in such abundance as his own backyard. Worthington has created his own three-acre sculpture park and filled it with aluminum sculptures out under the trees.

Worthington's creations span the range from purely aesthetic to functional. His sculptural works have titles like *Cherry Poppin*, *Tired Feet Aren't Fireproof*, and *Sunbather in December*, but they're more abstract than literal. His functional pieces include strangely shaped coffee tables, chairs, and desks. Are you looking for some furniture? If so, go look in the woods.

5935 Houseman Rd., Ostrander, OH 43061

(740) 363-3100

Hours: Daily Noon–Dusk

Cost: Free

www.macworthington.com

Directions: Northeast of town on Rte. 257, turn west on Rte. 37, then left at the first
road (Houseman Rd.) and a quarter mile ahead, on the left.

Port Clinton
African Safari Wildlife Park

Real zoos are nice enough, but there's something special about a free-range, drive-through wildlife park that makes a visitor feel as if he or she is on safari, rolling across the Serengeti in a Land Rover while lions roar and monkeys chatter. Of course, getting caught in a minivan traffic jam while a pooping wildebeest blocks the road kind of ruins the effect. So do the teenagers in cages hawking bundles of carrots every 300 yards—where would you find *them* in a game preserve?

The African Safari Wildlife Park is actually only a quarter African; the park is divided into four zones—North America, South America, Asia, and Africa—each filled with a collection of indigenous, tame critters and separated from the other continents by a sturdy fence. To move from one zone to the next you pull your vehicle into a double-gated car pen. Once trapped between continents, a teenager asks if you'd like more carrots or cornmeal, which of course you accept. The kid will then remind you of how to feed the hungry animals: place the carrot into the plastic cup and hold the cup out the window, but DO NOT hold the carrot in your hand—fingers look like carrots. And whatever you do, don't allow an animal to get its head inside the window, but if it does, DO NOT roll up the window until it has extracted its head. Well, duh.

267 Lightner Rd., Port Clinton, OH 43452

(800) 521-2660 or (419) 732-3696

Hours: April–May and September–October, daily 10 A.M.–4 P.M.; June–August, daily
9 A.M.–7 P.M.

Cost: Summer/Spring and Fall, Adults $15.95/$12.95, Kids (3–6) $9.95/$6.95

www.africansafariwildlifepark.com

Directions: One block east of Catawba Rd. (Rte. 53) on Harbor Rd. (Rte. 163), turn
south on Lightner Rd., and follow the signs.

Put-in-Bay
Crystal Cave

It's not geologically accurate to call the hole found beneath Heineman's Winery a cave. It's actually a geode, one of those colorful, crystal-filled, egg-shaped rocks sold in New Age gift shops. At 30 feet in diameter, it is in fact the World's Largest Geode. Thirty people can easily stand inside it at the same time. These celestite (strontium sulfate) crystals are not formed by underground water, as are traditional caves, but grow in cavities in limestone and sandstone formations.

Heineman's Winery first opened its doors in 1888. Its owners did not know they were sitting atop this unique formation. When local quarries started uncovering geodes, Heineman's dug down 40 feet and ta-dah! Lucky for them, too. During Prohibition, the Crystal Cave kept business afloat with tourist dollars. Visitors were given unfermented grape juice at the end of the cave tour, a tradition that continues to this day. But thanks to the Twenty-first Amendment, you can now have wine if you prefer.

Heineman's Winery, 978 Catawba St., PO Box 300, Put-in-Bay, OH 43456

(419) 285-2811

Hours: Daily 11 A.M.–5 P.M.

Cost: Adults $5, Kids (6–11) $2

www.ohiowine.com

Directions: Three blocks south of the docks on Rte. 215 (Catawba St.).

"We have met the enemy, and they are ours."

On September 10, 1813, Admiral Oliver Hazard Perry scribbled those famous words on a note to William Henry Harrison, who was leading a group of 4,500 soldiers to fight the British at Detroit. The statement downplayed the significance of Perry's accomplishment. With only nine ships, the 28-year-old had defeated an entire British fleet, the first and only time that has ever happened.

Of course, the British played a part in their own demise; for some time leading up to the battle, Perry built ships and trained sailors near Buffalo while the British sat by and did nothing. When they finally engaged one another near South Bass Island, Perry charged the enemy with his flagship *Lawrence*, drawing most of the Brits' fire. The British blasted away at the *Lawrence* for two hours, killing or wounding all but 18 crew members and destroying all of the ship's cannons. Perry then hopped into a rowboat and headed for the *Niagara*, one of his fleet that had been hanging back (against Perry's orders) trying to avoid fire. Perry relieved the ship's commander as soon as he climbed aboard, then boldly sailed toward the enemy a second time. In the confusion, two British ships became entangled while the *Niagara* blasted away at them. In less than 10 minutes, the engagement was over. The Americans had won.

Perry's victory was honored with a 352-foot-tall monument—the World's Largest Doric Column, the third tallest monument in the United States—on South Bass Island, near where the bodies of dead British sailors washed ashore. It was erected on the battle's centennial. If you want to see timbers from the crippled *Lawrence*, visit the Great Inland Seas Maritime Museum in Vermilion (480 Main Street, (440) 967-3467, www.inlandseas.org). The *Niagara* still sails Lake Erie, but it is docked in Presque Isle, near Erie, Pennsylvania.

Perry's Victory and International Peace Memorial, PO Box 549, 93 Delaware Ave., Put-in-Bay, OH 43456

(419) 285-2184

E-mail: PEVI_Superintendent@nps.org

Hours: May and September–October, daily 10 A.M.–5 P.M., June–August, daily 10 A.M.– 7 P.M.

Cost: Free; Elevator, Adults $3, Kids (16 and under) Free

www.nps.gov/pevi/

Directions: Three blocks east of the docks, on the isthmus leading to the north side of the island.

PAULDING
Police are allowed to bite dogs to silence them in Paulding.

PORT CLINTON
New York City drops a ball in Times Square each New Year's Eve, but Port Clinton drops Captain Wylie, a 20-foot-long fiberglass fish, from the roof of a downtown building. The ceremony marks the end of the annual Walleye Festival (www.walleyefestival.com).

Wouldn't you expect Jamie Farr's buns to be hairier?
Photo by author, courtesy of Tony Packo's

Toledo
Tony Packo's and the Bun Museum

Tony Packo's might have been just another Toledo hot dog joint were it not for Burt Reynolds and Jamie Farr. Reynolds was in town in 1972, appearing in a production of *The Rainmaker*, when he was invited by Packo's daughter Nancy to stop by after the show. To everyone's surprise, he did. At the end of the meal, the crew wanted his autograph to hang on the wall, yet couldn't find a suitable scrap of paper. But somebody did find an old hot dog bun, and a tradition was born.

The restaurant soon learned that stale buns don't last forever, so they switched to Styrofoam replicas. Believe me, you won't be able to tell the difference. More than 1,000 autographed buns now line the walls of Tony Packo's, including five from U.S. presidents and almost everyone that has ever appeared on *The Love Boat*.

Of course, Tony Packo's has hometown boy Jamie Farr to thank for spreading the word about its establishment outside northeast Ohio. Farr (as Corporal Klinger) improvised a plug for the eatery in an episode of *M*A*S*H* that aired February 24, 1976. Soon folks were coming from all over. The restaurant figured in several episodes, including one where the operating room crew used its sausage casings to repair a blood filter. Yum!

Tony Packo's still serves up the same Hungarian-style dogs that it has since 1932: smoked sausage split down the middle with onions and chili over the top. It's also known for its deep-fried pickles and chili sundaes.

1902 Front St., Toledo, OH 43605

(419) 691-6054

E-mail: eat@tonypackos.com

Hours: Monday–Thursday 11 A.M.–10 P.M., Friday–Saturday 11 A.M.–11 P.M., Sunday Noon–9 P.M.

Cost: Meals $6–$12

www.tonypackos.com

Directions: One block east of I-280 at the Front St. Exit, south of the river.

BIG BOY BROUHAHA

Is nothing sacred? Sometime during the night of March 17, 1995, a clandestine gang calling themselves Pimps of Pimplyness kidnapped a six-foot, 300-pound Big Boy from in front of a Toledo Big Boy restaurant. Over the next several days, dismembered body parts were found at other restaurants around the city, along with lists of demands.

Toledo police eventually caught up with the Pimps, and the restaurant has since glued the 10 pieces back together, and remounted Big Boy in front of the establishment. This time, though, his feet are encased in cement.

BORN IN TOLEDO

Here are a few stars born in Toledo:

Anita Baker	January 26, 1958
Jamie Farr (Jameel Joseph Farah)	July 1, 1934
Gloria Steinem	March 25, 1934
Charlie Weaver (Cliff Arquette)	December 28, 1905

RAWSON

If you want to throw rotten eggs in Rawson, you must be alone, according to the law.

SIDNEY

It is illegal to bring Spanish peanuts to political rallies in Sidney.

TIFFIN

Tiffin's St. Paul's United Methodist Church (46 Madison Street) was, in 1874, the first public building in the world to be wired for electricity.

TOLEDO

It is illegal to throw reptiles at people in Toledo.

"Saturday night in Toledo, Ohio, is like being nowhere at all."
—John Denver

The Toledo Zoo (2700 Broadway, (419) 385-5721) boasts the world's only Hippoquarium. To check out what's happening there at any time of day, try www.toledo.com/zoocams.

A swarm of mayflies smothered a Toledo power plant in 1996, overheating the equipment and causing outages at 290,000 homes and businesses.

Toledo's Mildred Wirt Benson wrote 23 of the first 30 Nancy Drew mysteries under the pen name Carolyn Keene. She received a flat fee of $125 per book. Benson is buried in Toledo Memorial Park (6382 Monroe Street, Sylvania, (419) 882-7151).

Sixteen members of the Cal-Poly football team were killed when their Arctic Pacific Airlines chartered jet crashed near Toledo on October 29, 1960.

Toledo claims to be the Glass Capital of the World.

Wapokoneta
Neil Armstrong Air and Space Museum

When you approach the Neil Armstrong Air and Space Museum from the parking lot, you get the sensation that you are landing on a futuristic moon base; a dome rises between two hills and a string of blue landing lights mark your approach. When this museum opened in 1972, it seemed as if moon colonization might be a possibility, yet today a lunar base seems as far away as ever.

Well, now is not the time to dwell on it—you're here to celebrate the accomplishments of the first man to walk on the moon: Wapokoneta native Neil Armstrong. He was born on his family's nearby farm on August 5, 1930, and he learned to fly a plane before he could drive a car. The museum chronicles his journey from Ohio to the great beyond with an impressive collection of family artifacts and NASA junk, including:

➡ Armstrong's backup Apollo space suit

➡ a moon machete (no kidding)

➡ the *Gemini VIII* spacecraft, the first vehicle to rendezvous and dock in space

➡ a moon rock presented by Tricia Nixon (was she an astronaut?)

➡ a Jupiter rocket engine

➡ the 1946 Aeronca 7AC Champion in which Armstrong first learned to fly at age 15, and the bike he rode to the airport for his lessons.

Be sure to stay for a show at the spherical AstroTheater. Marvel at the endless stars in the Infinity Room, a glorified mirror trick using smoked glass and holiday lights. Imagine that you will one day fly through the void of space on an intergalactic journey, despite all the evidence that humans likely won't be leaving this Earth during *your* lifetime.

Sorry, *Star Trek* fans.

500 S. Apollo Dr., PO Box 1978, Wapokoneta, OH 45895

(800) 860-0142 or (419) 738-8811

E-mail: namu@ohiohistory.org

Hours: Monday–Saturday 9:30 A.M.–5 P.M., Sunday Noon–5 P.M.

Cost: Adults $6, Kids (6–12) $2

www.ohiohistory.org/places/armstron/

Directions: Take the Bellefontaine Rd. Exit west from I-75, then follow the signs.

West Liberty
Ohio Caverns

There's no beating a cavern tour on a hot summer day, or a freezing winter day for that matter. January or July, at Ohio Caverns you can be sure that it'll be 54°F below the surface, no matter what it's like outside. While you're down there, you'll see stalagmites and stalactites in the Palace of the Gods, the Crystal Sea, and the Big Room.

Ohio Caverns opened in 1897 and has a nice selection of specially named formations, such as the Old Town Pump, the Caveman's Couch, and the Devil's Tea Table. Most impressive, however, is the five-foot-long Crystal King stalactite located in the Big Room—that one didn't grow overnight!

The caverns offer a special historic tour to areas that have been closed to the public since 1925, including the Palace of Natural Art. If you've got an extra five dollars and a half-hour, it's well worth the trip.

2210 E. Rte. 245, West Liberty, OH 43357

(937) 465-4017

E-mail: ohiocaverns@caverns.com

Hours: April–October, daily 9 A.M.–5 P.M.; November–March, daily 9 A.M.–4 P.M.

Cost: Regular Tour, Adults $9.50, Kids (5–12) $5; Historic Tour, Adults $15, Kids
  (5–12) $9.50

www.ohiocaverns.com

Directions: Head east out of town on Rte. 287, turn south on Rte. 245, and follow the signs.

UPPER SANDUSKY
The grave of Christianna Haag at the Wyandott Indian Mission in Upper Sandusky lists her date of death as February 31, 1862.

VAN WERT
Van Wert is the Nation's Peony Center.

OTHER OHIO HOLES

★ **Olentangy Indian Caverns** (1779 Home Road, Delaware, (740) 548-7917, www.olentangyindiancaverns.com) These caves were first used by the Wyandotte Indians for shelter, and it was here at the entrance that Chief Leatherlips was murdered by his own tribe members. The caverns were later "discovered" by settler J. M. Adams in 1821 when one of his unfortunate oxen plunged through the surface to its death below. Formations here include the Crystal Room, Cathedral Hall, Bell Tower, Indian Lover's Bench, and Fat Man's Misery.

★ **Perry's Cave** (979 Catawba Avenue, Put-in-Bay, (419) 285-2405, www.perryscave.com) When he was preparing to attack the British Navy, Admiral Perry discovered the cave that now bears his name, 52 feet beneath the surface of South Bass Island. The cave's Underground Lake is connected to Lake Erie, and rises and falls with the lake. Perry's Cave offers a private, after-hours lantern tour that is a little more expensive, but you get a nifty T-shirt.

★ **Seneca Caverns** (15248 E. Thompson, TR718, Bellevue, (419) 483-6711, www.senecacavernsohio.com) Seneca Caverns bills itself as "The Caviest Cave in the USA," whatever that means. It was discovered in 1872 by two boys when their dog disappeared into a bush after a rabbit but didn't come back out. Both boys fell through the same hole as their dog, but they managed to crawl back out. These subterranean caves were carved out over the years by the Ole Mist'ry River.

★ **Zane Shawnee Caverns** (7092 Route 540, Bellefontaine, (937) 592-9592, www.zaneshawneecaverns.org) These caverns have been owned and managed by the Shawnee Nation since 1995, which means you won't be hearing some hokey story during the tour about a jilted Indian maiden throwing herself down the bottomless pit. You may hear all about the unique cave pearls that form here, however, as well as about the many bats who call this hole home.

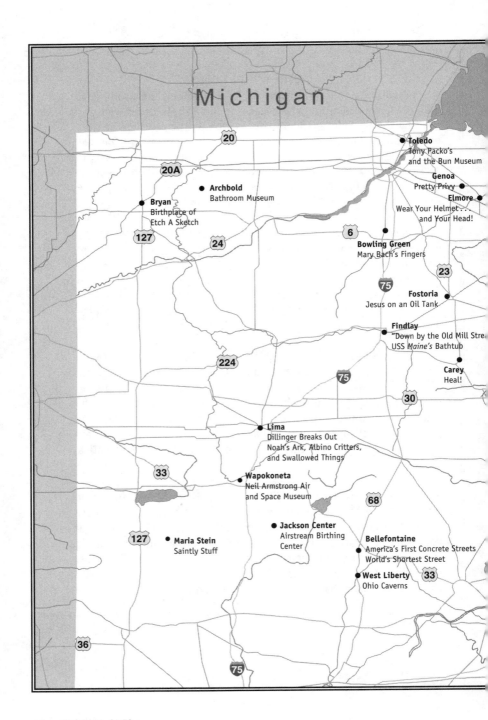

Michigan

20

20A

● **Toledo**
Tony Packo's
and the Bun Museum

Genoa
Pretty Privy ●

Archbold
Bathroom Museum

Elmore ●
Wear Your Helmet . . .
and Your Head!

● **Bryan**
Birthplace of
Etch A Sketch

127

24

6

Bowling Green
Mary Bach's Fingers

23

75

Fostoria
Jesus on an Oil Tank ●

Findlay
"Down by the Old Mill Stre
USS *Maine's* Bathtub

224

Carey
Heal! ●

75

30

● **Lima**
Dillinger Breaks Out
Noah's Ark, Albino Critters,
and Swallowed Things

33

● **Wapokoneta**
Neil Armstrong Air
and Space Museum

68

127

● **Maria Stein**
Saintly Stuff

● **Jackson Center**
Airstream Birthing
Center

Bellefontaine
America's First Concrete Streets
World's Shortest Street

● **West Liberty**
Ohio Caverns

33

36

75

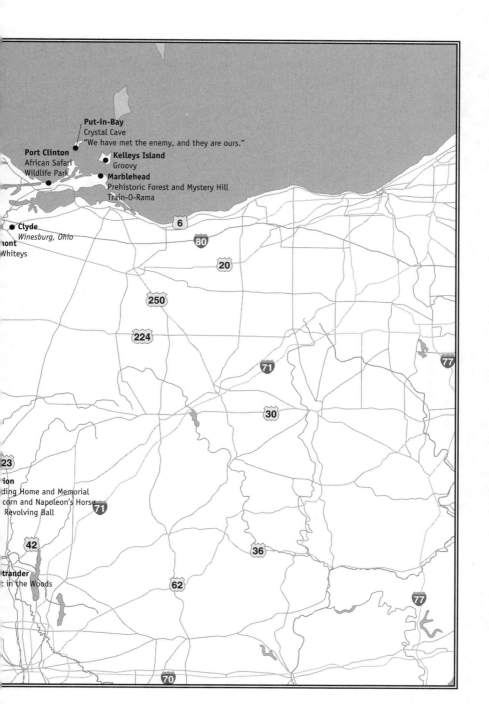

Put-in-Bay
Crystal Cave
"We have met the enemy, and they are ours."

Port Clinton
African Safari
Wildlife Park

Kelleys Island
Groovy

Marblehead
Prehistoric Forest and Mystery Hill
Train-O-Rama

Clyde
Winesburg, Ohio

nont
Whiteys

6

80

20

250

224

71

77

30

23

ion
ding Home and Memorial
corn and Napoleon's Horse
Revolving Ball

71

42

36

trander
t in the Woods

62

77

70

2

THE NOrtheast

*I*f you're looking for Ohio's Western Reserve, don't look to the western part of the state. Look to the *northeast*. This name wasn't as confusing to Revolutionary War veterans from Connecticut; they had been told this land to their west had been "reserved" for them, and the region's name is still used.

So you think a northeastern Western Reserve is a little bass-ackwards? You haven't heard anything yet. Do you want to see a cuckoo clock the size of a small home? It's here. So is a motel built in an old grain silo, a robotic president, and an Amish SUV. What next? Elvis Presley landing an X-Wing Fighter outside a Kent eatery?

As a matter of fact, yes.

Count 'em—there are 12 steps.

Akron
Birthplace of Alcoholics Anonymous

Well, it appears the founders of Alcoholics Anonymous aren't so anonymous any more. Here's their shorthand story. Stockbroker William Wilson came to Akron in the spring of 1935 to take control of the National Rubber Machinery Corporation, but the proxy fight failed. With only $10 in his pocket, he had no way of returning home to Vermont. He eventually found himself at the home of Robert and Anne Smith. Anne asked Wilson to stay and keep an eye on her husband who was trying to sober up. On June 10, Robert Smith swore off booze forever, and AA was born.

In the months that followed, Smith and Wilson wrote up the basic framework for AA, a tenet of which was the anonymity of its members; Smith and Wilson thus became "Dr. Bob" and "Bill W." Dr. Bob's home served as the halfway house for new members after being detoxed at the Akron City Hospital (525 E. Market Street). The stories of these recovering alcoholics formed the backbone of *The Big Book*, which was written to inspire those in recovery.

Volunteers have restored Dr. Bob's former home to its 1935 appearance, complete with Smith family furniture (a little the worse for wear), a few of Dr. Bob's empty bottles found in hiding places and around the home's foundation, and first editions of *The Big Book* and other AA publications. In the basement, where Dr. Bob parked his Buick, there's a gift shop where you can buy T-shirts and caps, but where you *won't* find monogrammed shot glasses or foam beer can holders. For those of you interested in the complete Akron AA tour, the museum has free maps to direct you to Dr. Bob's grave, the Akron City Hospital, and the former site of Kistler's Donuts (torn down) where the tradition of doughnuts at meetings first began.

Dr. Bob's Home, 855 Ardmore Ave., Akron, OH 44302

Contact: Founders Foundation, PO Box 449, Akron, OH 44309

(330) 864-1935

Hours: Daily Noon–3 P.M.

Cost: Free

www.drbobs.com

Directions: Between Exchange St. and Market St. (Rte. 18), two blocks west of Portage Path.

BORN IN AKRON

Akron isn't just the birthplace of Alcoholics Anonymous and televangelism. There are a number of celebrities who hail from this town:

John Dean	October 14, 1938
Hugh Downs	February 14, 1921
Chrissie Hynde	September 7, 1951
Thurmon Munson	June 7, 1947
Ara Parseghian	May 10, 1923

Birthplace of Televangelism

It was a marriage made in heaven or, as some would have you believe, a marriage blessed by heaven: television and evangelism. Televangelism.

Television was still in its infancy in 1952 when Arkansas preacher Rex Humbard was passing through Akron with his tent revival, the Gospel Big Top. While strolling downtown one evening, he noticed a crowd pressed against the window at O'Neil's Department Store. They were watching a baseball game between the Cleveland Indians and the New York Yankees. Humbard knew that if this small electric box could attract sports fans it could certainly attract the unsaved. He decided to launch a television ministry. To that end, he purchased the Ohio Theater, just across the river in neighboring Cuyahoga Falls.

Humbard's new church was named Calvary Temple, and it did more than just broadcast its services; it played wholesome movies on Saturday nights, taught Bible classes, and inaugurated a Dial-a-Prayer phone line where uplifting messages were changed every day. But it was clear that the television broadcasts were the way to reach the masses. And those TV masses donated enough money to expand the ministry even further: by 1958, Rex had enough cash to build the Cathedral of Tomorrow (2700 State Road, Cuyahoga Falls), the first cathedral built specifically for broadcasting. Many locals refer to it as Rex's Erection.

During the 1960s, Humbard launched the *Sunshine Party Show*, a title designed to soft-pedal the show's true nature. Humbard admitted it was intended to be "an old-fashioned, Holy Ghost, God-sent, soul-savin', devil-hatin' revival!" True enough. At its peak, Humbard's programs were broadcast on 60 stations in the United States and 2,000 worldwide, in 97 different languages. Rex Humbard Ministries is still around today, but it hardly has a monopoly on the market it helped create. The Cathedral of Tomorrow was sold to the Reverend Ernest Angley and is now the Grace Cathedral (see page 65).

Roetzel and Andress (former O'Neil's Department Store), 222 S. Main St., Akron, OH 44308

Contact: Rex Humbard Ministries, PO Box 100, Akron, OH 44309

(330) 923-4956

Hours: No longer visible; torn down

Cost: Free

www.rexhumbard.com

Directions: At the corner of State and Main Sts. in downtown Akron.

Gentlemen, start your gravity.

Derby Downs

Though Akron has played host to the All-American Soap Box Derby since 1937, the Depression-era sport was not born here. It actually started on a Dayton street in 1933. It was a slow news day when Myron "Scottie" Scott, a photographer for the *Dayton Daily News*, spotted three boys racing homemade cars down a local street. To generate a little news, he decided to organize a race for later in the week. Nineteen contestants showed up. A photo of the winner, Robert Gravett, made papers across the nation. Based on the overwhelming response to the photo, the paper decided to fund a widely publicized third race, which was held on August 19, 1933. This competition had 362 participants. The Soap Box Derby was born.

The race moved to Akron in 1935, where it was run on Tallmadge Hill. But after a driver plowed into big-name sports announcer Graham McNamee while newsreel cameras rolled, organizers knew they needed to create a safe permanent track. The WPA stepped in to construct Derby Downs, a three-lane, 989-foot track with an 11 percent grade on the eastern side of the Akron Airport. It has remained the race's home ever since.

Each August kids from around the country compete by rolling down the hill. By the time the racers cross the finish line 29 seconds later, they're traveling 30-some miles an hour, not exactly warp speed, but fast enough to cause injury. Winning cars are donated to Derby Downs' growing collection. The organization plans to build a museum someday, but until it's finished you can only see the cars during Derby Days, or by making an appointment.

Derby Downs, George Washington Blvd., Akron, OH 44306

(330) 733-8723

Hours: Early August, or by appointment

Cost: Free

www.aasbd.org

Directions: North of Rte. 224 (Waterloo Rd.) on Rte. 241 (George Washington Blvd.),
   on the east side of the airport.

Goodyear's World of Rubber

To get to Goodyear's World of Rubber you must first sign in with security, take a walnut-paneled elevator to the fourth floor, then wend your way down an eerily quiet corridor . . . but is it ever worth it. All hail vulcanized rubber!!!

A bronze statue of Charles Goodyear greets you in the rotunda. So what if he died penniless 38 years before Goodyear Tire & Rubber was founded. Big deal that neither he nor his descendants are at all involved in the company that bears their name. Goodyear discovered a method of transforming natural rubber, which easily cracks in the winter and melts into goo in the summer, into the pliable, multiuse material we know and love today: just add sulfur and heat.

You'll learn all about it on the self-guided tour, which starts as all natural rubber starts: in a rubber tree forest. Unlike a real rain forest, the trees at the museum go on forever, an optical illusion created by two parallel mirrors and half a dozen fake trees. The multimedia magic continues with wall-size, neon-lit industrial flow diagrams that show "How Synthetic Rubber Is Made" and "How a Radial Tire Is Made." Fascinating! Next, check out the spare Moon Tire left over from the Apollo missions, and see a replica of an artificial flipper built for Lucky the Sea Turtle. Marvel at the 300,000,000th tire made by the company, which rolled off the assembly line on August 9, 1939. And for you ATV fans, check out the jumbo tires made for Admiral Byrd's 1940 Antarctic-mobile. Want more info? Just punch the start button on any of the 1970s-era Videotronic Projectors scattered throughout the museum and a warbling fuzzy film will mesmerize you with the wonders of rubber, rubber, rubber. Thus brainwashed, you will find yourself inextricably drawn to the Goodyear Gift Shop on the way back to the elevator.

Goodyear Hall, 1144 E. Market St., Akron, OH 44316

(330) 796-7117

Hours: Monday–Friday 8 A.M.–4:30 P.M.

Cost: Free

www.goodyear.com

Directions: Just north of I-76 on Rte. 18 (Market St.) at Goodyear Blvd.

One of the Goodyear Company's biggest accomplishments is too large to fit into this museum: the Goodyear Blimp. There was a time when Goodyear was in the blimp-building business, and to build those blimps it built a big blimp building. When it was constructed in 1929, the Goodyear hangar was the largest building in the world without internal supports. At 211 feet tall, 320 feet wide, and 1,175 feet long, it encloses 55,000,000 cubic feet of air and, depending on atmospheric conditions, can generate its own weather systems inside, including cloud formations and rain. It was sold off years ago when Goodyear got out of the business, and today it is called the Lockheed-Martin Airdock. It is not open to the public, but you certainly can't miss it from the road.

The Goodyear Tire & Rubber Company still uses blimps for PR. It has three aircraft in its fleet. One, the 192-foot *Spirit of Goodyear*, is based at the Wingfoot Lake Airship facility in neighboring Suffield (www.goodyearblimp.com/b_goodyear.html).

Kelly Ave. and Exeter Rd., Akron, OH 44306

Private phone

Hours: Always visible

Cost: Free

Directions: On the southwest side of the Akron Fulton International Airport; best viewed from Kelly Ave., coming from the north.

NO GOOD INVENTION GOES UNPUNISHED

Charles Goodyear's discovery of vulcanization should have made him rich, but it turned out to be a curse. For 10 years leading up to his breakthrough and the patent, Goodyear's fortune hovered between poverty and bankruptcy. What little money he was able to scrounge up he plowed back into his research, much to the detriment of his poor wife and suffering children. Goodyear was thrown into debtors prison on numerous occasions, but the moment he got out he spent money he could not spare on more experiments.

After being awarded a patent in 1844, his troubles compounded. He licensed the process to American manufacturers for much less than the rights were worth, concerned more about the benefits to humankind than his personal fortune. A British inventor patented Goodyear's rubber in England as his own. So did the French government, but Napoleon III did thank Goodyear by awarding him the Cross of the Legion of Honor . . . while Goodyear was serving time in debtors prison. Still, Goodyear developed new uses for his wonder material, including rubber bands, life preservers, and rubber gloves. Manufacturers shamelessly ripped off each and every new design. By the time Goodyear died in 1860, he was $191,000 in debt, having cleared only $19,000 in profits over the previous 16 years. His wife and seven of his twelve children beat him to the grave, all from curable conditions compounded by the family's poverty.

Invent Now

Although the U.S. Patent and Trademark Office sponsored the development of this five-story $38 million museum, it is anything but a bureaucratic bore. Not satisfied simply to honor famous inventors of the past, this hands-on museum aims to inspire future inventors. Its Inventors Workshop has tools, machines, and materials you can use to solve various problems posed in the exhibits. In the Take Apart Room you're allowed to fulfill those childhood urges to disassemble old appliances to see what makes them tick—and your parents won't yell at you. The museum also sponsors workshops and summer camps aimed at improving the art of creative problem solving.

Invent Now honors inventors as well. Ohio native Thomas Alva Edison was the first (and only) inductee to the Hall of Fame in 1995, its premier year. With 1,093 patents to his credit, he earned it. To date, the Hall has inducted more than 150 inventors.

National Inventors Hall of Fame, 221 S. Broadway, Akron, OH 44308-1505

(800) 968-4332 or (330) 762-4463

Hours: Tuesday–Saturday 9 A.M.–5 P.M., Sunday Noon–5 P.M.

Cost: Adults $7.50, Seniors (65+) $6, Kids (18 and under) $6

www.invent.org

Directions: Downtown, at the intersection of Broadway and University Ave.

AKRON

Devo was founded in Akron during the late 1970s by Bob and Mark Mothersbaugh, Bob and Jerry Casale, and Alan Myers.

The ghost of Eula Bonham, a matron killed by girls at Akron's Summit County Juvenile Detention Home on November 27, 1955, is said to walk the facility's halls, still confiscating contraband cigarettes.

Abolitionist **John Brown** lived in Akron for two years, from 1844 to 1846, where he worked with Colonel Simon Perkins to raise Merino sheep for wool (514 Copley Road, (330) 535-1120).

Sleep in a Silo

Not everything in the Rust Belt is still rusty. Take, for example, this former Quaker Oats factory in downtown Akron. Back in the mid-1970s, developers made it into a mall without changing the infrastructure too much.

Its best feature is the hotel it made from the plant's 36 turn-of-the-century grain silos. Each round room is 24 feet in diameter and gives you a sense of what an ant must feel after it falls inside a soda can. That's not to say the rooms are claustrophobic; though the original walls were made of concrete several inches thick, they've cut balconies into them to give guests panoramic views of Akron. If you visit with the kids and they start to misbehave, punish them by making them stand in the corner. That'll keep them occupied.

Sleep in a silo.

Crowne Plaza Quaker Square Hotel, 135 S. Broadway, Akron, OH 44308
(330) 253-5970
E-mail: sales@cpquakersquare.com
Hours: Always visible
Cost: Free; Rooms $99 and up
www.quakersquare.com/sleep_fr.htm
Directions: Two blocks south of Rte. 18 (Market St.) on Rte. 261 (Broadway).

You would have thought this would be in Youngstown. . . .

World's Largest Cockroach

When you see the 15-foot-long cockroach crawling on the outside of TNT Exterminating's headquarters, you'll almost wonder if they use TNT to do the job. Clearly this big-ass bug wouldn't be felled by a standard hand sprayer, unless you clubbed it over the head with the canister.

TNT Exterminating has been part of Akron's pest-killing scene since it first opened its doors in 1936. Considering the size of this insect, can you imagine what things were like around here *before* they showed up?

TNT Exterminating, 92 N. Main St., Akron, OH 44308

(330) 535-6411

Hours: Always visible

Cost: Free

www.tntexterminating.com

Directions: Just north of Perkins St. on the northeast side of downtown.

Alliance
Dead-End Town

It's more than a little unusual trying to get out of downtown Alliance. Head east on Main Street and you reach a dead end at Webb Avenue. If you turn around and head west, you dead-end into Sawsburg Road. What's going on here?

No mystery, just a unique example of urban planning: Alliance is the only town in America that has a Main Street with two dead ends. Whether or not this was part of some civil engineer's master plan to keep folks from ever leaving, we may never know. But looking around Alliance, it's clear that some citizens figured out the secret long ago.

And they left.

Main St., Alliance, OH 44601

No phone

Hours: Always visible

Cost: Free

www.alliance.oh.us/home.htm

Directions: Two blocks south of Ely St. (Rte. 84).

Ashtabula
Dead Passengers and Missing Gold

If there is a lesson to be learned from the Ashtabula train disaster it's that you don't want to experiment with an innovative bridge on a passenger rail line. The newfangled truss bridge designed by Amasa Stone was barely given a once-over by the Lake Shore & Michigan Southern's president, Charles Collins, before construction began. Still, for 11 years the bridge soared 82 feet above the deepest part of "The Gulf" where Ashtabula Creek dumps into Lake Erie.

All that ended on December 29, 1876. During a raging blizzard, the Pacific Express Number 5 was creeping over the trestle at a manageable speed when the train's engineer noticed that the light beam from his engine lamp was slowly rising off the snowy tracks. That could mean only one thing: the bridge was sinking behind him! He opened the throttle and tried to make it to the opposite end of the bridge, but only his engine made it to the abutment; the rest of the cars and another engine plunged into the chasm.

In all, 92 passengers and crew perished, most of them burned alive in the wreck as the stoves in the cars ignited the splintered train. Local thieves picked over the smoking mass late into the evening, and more than a few pieces of jewelry were pulled from charred corpses. There was even talk that $2 million in gold had sunk to the bottom of the creek, but nothing was ever recovered. Most think the gold story an urban legend, but you never know.

Rumors also circulated that rescue workers were discouraged from dousing the flames in order to exterminate any surviving witnesses. If this was true, it certainly didn't discourage a formal investigation. The evening after LS&MS's Collins faced grueling questioning, the president went home (to 3rd Street and St. Clair Avenue in Cleveland) and, in a rare gesture of corporate accountability, put a bullet in his head. Stone, the bridge's designer, killed himself a few years later.

Twenty-five unidentified crash victims were buried in 19 plots at the Chestnut Grove Cemetery (Grove Drive, (440) 997-9551). Ghost hunters have spotted glowing orbs hovering over the monument. President Charles Collins is also interred at Chestnut Grove, but he's in a comfy mausoleum.

3200 Lake Ave., Ashtabula, OH 44004

No phone

E-mail: arhf@alltell.net

Hours: Always visible

Cost: Free

home.alltel.net/arhf/

Directions: Just east of the intersection of 32nd St. and Lake Ave.

ASHTABULA

Actor **Don Novello**, best known as Father Guido Sarducci, was born in Ashtabula on January 1, 1943.

You should see how big Grandma is!

Austinburg
World's Largest Rocking Chair

Lily Tomlin's character Edith Ann had a large rocking chair on *Laugh-In*, but it was nothing compared to the rocker on the north side of Austinburg. It is owned by Country Cousins, a builder and distributor of cedar log furniture, the kind you put on your deck, not inside your house.

Contrary to what you might have guessed, Country Cousins did not build the World's Largest Rocking Chair; this superseat has been part of the Austinburg commercial landscape longer than Country Cousins and several businesses before it. Somebody built it back in the 1960s, but nobody seems to know quite who. The chair is too cumbersome to move and too fabulous to bulldoze. So here it sits, and here it will remain, for eternity.

Country Cousins, 1933 Rte. 45, PO Box 288, Austinburg, OH 44010

(440) 275-1226

Hours: Always visible

Cost: Free

Directions: Two blocks north of Rte. 307 on Center Rd. (Rte. 45).

Barberton
Mary Gets Around

Anthony Fernwalt was just another volunteer at the Shrine of St. Jude when, on March 10, 1992, he bumped into somebody famous. Who? None other than the Virgin Mary, *Mother of God*! Fernwalt had come to clean the shrine, but he found a woman in her late teens who had a glow about her and who bragged about giving birth to Jesus Christ. She also warned him about world government and predicted an impending invasion of Israel from the north.

Fernwalt immediately ran to get the shrine's pastor, Father Roman Bernard, but by the time the pair returned, Mary had split. Father Roman might have dismissed Fernwalt as a crackpot, but he noticed that one of the shrine's icons, a painting of Mary on plywood titled *Our Lady of the Holy Protection*, had begun shedding tears. Bingo!

Word got around and soon cars full of the faithful were arriving at the tiny 24-seat chapel built from a converted barbershop. Some claimed to smell roses when no flowers were present, and others had their rosaries turned from silver to gold. The weeping icon even cured a gangrenous ulcer on the leg of 85-year-old Irma Sutton, or so she said.

Fernwalt and Father Roman had a falling out a week after all the craziness began. Fernwalt fled to Steubenville, and later Kilgore, with a band of followers. Then, in March 2003, federal agents arrested Fernwalt for providing fake U.S. passports to Indian and Pakistani nationals. Antiterrorism agents had also received tips that he was planning a sarin gas attack, but no chemical evidence was ever found on his property.

Now what would Barberton's Virgin Mary think of that?!?? Well, she still weeps from time to time.

Shrine of St. Jude (St. Jude Orthodox Church), 594 Fifth St. NE, Barberton, OH 44301

(330) 753-1155

Hours: Daily 11 A.M.–1:30 P.M., or by appointment

Cost: Free

Directions: Two blocks south of Rte. 619 (Wooster Rd.), just west of State St.

JESUS GETS AROUND

The Virgin Mary isn't the only one to have shown up in northeast Ohio—Jesus has made an appearance here as well. In the early 1990s, the Messiah's bearded face appeared on the cash register at the James Dean Bar & Grill (786–800 Lovers Lane) in Akron. Doubters claimed it was created by a coin rubbed on the machine, but believers begged to differ. Whatever the case, he's no longer there; the bar has since closed and the cash register is gone . . . or has it been resurrected?

Bellevue
World's Largest Collection of Postmarks

Some folks collect stamps, but darn few people collect postmarks. So few, in fact, that there's only one museum in the world dedicated to this unique hobby, and it's only a small part of an even larger museum complex. The Postmark Collectors Club has the bulk of its collection on display in 600 binders in Historic Lyme Village's old Groton Township Hall. These binders contain more than a million examples of those little cancellations in the upper right corner of your envelopes.

Underimpressed? Perhaps the size of this collection hasn't quite sunk in. Think of it this way: if you were to look at 600 postmarks an hour (10 per minute) during the 350-odd hours this museum is open each year, it would take you almost five years to see them all. By then the club will probably have added a half-million more.

Post Mark Collectors Club Museum, Historic Lyme Village, 5001 Rte. 4, Bellevue, OH 44811

(419) 483-4949

Hours: June–August, Tuesday–Sunday 1–5 P.M.; May and September, Sunday 1–5 P.M.

Cost: Adults $7, Seniors $6, Kids (6–12) $3

www.lymevillage.com

Directions: Northeast of town near the intersection of Rtes. 113 and 4.

Berlin
The Amish SUV

It's bad enough that every urban jackass wants an SUV, but now the *Amish* are getting into the act? Yep, it appears *somebody's* trying to keep up with the Yoders. Housed inside Wendell August Forge is the biggest, baddest buggy you ever did see: 10 feet, 1½ inches tall; 13 feet, 9 inches long; and 7 feet, 4 inches wide. This buggy tips the scales at 1,200 pounds and has five-foot tall wheels. If it has a saving grace, it's that nobody can accuse its owner of driving a gas guzzler. A hay guzzler, perhaps.

Wendell August Forge, 7007 Rte. 62, Berlin, OH 44610

(800) 923-3713 or (330) 893-3713

Hours: Monday–Saturday 9 A.M.–6 P.M.

Cost: Free

www.wendellaugust.com

Directions: Northeast of town along Rte. 62.

The Cyclorama

It sounds so futuristic—*The Cyclorama*—yet it's anything but. Remember, this is Amish country. The Cyclorama is a 10-foot by 265-foot painting by artist Heinz Gaugel that traces the history of the Amish, Mennonites, and Hutterites, from their founding to the present. The work took 14 calendar years to complete, and is housed in its own building attached to the Mennonite Information Center east of Berlin. The painting hangs in a circle and stops where it started, hence the name.

Gaugel titled his painting *Behalt*, meaning "to keep or remember." Given the history of the Anabapist movement, it seems like it would be awfully hard to forget. From its first days in Zurich, Switzerland, in 1525 these folks have been persecuted, tortured, and chased across the globe for their faith. You'll learn all about it on the guided tour: who was burned at the stake, who was killed with a red-hot poker, who was beheaded, and who was held under water until they renounced their beliefs (which they never did). The images on the painting can be quite gruesome, and you won't be bored.

The building that holds the Cyclorama is filled with chairs you can sit on during the lecture. One seat, however, is off limits: Christ's Chair. This wooden throne was built without nails in 1809 by local eccentric Jonas Stutzman. Most folks called him White Jonas because he didn't wear the traditional black garb. White Jonas was convinced that Jesus was going to return, so he built him a place to sit. Jesus never arrived, but who knows what the future holds? If the Messiah ever does come back, folks in Berlin will be ready.

Mennonite Information Center, 5798 Rte. 77, PO Box 324, Berlin, OH 44610

(330) 893-3192

E-mail: behalt@sssnet.com

Hours: June–October, Monday–Thursday 9 A.M.–5 P.M., Friday–Saturday 9 A.M.–8 P.M.;
   September–May, Monday–Saturday 9 A.M.–5 P.M.

Cost: Adults $5.50, Kids (6–12) $2.50

http://pages.sssnet.com/behalt/index.shtml

Directions: South of Rte. 62 on Rte. 77, northeast of town.

A CHEESY MURAL
If you're looking for a more secular mural than *Behalt*, or at least one with fewer beheadings, drive on over to Heini's Cheese Chalet (Route 77 at Route 62, (330) 893-2131). There you'll find a smaller (but still impressive) painting tracing the history of cheese, all the way back to the Egyptians. Heini's is the place to go for anything cheesy. It calls itself the Home of the Famous Mini-Cheese Wheels. It was once home to a 10-ton cheese wheel—the world's largest—but the colossal curd is now kaput.

Canton
Johnny Carson's DeLorean

For years Ed McMahon had to endure Johnny Carson's jokes about being a lush, so it must have been a bit of a vindication when, in October 1982, the *Tonight Show* host was picked up for DUI in Los Angeles. Carson was driving his 1981 stainless steel DeLorean, a half-million-dollar gift from John DeLorean for helping to get his auto company off the ground. Carson pled no contest to the charge, paid a $603 fine, received a three-year suspended sentence, and was ordered to take a defensive-driving class.

Carson eventually sold his DeLorean Drunkmobile and it ended up here, in one of the best auto museums in Ohio. The Canton Classic Car Museum is housed in the former home of the nation's second Ford dealership. Its collection includes the 1928 Lea Francis seen in the movie *Those Daring Young Men in Their Jaunty Jalopies*, Amelia Earhart's 1916 Pierce-Arrow, the only 1914 Benham known to exist, and the Queen Mother's 1939 Lincoln (probably driven by a man named Jeeves).

Canton Classic Car Museum, 555 S. Market St., Canton, OH 44702

(330) 455-3603

Hours: Daily 10 A.M.–5 P.M.

Cost: Adults $7.50, Seniors $6, Kids (6–18) $5

www.cantonclassiccar.org

Directions: Take the 6th St. exit from I-77, head east until you get to Market St.

BARBERTON
Barberton hosts a Chickenfest every September.

CANTON
TV host **Jack Paar** was born in Canton on May 1, 1918.

COSHOCTON
A Coshocton woman reported that she awoke on January 2, 1988, to find Bigfoot staring through a bedroom window at her. It had red eyes and stood about 7½ feet tall. The woman believed it had been attracted by the sound of her crying baby, perhaps thinking it was food.

More lifelike than the original.
Photo by author, courtesy McKinley National Memorial and Museum

Presidential Robot

Poor William McKinley. He was born a century too early. Had the robot in this Canton museum been available at the Pan-American Exposition in Buffalo, New York, perhaps anarchist Leon Czolgosz would have shot it instead of the flesh-and-blood president. No such luck; on September

6, 1901, the second-term Republican was greeting well-wishers when a not-so-well-wishing Czolgosz fired two shots at him from beneath a fake hand bandage. One bullet missed, but the other pierced the president's stomach. Eight days later, on September 14, McKinley expired.

However, through the miracle of animatronics, McKinley and his wife Ida have been resurrected to greet modern-day visitors just down the hill from their humongous tomb. An electric eye tips them off when you arrive, and they ramble on and on about his legacy. Somebody's got to do it—McKinley is the only U.S. president whose prepresidency residences have all been destroyed. His birthplace in Niles, where he burst upon the world on January 29, 1843, burned to the ground in 1935 and was replaced by the McKinley Federal Savings and Loan (36 S. Main Street). To make up for it, Niles built a McKinley Memorial Library (40 N. Main Street, (330) 652-1704, www.mckinley.lib.oh.us) as a repository for his personal and professional papers.

McKinley National Memorial and Museum, 800 McKinley Monument Dr., NW, Canton, OH 44708

(330) 455-7043

E-mail: mmuseum@neo.rr.com

Hours: Tomb, Monday–Saturday 9 A.M.–5 P.M., Sunday Noon–5 P.M.

Cost: Tomb, Free; Museum, Adults $6, Seniors $5, Kids (3–18) $4

www.mckinleymuseum.org

Directions: East of I-77 on 12th St. SW, turn south on Stadium Park Dr., then right (north) on Monument Dr.

Cuyahoga Falls
Cathedral Buffet and the Life of Christ Display

When Rex Humbard sold the Cathedral of Tomorrow to Ernest Angley, little did he know that Angley would transform the complex from the Birthplace of Televangelism (see page 48) to the Birthplace of Banquetvangelism. Angley, known to television viewers for his white-bread miracles (viewers were sometimes asked to press slices of bread to their television sets to receive a blessing) has now opened a 1,000-seat banquet hall where, presumably, all the bread is holy.

But a large, banquet-style restaurant wouldn't be worth visiting were it not for the remarkable Life of Christ display open to Cathedral Buffet diners of all faiths. Each of the 13 miniature scenes took sculptor Paul Cunningham a year to complete. They combine the elements of model railroad building with a biblical twist. Cunningham used everything from frayed rope to human fingernails to give his creations an authentic feel.

2690 State Rd., Cuyahoga Falls, OH 44223

(330) 922-0467

Hours: Tuesday–Thursday 11 A.M.–8 P.M., Friday 11 A.M.–5 P.M., Saturday 11 A.M.–
   7 P.M., Sunday 1:30–5 P.M.

Cost: Free

www.cathedralbuffet.com and www.ernestangeley.org/LifeOfChrist/loc.htm

Directions: One block south of Portage Trail on State Rd. (approximately 22nd St.),
   northwest of downtown.

CUYAHOGA FALLS

Forty-three riders and crew on an interurban doodlebug were incinerated on July 31, 1940, after their commuter car collided with a Pennsylvania Railroad freight train at the Front Street crossing in Cuyahoga Falls.

DOVER

The skull of Confederate terrorist **William Quantrill** is buried in Dover's Fourth Street Cemetery (Poplar and Fourth Sts.), in the town where he was born. The rest of his body is buried elsewhere.

EAST LIVERPOOL

East Liverpool is known as America's Crockery City.

The **Klondike Bar** was invented by Isaly's Dairy in East Liverpool around 1922.

Dennison
Dreamsville

The Dennison Depot might look a little plain today, but to the 1.5 million GIs who passed through here on the Pennsylvania Railroad during World War II, it was Dreamsville. Starting on March 19, 1942, local volunteers rolled out the red carpet for the troop trains, organizing a canteen to rival any found in New York or San Francisco. Over the next four years, a total of 3,987 volunteers kept the canteen open 24 hours a day, seven days a week. The canteen was nothing fancy, just a nice spot for soldiers to get off the train and stretch their legs, and get a cup of coffee and a warm sandwich.

With the war over, Dreamsville closed its doors on April 8, 1946. The depot eventually fell into disrepair, and was slated for demolition in 1984. A nonprofit group saved it from the wrecking ball and reopened it as a museum in 1989 after extensive restoration.

Dennison Railroad Depot Museum, 400 Center St., PO Box 11, Dennison, OH 44621
(877) 278-8020 or (740) 922-6776
E-mail: depot@tusco.net
Hours: Tuesday–Saturday 10 A.M.–5 P.M., Sunday 11 A.M.–3 P.M.
Cost: Adults $3, Seniors $2.75, Kids (3–12) $1.75
www.dennisondepot.org
Directions: Two blocks east of 2nd St., along the railroad tracks.

Dover
Warther Museum

Ernest "Mooney" Warther wasn't the type of person who loafed around. He dropped out of school in the second grade and went to work herding dairy cows. One day he found a penknife and started whittling to pass the time. A wandering hobo taught him how to carve a pair of wooden pliers out of a single block of wood using only 10 cuts, and the rest is carving history.

Warther carved every time he got the chance. At the age of 14 he went to work in the American Sheet and Plate Company's steel mill where he learned about machinery and how to forge metal. This would come in handy as his carving skills soon surpassed the tools that were available to him. No problem, he just forged his own. (His knife-making grew into the family's Warther Kitchen Cutlery business today.)

The Warther Museum contains Warther's life's work. Most of his carvings are of steam locomotives and train cars; there are 64 in all. The collection includes his largest, the Great Northern locomotive (which has 7,752 individual pieces whittled from ivory, walnut, and ebony), and the *Empire State Express*, the World's Largest Ivory Carving. The centerpiece of the exhibit, however, is an eight-foot-long rendering of Abraham Lincoln's funeral train, complete with a lighted car that houses the president's teeny casket. Warther completed it on the one-hundredth anniversary of the assassination. Each train has a time capsule built into its coal or wood bin, which contains notes from local children and the last scrap of sandpaper Warther used to finish the job, inscribed with the date of completion.

One of the strangest items on display is Warther's Plier Tree, a variation on the hobo's original design. Warther carved a second and third pair of pliers from the first pair's handles, then more pliers from their handles, and so on until he had 511 interlocking pliers from the original block of wood. Warther also created an educational exhibit tracing the history of steam power and a diorama of a steel mill where he once worked. The scene has dozens of working parts, except for the one employee who can be seen napping on the job; Warther carved a grumpy boss to yell at him.

Frieda Warther, his wife of 62 years, was no layabout either. She was a button fanatic on an endless search for clothes fasteners of every shape and size. Frieda arranged and mounted her buttons into flowers and stars, which she eventually placed in their own minimuseum on the grounds. The folks here claim that none of the 73,282 buttons are exactly the same—sorta like snowflakes. Then again, who would challenge such a statement, and how could anyone realistically prove the curators wrong?

The Warther carvings attracted the attention of Henry Ford. He offered to buy Warther's work and put him on salary; Mooney told Ford to take a hike: "My roof doesn't leak, my family is not hungry, and my wife has all her buttons." What more could anyone ask for?

331 Karl Ave., Dover, OH 44622

(330) 343-7513

Hours: March–November, daily 9 A.M.–5 P.M.; December–February, daily 10 A.M.–4 P.M.

Cost: Adults $8.50, Kids (6–17) $4

www.warthers.com

Directions: Take Exit 83 from I-77, head southeast on Rte. 39, turn right on Tuscawaras Ave., right on 9th St., and right on Karl St.

East Liverpool
Pretty Boy Floyd Death Site

It was a rain-slick road that led to the demise of Charles Arthur "Pretty Boy" Floyd on October 22, 1934. Sure, the FBI gunned him down, but the mad-dog killer might not have been caught had he not run off Route 7 between Wellsville and East Liverpool two days earlier. His Ford struck a telephone pole and was damaged, so he asked Beulah and Rose Baird, the two molls he was traveling with, to take the car to a Wellsville mechanic. Floyd and accomplice Adam Richetti then set up camp along the road at Elizabeth Hill and waited for the women to return.

Several locals became suspicious of their campfire and called the cops. After a brief shootout, Richetti was captured, but Floyd escaped. He later forced a farmhand at gunpoint to drive him to Youngstown, but they ran out of gas before they got very far. (Depression-era farmers didn't keep full gas tanks—go figure.) Floyd commandeered another vehicle and another hostage and got as far as Lisbon, but there he met with a roadblock at the railroad tracks. They backtracked toward East Liverpool along Roller Coaster Road, chased by police. After a brief gun battle, Floyd took off on foot into Spence's Woods.

Back in a basement cell at Wellsville City Hall, Richetti snapped and revealed his identity, though he denied that his missing cohort was Pretty Boy. FBI agent Melvin Purvis, the guy who gunned down Dillinger in Chicago, knew better. He flew to Wellsville the next day to lead the 200-man posse.

On Sunday, October 21, unsuspecting farmer's daughter Mabel Wilson allowed Floyd to wash his face at her family's home, then sent him off with a sandwich, a few apples, and some ginger cookies. The posse talked to her not long after Floyd had left, and were able to tighten their dragnet. Floyd ate a second meal, this one at the home of Ellen Conkle the next day, and paid the woman one dollar.

The spareribs, potatoes, and rice pudding turned out to be his final meal. Purvis and his deputies drove by the Conkle farm and spotted Floyd sitting in a car next to the corncrib. Pretty Boy then took off on foot across a cornfield, but was shot by East Liverpool policeman Chester Smith, once in the elbow and once in the back. While he lay bleeding, Purvis asked if he was Pretty Boy Floyd. "I am Floyd," he admitted, then expired.

He always hated that nickname.

Beaver Creek State Park, Spruceville Rd., East Liverpool, OH 43920

(216) 385-3091

Hours: Always visible

Cost: Free

www.dnr.state.oh.us/parks/parks/beaverck.htm

Directions: Head south on Rte. 428 (Sprucevale Rd.), just north of (Rte. 961) Ware Rd.

Floyd's body was taken to the Sturgis Funeral Home in East Liverpool where employee Frank Dawson embalmed the body. Hearing rumors that the police were hot on the gangster's trail, Dawson had gone to the local barber earlier that afternoon and instructed him to "Give me a good haircut because I'll probably be in the newspapers." He was right.

Police used the $122 found on Floyd's body to pay the funeral home for its services. Floyd's muddy, bloody, blue suit was cut into swatches and passed out as souvenirs. That evening 10,000 citizens filed by his corpse to get a last look at the killer. Two local doctors performed a postmortem, and listed the cause of death as internal bleeding from three gunshot wounds.

Wait a second . . . *three*? Nobody ever cared to explain the discrepancy between the number of shots reportedly fired in the cornfield by Smith and the number of holes in the killer's body at the funeral home. Then, in 1979, Smith broke his silence to *Time* magazine: after failing to get a confession from Floyd for the Kansas City Massacre, Purvis ordered agent Herman Hollis to execute Floyd, and Hollis did.

The funeral home has recently been converted into a charming bed and breakfast. If you stay there, ask to visit the laundry room. There you will find Pretty Boy Floyd's death mask and the metal stand that cradled his head while he was being embalmed.

Sturgis House, 122 W. 5th St., East Liverpool, OH 43920

(330) 382-0194

Hours: Call for a reservation

Cost: $65–$95

www.sturgishouse.com

Directions: Three blocks north of Rte. 30 (2nd St.), east of Jackson St.

Who's a pretty boy now?
Photo by author, courtesy of Sturgis House

If you can't make it to East Liverpool but find yourself near Hanoverton, there's another copy of the death mask at the Spread Eagle Tavern and Inn.

Spread Eagle Tavern and Inn, 10150 Historic Plymouth St., PO Box 277, Hanoverton, OH 44423

(330) 223-1583

Hours: Lunch, daily 11:30 A.M.–2 P.M.; Dinner, Monday–Thursday 5–8 P.M., Friday–Saturday 5–10 P.M., Sunday 2–8 P.M.

Cost: Meals $8–$25

Directions: Two blocks north of Rte. 30 (Canal St.), one block east of Rte. 406 (1st St.).

Fernwood
Mary Hartman, Mary Hartman

When *Mary Hartman, Mary Hartman* hit the airwaves in 1976, it was both praised and reviled. It was a soap opera parody of a Fernwood, Ohio, homemaker (Louise Lasser) who, when she wasn't preoccupied by waxy yellow buildup on her kitchen floor, was plagued by the excesses of her family and neighbors. Her husband had trouble in bed, her trench coat–wearing grandfather was arrested as the Fernwood Flasher, and her mother Martha Shumway (Dody Goodman) was oblivious to it all. Hartman's friend Loretta Haggers (Mary Kay Place) was a little-known country-western singer at the Rosemont Bowling Alley's Capri Lounge until hitting it big with "Baby Boy." The mayor of Fernwood was caught with a prostitute, which was an embarrassment to his son, eight-year-old televangelist Jimmy Joe Jeeter. The child later died when a TV fell into his bathtub, leaving plans for the Condos for Christ development on the drawing board. Mary was eventually committed to the Fernwood Psychiatric Hospital after suffering a nervous breakdown.

The show was produced by 1970s sitcom powerhouse Norman Lear, but that didn't guarantee its success. When Lasser quit in 1977, the show struggled on for six more months. It was followed by the short-lived *Fernwood Forever*, and then by *Fernwood 2-Night*, which ran from 1977 to 1978. The latter series was a mock talk show on WZAZ-TV, Channel 6, hosted by Barth Gimble (Martin Mull) and his sidekick Jerry Hubbard (Fred Willard). They interviewed a bottomless list of bizarre guests interspersed with public service announcements for programs such as the Guns to Kids giveaway, part of the town's Kiddie Krime Korps.

Of course, there never was a Fernwood, Ohio, where this all took place. But there is a Fernwood in Ohio, a wide spot in the road southwest of Steubenville. It has no Capri Lounge, no mental hospital, and no television station. But it does have a couple of town signs for TV Land junkies to pose next to.

"343 Bratner Ave.," Fernwood, OH 43938

No phone

Hours: Never visible

Cost: Free

Directions: Along Solter Rd. (Rte. 2).

George Washington, you're a fraud!

Hartsgrove
John Hanson, Father of Our Country

Chances are you're one of the 250 million miseducated Americans who believe the lie that George Washington is the Father of Our Country. You poor, ignorant fool. Anyone who's studied the history of our nation, I mean *really* studied it, knows it was John Hanson of Maryland. He was named U.S. president by the congress in 1781 under rules outlined in the Articles of Confederation.

So was Washington the second president? My, my, my, somebody was asleep during social studies . . . and I bet it was *you*. The Articles of Confederation clearly stated that presidents were to serve one-year terms, with a maximum of three terms. So when Hanson stepped down, Elias Boudinot was named our second chief executive.

Ever hear of Thomas Miffin? You should; he was our third president.

I'd call you ignorant, but it's not your fault—everyone has been told the same lies, unless they've had a talk with Nick Pahys Jr., founder and curator of the Hartsgrove Presidential Museum, the smartest fellow you'll ever meet, and he doesn't mind telling you so.

And he will. *Plenty* of times.

Here are the rest: fourth president, Richard Henry Lee; fifth, John Hancock; sixth, Nathaniel Gorham; seventh, Arthur St. Clair; eighth, Cyrus Griffin; and *ninth*, George Washington, the first president elected under the new *federal* constitution. You probably know the rest after him.

Or at least most of them.

OK . . . maybe *10* of them?

Pahys has been engaged for decades in the Sisyphean task of correcting Americans' ignorance, one person at a time. If you've got an hour or so to spare, stop on by the Hartsgrove Emporium; the museum is on the second floor. Pahys, who has the world's longest list of honorary titles after his name—DDG-CH-AdVS-A.G.E.-LDA-FIBA; whatever you do, *don't* ask—will correct not only your understanding of the executive branch, but any other topic that comes to mind. His mind, not yours. When you've reached the point where you can take no more of your own misperceptions, back away, ever so slowly, toward the door.

Hartsgrove Presidential Museum, Hartsgrove Emporium, 5269 Geneva-Windsor Rd., Hartsgrove, OH 44085

(440) 474-5369

E-mail: pahysltd@suite224.net

Hours: Thursday–Sunday 11 A.M.–5 P.M., or by appointment

Cost: Adults $5

www.OneandOnlyPresidentialMuseum.com

Directions: On the southwest corner of the town square, at the intersection of Rtes. 6 and 534.

GAMBIER

Students at Kenyon College in Gambier call the columns on either side of Middle Path the Gates of Hell, and claim a door to the Underworld can be found in the basement of Mather Hall.

HIRAM

Joseph Smith, founder of the Church of Jesus Christ of Latter Day Saints, was dragged from his home by a Hiram mob in March 1832. He was tarred, feathered, and beaten so badly that he was left permanently scarred.

Hinckley
Buzzard Sunday

Way back in 1818, Hinckley residents organized a hunt that still affects this small community. It was Christmas Eve, and everyone was looking for some fancy vittles for the big day. So about 600 men and boys encircled the township and moved inward and systematically slaughtered everything that moved, including 300 deer, 17 wolves, and 21 bears. As you can imagine, there were more leftovers than usual, and the smell of rotting carrion attracted a colony of buzzards—turkey vultures, actually—that set up a roost in what is today the Hinckley Reservoir Metropark.

The current 75-buzzard colony migrates between Ohio and Florida, always returning on March 15 (or so they say). In 1957, after hundreds of birdwatchers showed up for the birds' return, somebody got the bright idea to turn it into a fundraising event. On the first Sunday following March 15 each year the community hosts a pancake breakfast and celebration. Vendors hawk T-shirts and a Buzzard Queen is crowned. As you might expect, it is not entirely a beauty contest. To win, contestants need not have a hooked beak or eat dead animals, but it couldn't hurt. All this fun is a great distraction for the birds' often less-than-punctual arrival at Whipp's Ledge.

Whipp's Ledge, Hinckley Reservoir Metropark, Hinckley, OH 44233

Contact: Hinckley Chamber of Commerce, PO Box 354, Hinckley, OH 44233

(330) 278-2066

Hours: First Sunday after March 15

Cost: Free

www.hinckleytwp.org/buzzardday.html

Directions: Between Ledge Rd. and Bellus Rd. on State Rd.

Hiram
SSSSH

What, you ask, is SSSSH? It's the Secret Society of Serendipitous Service for Hal, formed to honor the memory of Hal Reichle, an Army helicopter pilot who died in 1991 during Operation Desert Storm. Reichle was known around Hiram as an anonymous do-gooder, a man who would help out neighbors and strangers alike with simple acts of kindness, then deny it.

Groceries would appear on a struggling family's front porch. An elderly person's rundown garage would get a fresh coat of paint in the middle of the night. A bank would inexplicably change a used-car loan application from Denied to Accepted. Locals called these mysterious events "Reichles," but Hal would only respond with a "Who, me?" deadpan.

Today, SSSSH continues the tight-lipped tradition in northeast Ohio. Members pay no dues and never meet. There is not even a membership list. If anyone pulls a Reichle, he or she describes the act in a letter and sends it to Reichle's old buddy Roger Cram, who publishes it in a periodic newsletter documenting the deeds. But if the letter comes with a signature or return address, Cram crams it into the trash—Hal wouldn't have taken credit, so why should anyone else? That's why the group is called *SSSSH*.

So if you find yourself near Hiram, why not pull a Reichle of your own . . . on a complete stranger. Or better yet, pull a Reichle wherever you happen to find yourself.

Somewhere in Town, Hiram, OH 44234

No phone

Hours: Any time

Cost: Free

Directions: Nobody will say.

HURON

Huron calls itself the National Live Capture and Control Center for the Lake Erie Monster, sometimes called Lake Erie Larry, or South Bay Bessie. A local "scientist" claims that there are approximately 125 Loch Ness–type creatures in the lake, each about 35 feet long.

KINSMAN

Lawyer **Clarence Darrow** was born on April 18, 1857, in the octagonal house just north of the town square in Kinsman, where Routes 5 and 7 meet.

Jefferson
Prams

Do baby buggies really have rubber bumpers? If anyone knows the answer to that question it's Judith Kaminski or Janet Pallo, twin sisters and curator/owners of America's only museum dedicated to baby carriages. Their collection fills the building's nine rooms, and includes the baby buggy from *Gone With the Wind*, an 1870 Wakefield rattan twin carriage, a 200-year-old high chair, and a gondola carriage from the 1880s, to name just a few. Because it can be rather costly to keep babies on staff to demonstrate the perambulators, dolls have had to suffice. In fact, even if you're not into baby buggies, there are more than enough dolls to keep you occupied.

The Victorian Perambulator Museum of Jefferson, 26 E. Cedar St., Jefferson, OH 44047
(440) 576-9588

Hours: September–May, Saturday 11 A.M.–5 P.M.; June–August, Wednesday and
Saturday 11 A.M.–5 P.M.

Cost: Adults $3, Kids $2.50

Directions: One block east of Rte. 46. (Chestnut St.), one block north of Rte. 407
(Mulberry St.).

LORAIN
On June 28, 1924, a tornado killed 78 Lorain residents and injured 1,200 more.

Author **Toni Morrison** was born Chloe Anthony Wofford in Lorain on February 18, 1931.

LOUDONVILLE
Many Loudonville residents report seeing a vision of New Jerusalem on March 12, 1890, just outside of town. Others claim it was a mirage of Sandusky, which is some 60 miles away.

Now that you can hear, we have to tell you: that hat looks ridiculous.

Kent

Hearing Aid Museum

What's that you say? Never heard of the Hearing Aid Museum? Perhaps you ought to pick up a hearing aid yourself.

The Kenneth W. Berger Hearing Aid Museum and Archives lines two long walls of a corridor in Kent State's Music and Speech Building. The museum contains everything from low-tech ear trumpets to state-of-the-art implants. It's probably not surprising that hearing aids have become less cumbersome over the years, but it is interesting to see just how many different strategies have been used to assist the hearing impaired. They've got devices that were hidden in eyeglasses, hats, and vest pockets, as well as instruments used by doctors to test their patients' hearing.

The museum has 3,000+ artifacts on display, but that number keeps growing. The hallway isn't getting any longer, though, so the devices are starting to pile up. You might want to see them before the museum does some housecleaning.

Kenneth W. Berger Hearing Aid Museum and Archives, Music and Speech Building, Kent State University, Kent, OH 44242

(330) 672-2672

Hours: Monday–Friday 8 A.M.–5 P.M.

Cost: Free

http://dept.kent.edu/hearingaidmuseum/

Directions: On the north campus, south of Main St. and east of Midway.

Kent State

When the Ohio National Guard opened fire on students at Kent State on May 4, 1970, it confirmed suspicions that the country was slipping further into a police state under President Richard Nixon. The cover-up that followed made it even clearer.

How did it happen? It actually started five days earlier on the other side of the globe. Nixon announced on April 30 that he was expanding the war in Southeast Asia into Cambodia. Activists across the nation mobilized, even at Kent State, a college once dismissed as "a hotbed of student rest." On Friday, May 1, a riot broke out in downtown Kent along North Water Street; 50 shop windows were broken and a jewelry store was looted. Though it had less to do with Vietnam and more to do with excessive alcohol consumption (mostly by nonstudents), Governor Rhodes called up the Ohio National Guard and ordered them onto the campus.

On Saturday, a campus demonstration ended when several students burned the ROTC building (on the western side of the Commons) to the ground. An athletic department shed was also torched. Curiously, though the buildings started burning around 8 P.M., police did not arrive until 9:15 P.M. When it was later learned during the investigation that police had dozens of undercover officers *at the scene*, pretending to be students, many suspected the police may have been partially responsible for encouraging a melee that was used to justify the guard's presence.

The campus was relatively calm on Sunday, and on Monday, May 4, classes resumed. Around lunchtime there was a confrontation between student demonstrators and the guardsmen on the Commons. Pelted by rocks, the soldiers retreated up Blanket Hill to a high point just in front of Taylor Hall. From that vantage point, they opened fire at 12:24 P.M., killing students Allison Krause, Jeffrey Miller, William Schroeder, and Sandra Scheuer, and wounding nine others.

The 28 shooters later testified that they believed their lives were in immediate danger, but the FBI (under the direction of Herbert "No-Friend-of-Hippies" Hoover) later discovered that the guardsmen had gotten together after the shootings to agree on that story. Though no evidence was ever found that any student even got within 60 yards of the guardsmen, no guardsmen were indicted by the state grand jury investigating the case. The grand jury did, however, indict 25 people linked to the campus demonstrations. Apparently they sided with special prosecutor Seabury Ford, chairman of the Portage County GOP and appointee of Governor Rhodes, who let his feelings be known: "The National Guard should have shot all the troublemakers." Welcome to Amerika.

Several National Guardsmen were acquitted of wrongdoing in a 1974 federal trial. In 1979, the victims' families received a whopping $15,000 each for their dead children. When the university announced it was going to build a gym on the killing site in the 1980s, the plan sparked protest and the blueprints were scrapped. A monument was erected instead, dedicated on May 4, 1990, the twentieth anniversary of the murders. A candlelight vigil is held there on May 4 each year.

Kent State University, Kent, OH 44242

(330) 672-3000

Hours: Always visible

Cost: Free

www.kent.edu/history/may4_1970.cfm or www.May4.net

Directions: On the north campus, near the parking lot to the east of Taylor Hall.

Calling all nerds . . . come in, nerds . . .

X-Wing Fighter

Whaaaat? Did Luke Skywalker stop by for a bite? Don't be silly. Luke would never park his X-Wing Fighter in a handicapped zone. Darth Vader, definitely, but never Luke. This true-to-"life" spaceship is actually not a relic from long ago, nor from a galaxy far, far away; the menu at Mike's Place explains where it came from: Elvis parked it here. It's never been moved because the King is currently working as this restaurant's cook.

And what a menu Elvis has dreamed up! Try the foot-long hot dog, the Dirk Diggler—"You WILL need two hands for this 12-incher"—or the Twin Peaks—"Not one teeny tiny bosom but two voluptuous chicken breasts." Elvis was never known for his subtlety.

Owner Mike Kotensky runs this restaurant with the same bang-you-over-the-head panache. A sign warns parents that Mike's is a family-friendly place, within limits: "Thou shalt control thy children, or we will provide duct tape." A few other restaurants should adopt this policy.

Mike's Place, 1700 Water St., Kent, OH 44240

(330) 673-6501

Hours: Always visible

Cost: Free; Meals $4–$12

Directions: On the southwest corner of Rte. 43 (Water St.) and Rte. 261.

Lucas
Bogart and Bacall's Wedding Site

When Humphrey Bogart (age 45) married Lauren Bacall (age 19) on May 21, 1945, it wasn't in some fancy-schmancy Hollywood ceremony. No, it was right here, in the heart of the Midwest, at Malabar Farm. You can still see their nuptial beds. That's right, their honeymoon suite contains two four-poster twin beds. It is probably safe to assume that they used only one, though it is considered tacky to ask the tour guide which one. The beds did, however, have wheels on them—so the possibilities were endless.

Why did the pair tie the knot at Malabar Farm? Author Louis Bromfield, the farm's owner, had cultivated an impressive list of Hollywood friends who, when they came to Ohio, usually stopped by for a visit. James Cagney, Dorothy Lamour, Tyrone Power, William Powell, Shirley Temple, Carole Lombard, Hedy Lamarr, and Errol Flynn were among those who spent a night or two here. Bromfield didn't believe in coddling his superstar guests; he lived by the motto, "Them that works, eats!" Cagney was told to go sell apples at the local stand, and he did.

Malabar Farm State Park, 4050 Bromfield Rd., Lucas, OH 44843

(419) 892-2784

Hours: September–April, Tuesday–Saturday 11 A.M.–4 P.M., Sunday Noon–4 P.M.; May, Tuesday–Saturday 10 A.M.–5 P.M., Sunday Noon–5 P.M.; June–August, daily 9 A.M.–5 P.M.

Cost: Adults $4, Seniors $3.60, Kids (6–18) $2

www.malabarfarm.org

Directions: Moffet St. (Rte. 330) south to Pleasant Valley Rd. (Rte. 303), east to Bromfield Rd., turn south.

ANOTHER HOLLYWOOD DUO TIES THE KNOT

Actors **George Burns** and **Gracie Allen** were married in Cleveland on January 7, 1926, where they were appearing at Play House Square. Their marriage license can be seen at the Cuyahoga County Archives (2905 Franklin Avenue, Cleveland, (216) 443-7250).

Mansfield
Living Bible Museum

The last few decades have been pretty hard on this nation's wax museums. Those once-plentiful tourist traps have melted away to make way for a new generation of attractions—bungee jump towers and water parks—and isn't that a shame?

Well, the average tourist's loss is the Living Bible Museum's gain . . . and yours if you visit. Since the 1970s, under the direction of Pastor Richard Diamond, the museum has been snagging up waxy celebrity mannequins and recasting them to fit into dioramas of the Bible's best-known stories—add a beard here or a head scarf there and nobody would suspect that those guys on the crosses were once *Welcome Back, Kotter* sweathogs. Well, almost nobody would suspect. More than 175 figures are now scattered through 41 scenes divided among four different tours.

First up, just as in the Bible, is the **Miracles of the Old Testament Tour**. It starts predictably with Adam and Eve frolicking in the Garden of Eden, each covered quite modestly by a bushel of fig leaves. Satan appears as a serpent, his red eyes flashing as he speaks, and everything goes downhill for humanity from then on. Cain and Abel (who looks like a recycled John Paul II) make sacrifices to the Almighty, but the narrator cuts away before the jealous Cain clubs the Pope. Elizabeth Taylor, as Pharaoh's daughter, rescues Moses from his basket when it snags in the reeds along the Nile. Later, Moses brings the Ten Commandments down from the mountain; each rule lights up in sequence on the high-tech tablet as the narrator translates from the original Hebrew.

Next up, a slimy Jonah sprints away from the jaws of a large whale that has just regurgitated him onto a beach. King Nebuchadnezzar throws Shadrach, Meshach, and Abed-nego into a blazing oven, but when Jesus appears (a little prematurely, I might add), to protect them from the fire, the king has a change of heart. Around the corner David battles Goliath who, though he is a giant, has a very tiny head. Sampson is betrayed by Karen Carpenter, er, *Delilah*. Lot's wife turns to a pillar of salt while looking back on Sodom and Gomorrah. Noah loads kangaroos, turtles, pheasants, and squirrels into the ark. Job, covered in festering sores, wallows around in an enormous pile of poop. This stuff is *cool*!

The tour ends just as *Raiders of the Lost Ark* does, only in this tale it isn't Indiana Jones who appears from behind the curtains, but Jesus Christ. A hint of things to come?

Cost: Adults $4.50, Seniors (50+) $4.25, Kids (6–18) $3.50, Families $20

Time: 1 hour

That's right, the New Testament is the focus of the next tour: **The Life of Christ**. It starts when the Angel Gabriel appears to Mary, and before you know it John the Baptist is dunking the Savior in the river. Where did the manger and the shepherds and the Magi go? Who knows! Soon, Jesus is sitting on a rock under a tree while the children of the world gather round; there's a little Dutch girl, a young boy in a Tyrol hat, a geisha, a young Donna Summer, and an evil-eyed blond child of an indeterminate gender.

By the time Jesus gets to Gethsemane, things start to get strange. The garden is bathed in heavy-metal black light. When Roman guards whip Jesus, Ann-Margret cheers them on. Blue lightning flashes as Jesus dies on the cross. Sigfried waits outside Christ's tomb, but when the rock rolls back, neither Jesus nor a white tiger are seen anywhere. Take that, Vegas!

Ah, but Jesus *does* appear . . . in the very next diorama . . . blasting off to heaven in a Space Shuttle–like plume of smoke. Of course, not everyone goes to heaven. Around the corner you find Jesus again, this time sitting on a massive throne, streets of gold to his right and the fiery pits of hell to his left. Take your pick!

Cost: Adults $4.50, Seniors (50+) $4.25, Kids (6–18) $3.50, Families $20

Time: 1 hour

Compared to the two tours that precede it, the **Christian Martyrs** is somewhat anticlimactic. The scenes are all fairly tame, so you're left to imagine folks being burned at the stake, fed to the lions, and having their tongues ripped out with tongs. Narrators supply you with the gory details, though.

Cost: Adults $3.75, Seniors (50+) $3.50, Kids (6–18) $2.75, Families $10

Time: 30 minutes

The Reformers is similarly tame, but they do show John Huss tied to a post, moments away from being burned at the stake in 1415. You're also told the story of John Wycliffe whose body was incinerated in 1428 and his ashes scattered in a river, even though he had been dead since 1384. Finally, the Pilgrims bring Christianity to the New World while the Indians wait in the wings, anticipating trouble.

Cost: Adults $3.75, Seniors (50+) $3.50, Kids (6–18) $2.75, Families $10

Time: 30 minutes

Last, but certainly not least, the Living Bible Museum has a room filled with votive folk art, an Old World tradition where parishioners would bring precious heirlooms—jewelry, silverware, and such—that an artist would glue together to form an elaborate religious sculpture. If you ever wanted to see Jesus walk on an ocean of jewels, this is the place.

Diamond Hill Cathedral, 500 Tingley Ave., Mansfield, OH 44905

(800) 222-0139 or (419) 524-0139

E-mail: lbmjulia@richnet.net

Hours: April–December, Monday–Friday 10 A.M.–5 P.M., Saturday 10 A.M.–7 P.M., Sunday 3–7 P.M.; January–March, Saturday 10 A.M.–7 P.M., Sunday 3–7 P.M.

Cost: All four tours, Adults $15.50, Seniors (50+) $14.50, Kids (6–18) $11.50, Families $55

www.livingbiblemuseum.org

Directions: North of Rte. 30 on Rte. 545 (Olivesburg Rd.), turn right before the top of the hill onto Tingley Ave.

MADISON

A triangular UFO hovered over a Madison home for 30 minutes on November 15, 1957. The woman who witnessed the event broke out in a severe rash the next day.

MANSFIELD

Actor **Luke Perry** was born Coy Luther Perry III in Mansfield on October 11, 1966. He changed his name after seeing *Cool Hand Luke* when he was five.

Quack now or forever hold your bills.
Photo by author, courtesy of Mansfield Memorial Museum

Mansfield Memorial Museum

It's rare to find a real *museum* museum—a museum the way museums used to be: cluttered, weird, and without any apparent theme. The Mansfield Memorial Museum fits that mold; little has changed since it first opened more than a century ago. The building was constructed in 1889 and served as a meeting hall for Civil War veterans. Soon, a small zoo moved into the third floor. As members of this menagerie died, Edward Wilkinson (the museum's original director) stuffed the critters and added them to his growing collection of goodies. In addition to the animals, he had a scrap of wood from Admiral Perry's flagship *Lawrence* (see page 34), two trees planted by Johnny Appleseed, a post from California's Fort Sutter where gold was first discovered in 1849, a cutting from the 1858

Transatlantic Cable, and a sharpened pike used by John Brown during his raid at Harpers Ferry on October 16, 1859. All of it is still here.

As wonderful as all that historic stuff is, the real reason this place is worth visiting is the display cases filled with anthropomorphic critters. Wilkinson believed in elevating the cultural level of the lower species he stuffed. His first creation, a tea party for ducks and chickens, was completed in 1877. He then went on to organize Gideon's Band, a musical revue featuring squirrels and rats with a muskrat on bass and a frog at the piano. In the same display case, Doctor J. W. Craig, a large drake, presides over a duck wedding. Apparently Victorian ducks tied the knot before moving in together, unlike today's shacked-up quackers.

34 Park Ave. W., Mansfield, OH 44902

(419) 525-2491

Hours: June–August, Wednesday 1–4 P.M., Saturday–Sunday 1–5 P.M.; September–May, Saturday–Sunday 1–4 P.M.

Cost: Free; donations accepted

www.mansfieldtourism.org/pages/attract.html

Directions: One block west of Rte. 42 (Main St.) on Rte. 430 (Park Ave.)

MANSFIELD

A glowing, armless creature was spotted around Charles Mill Lake near Mansfield from 1959 to 1963.

MASSILLON

You are allowed by law to kill your neighbor's chickens in Massillon, but only if you get the permission of the majority of residents who live within 500 feet of the offending birds.

MOUNT VERNON

Mount Vernon dentist William Semple was awarded the world's first patent for chewing gum in 1869. He called his invention red rubber.

The Shawshank Redemption Prison

If you really have to go to prison, consider this place. That's what Tim Robbins did. And Morgan Freeman. And Sylvester Stalone and Kurt Russell. Of course, they didn't have to worry about getting stuck with a shiv in the exercise yard—they were filming movies! That's right, the Mansfield Reformatory is not an active prison, at least not as far as inmates are concerned.

This elaborate, spooky structure was built in 1886 to house juveniles; it was later converted to an adult facility. It contains the world's largest free-standing steel cellblock, with 550 cells spread out over six tiers and twelve ranges. It was closed in 1990 because of reports of inhumane conditions . . . and because a new prison had been finished just down the road.

A nonprofit group bought the abandoned structure in 1996 for one dollar. The group advertised the place as a perfect film set (since it already had been used successfully for several previous productions), and Hollywood took them up on the offer more than once. Mansfield doubled as Russia's Jurgen Prochnow Prison in *Air Force One*, and appeared in *Tango and Cash* and *Men in Black*. Lesser known films and TV specials have also been shot here, such as the hard-to-find 28-minute performance of a contemporary dance troupe from Dayton titled *Tiny Sisters in the Enchanted Land*.

But perhaps the best use of the old clink was in the 1994 movie *The Shawshank Redemption*, in which the Mansfield Reformatory passed for a Maine prison. The cells seen in the movie, however, were actually built from scratch in an old warehouse downtown; this was because Mansfield's cells are arranged back to back, not facing one another. This is just one of the zillions of interesting tidbits you'll learn on the informative Hollywood Tour. Guides also offer other themed tours, such as the Tower Tour, the Easy Time Tour, the Dungeon Tour, the Ghost Tour, and, each October, the Halloween Tour.

The Mansfield Reformatory, PO Box 8625, 100 Reformatory Rd., Mansfield, OH 44906

(419) 522-2644

E-mail: info@mprs.org

Tour hours: June–August, Tuesday–Friday 2 P.M. only; May–September, Sunday 1–
 4 P.M.; call ahead for special tours

Cost: Adults $8, Kids (7–17) $6

www.mrps.org

Directions: Just north of Rte. 30 on Rte. 545 (Olivesburg Rd.).

Milan
Get It in a Caboose

Need to add a little spice to your love life? How about doing it in a caboose? No, not in *your* caboose—not that there's anything wrong with that—*a* caboose. Remember, those fun little railcars that you used to see at the end of a train? The Erie Metroparks have converted one of them, a boxcar, and a train station into a train-themed bed and breakfast. The suites are more luxurious than they were when they were in service, so don't think you'll be bunking on straw in some hobo hotel. But if you choose to stay in the caboose, be forewarned that the bathroom is in the train station, not in your suite.

The Coupling Reserve, Mudbrook Rd., Milan, OH 44846

Contact: Erie Metroparks, 3910 E. Perkins Ave., Huron, OH 44839

(419) 625-7783

Hours: By appointment

Cost: $80–$110/night

www.erie-county-ohio.net/metro

Directions: North on Rte. 250 (Milan Rd.), then turn northeast onto Rte. 13
   (Mudbrook Rd.).

Thomas Alva Edison's Birthplace

Born in this brick home on February 11, 1847, Thomas Alva Edison spent his first seven years getting into trouble around Milan for his inquisitive nature . . . or so the stories go. One tale has him sitting on eggs behind the barn, trying to hatch a nest of baby chicks. Another has him burning down the same barn while exploring the properties of fire. (That anecdote is true; as punishment, young Thomas was beaten by his father in the town square in front of all the boys from his school.) You'll hear these tales and more from your tour guide.

One of the best features of the tour, however, is seeing the museum's collection of little-known Edison inventions, and hearing about others: the chalk telephone receiver, the talking doll, the folding pole ladder, the electric pen, wax paper, the mimeograph machine, and a device being developed for talking with the dead. (If you're out there, Thomas Edison, please give the museum a ring.) When Edison passed away in 1931, his obituary in the *New York Times* ran four and a half pages. It was the only way to do justice to his accomplishments, which included 1,093 U.S. patents, more than any inventor before or since.

Edison's birthplace is one of the few important structures from the inventor's life that has not ended up in Henry Ford's Greenfield Village. That in itself is an accomplishment. Ford and Edison visited this home in 1923, only to find it still being lit by candles.

9 N. Edison Dr., PO Box 451, Milan, OH 44846

(419) 499-2135

Cost: Adults $5, Seniors $4, Kids (6–12) $2

Hours: February–March and December, Wednesday–Sunday 1–4 P.M.; April–May and September–October, Tuesday–Sunday 1–5 P.M.; June–August, Tuesday–Saturday 10 A.M.–5 P.M., Sunday 1–5 P.M.

www.tomedison.org

Directions: Two blocks east of Rte. 601 (Main St.) on Rte. 53 (Edison Dr.).

MOUNT VERNON

Yankee songster **Daniel Decatur Emmett** was born on S. Main Street in Mount Vernon in 1815, and went on to write the 1859 song "I Wish I Was in Dixie."

NEW RUMLEY

General George Armstrong Custer was born near New Rumley on December 3, 1839, on his parents' homestead (www.ohiohistory.org/places/custer).

NILES

Niles resident Harry M. Stevens introduced the world's first hot dog bun at the Louisiana Purchase Exposition of 1904. He also is credited with coming up with the name "hot dog" after seeing a cartoon of a dachshund in the *New York Daily Times*. Stevens is buried in Niles Union Cemetery.

OBERLIN

Oberlin College was the first in the nation to go coed in 1837, admitting four female students. They were not entirely liberated, however; the women were required to clean the rooms of male students for 2¾¢/hour.

Is it gourd, or is it art?

Mount Giliad
Ohio Gourd Show

On the first full weekend in October each year, the folks of Mount Giliad turn into a single-minded bunch: they go gaga for gourds. They're cuckoo for curcabits. It's the annual Ohio Gourd Show—the largest festival of its type in the world!

So are they only interested in exhibiting their gardens' recent crops? Hardly! There are seminars on growing gourds, drying gourds, decorating with gourds, cooking with gourds, building birdhouses with gourds, and making gourd-themed floral arrangements, you name it.

Each year the Ohio Gourd Society chooses a different theme for its popular Gourd Art Contest, where participants paint, modify, and decorate their gourds to look like cartoon animals, patriotic displays, or dolls. Each year there's also a Gourd Hat Contest, an art show in its own right, which is as much about performance as it is about design. And when you've just about gorged on gourds, pull up a seat at the World Festival of Gourd Music. But be sure to bring your maracas so you can shake, shake, shake along.

Contact: Ohio Gourd Society, PO Box 274, Mount Giliad, OH 43338

(419) 362-6446

Hours: First full weekend in October

Cost: Adults $4

www.orgs.muohio.edu/ohiogourdsociety/

Directions: At the Morrow County Fairgrounds on Rte. 42, at the south end of town.

Mount Vernon and Amity
Paul Lynde's Hometown and Grave

Though he seemed too cynical, quick-witted, and flamboyant to be from Middle America, Paul Lynde was indeed born in the most typical Ohio small town imaginable, Mount Vernon, on June 13, 1926. The son of Hoy, the Knox County sheriff and later butcher, and Sylvia, a woman who Lynde said "fried everything, even the coffee," young Paul long dreamed of a more glamorous life away from his five siblings. At six years old, he would sit on the steps of the largest mansion in town and wave to passersby, hoping they'd think he lived there. (At the time, the family lived in the sheriff's residence over the local jail.) He also put his baby brother Johnny in a basket and tried to sell him to the nuns at the hospital. They weren't buying.

At the age of 10, Paul was bedridden for a year with peritonitis. He was nearly paralyzed, and his mother entertained him with food. By his eleventh birthday he was 100 pounds heavier. Lynde battled with weight issues most of his life, but in a sense, his teenage obesity was a blessing

A long way from the center square.

in disguise; to combat the grief he received from other kids he sharpened his witty claws.

In high school Lynde was known to classmates as "chicken plucker" because he helped dress and sell poultry with his father. After he graduated from Mount Vernon High School in 1944, he headed off to Northwestern to major in drama. The quote he chose to accompany his senior picture in the Mount Vernon yearbook was, "A well-governed appetite is a great part of liberty."

Teenage Home, 714 Coshocton Ave., Mount Vernon, OH 43050

Private phone

Hours: Always visible; view from street

Cost: Free

http://home.columbus.rr.com/paullynde/

Directions: Just east of Center St. on Rte. 36 (Coshocton Ave.) on the northeast side of town.

The trouble with Paul Lynde, however, was not sufficiently governing his appetites, in particular, his appetite for booze. If his friends remember him for anything, it was that you didn't want to be around him if he was drunk and angry, two conditions that often went hand-in-hand. But if you stayed on his good side, he was always the life of the party, on and off screen. Looking back at *Hollywood Squares*, he now seems a whole lot gayer than anyone remembers, and though he never discussed his sexual orientation publicly, he did kick the inside of his closet door fairly loudly on national television at a time when it wasn't in to be out.

After he died of a heart attack on January 10, 1982, the coroner discovered Lynde had the hardened arteries of an 85-year-old. His body was cremated and shipped to the Grohe Funeral Home in Mount Vernon. A memorial service was held at St. Paul Episcopal Church (100 E. High Street) and, once the ground thawed, his ashes were taken to nearby Amity and buried in the family plot.

Amity Cemetery, Gilchrist Rd., Amity, OH 43050

No phone

Hours: Always visible

Cost: Free

Directions: Between Wooster Rd. (Rte. 3) and Danville-Amity Rd. (Rte. 14) on Gilchrist Rd.

North Benton
God Works in Slithery Ways

Correct me if I'm wrong, but isn't it the *Devil* who hangs out with the snakes? No matter, many in North Benton see snakes as nothing less than a sign from the Almighty. It all started in the early 1900s when aging local agnostic Chester Bedell started making plans for his eventual burial. He commissioned a bronze statue of a man crushing a scroll with "Superstition" written upon it, while the figure uplifts another uncrumpled scroll that reads "Universal Mental Liberty."

In 1908, the 82-year-old Bedell was on his deathbed and in a final defiant gesture he challenged God. "If you exist, fill my grave with snakes," he demanded. And if you believe the locals, God did. Gravediggers had trouble opening the hole because there were so many snakes around. After Bedell was planted, snakes continued to rise from the ground around his body. It became a Sunday tradition in North Benton to head over to the cemetery after church and look for vipers, proof of God's existence. They appeared most often on October 30, the anniversary of Bedell's death.

Feel free to pay a visit, but don't say you weren't warned.

12th St., North Benton, OH 44449

No phone

Hours: Always visible; best on October 30

Cost: Free

Directions: On Rte. 23 (12th St.).

North Canton
Chocolate Hall of Fame

Have you always longed to tour a chocolate factory, but never found that Golden Ticket? Well, you don't need one—just come on by Harry London Candies, where three bucks will buy you a 45-minute tour. This confectioner has been at it since 1922, and currently produces more than 500 varieties of bon-bons, truffles, and candy whatnots. The best part about its factory tour is the free samples, which vary from day to day, depending on what they're cooking up. The Chocolate Hall of Fame is also part of the tour, a hall of plaques where the world's Willy Wonkas get their proper due.

Harry London Candies, 5353 Lauby Rd., North Canton, OH 44720

(800) 321-0444 or (330) 494-0833

Hours: Store, Monday–Saturday 9 A.M.–6 P.M., Sunday Noon–5 P.M.; Tours,
   Monday–Saturday 9 A.M.–4 P.M.

Cost: Store, Free; Tours, Adults $3, Kids (3–18) $2

www.harrylondon.com

Directions: Take the Akron–Canton Airport Exit from I-77, head west to Lauby Rd.,
   turn north, and the factory is ahead on the right.

Hoover Historical Center

If this place didn't suck so much, believe me, cleaning your house would suck a whole lot more. It is here, in North Canton, that the modern vacuum cleaner was born in 1907. Janitor James Murray Spangler was sick and tired of the heavy machine his employer gave him to clean the rugs, so Spangler created his own out of a soapbox, a pillowcase, a fan motor, a broom handle, and a roller brush—a regular MacGyver!

A year later Spangler had a patent and began selling the Electric Suction Sweeper door-to-door. One of his first customers was his cousin, Susan Hoover, who was married to saddlemaker William H. "Boss" Hoover. The businessman knew Spangler had a good thing going, and convinced the janitor to sell him the patent. In short order, Hoover was manufacturing the Model O, the first commercially available vacuum, which weighed a mere 40 pounds.

You'll see the Model O and most of the Hoover Company's later models at this museum located at the Hoover family homestead. They've also got plenty of clunky pre-electric models made by other companies to show why Spangler's invention was so revolutionary. The only break in the history of these sucking machines came during World War II when Hoover's factories were used for manufacturing munitions.

Hoover Park, 1875 E. Maple (formerly Easton) St., North Canton, OH 44720

(330) 499-0287

Hours: Tuesday–Sunday 1–5 P.M.

Cost: Free

www.hoovercompany.org

Directions: Just west of Rte. 43 (Market Ave.), across the street from Walsh College.

Orrville
Pencils!

Don't even think that coffee mug full of pencils from places you've visited constitutes an impressive collection. At Orrville's Toy and Hobby Museum, how many pencils would you guess they have on display? Maybe 500? How about 1,000? Try 10,000—and they're adding more each year. Most of the collection serves the same basic purpose—to write with—but these babies are never used for that common task. Now they've become an archive of businesses, attractions, and individuals who have felt the need to have their names emblazoned on an office product.

The museum also has a collection of 4,500+ toy trucks, and more than 1,000 unique salt-and-pepper shakers. But let's face it: it's the pencils that are worth the price of admission.

Toy and Hobby Museum, 531 W. Smithville Rd., Orrville, OH 44667

(330) 683-TOYS

Hours: Monday and Friday 6:30–9 P.M., Saturday Noon–6 P.M., or by appointment

Cost: Adults $3, Kids $3, Families $10

Directions: Six blocks north of Rte. 502 (High St.), one block west of Rte. 57 (Main St.).

Sandusky
The Merry-Go-Round Museum

This place bills itself as the only museum in America with a working merry-go-round inside, but wouldn't you sort of expect that, considering the name? Housed in the city's former post office (shaped like a horseshoe, oddly enough), the Merry-Go-Round Museum isn't a musty repository of a dead art form. It's an active restoration facility. Figure collectors are encouraged to send their pieces in for repairs, if in exchange for the work they agree to let their carvings be put on display for two years. Not a bad deal.

Those familiar with carousel carving know the works of master craftsmen such as Gustav Dentzel, Charles Loof, Daniel Muller, M. C. Illions, and Allen Herschell. But the museum also has examples of work done by the hired hands, such as onetime carousel sander Dwight D. Eisenhower. What ever happened to him?

W. Washington and Jackson Sts., PO Box 718, Sandusky, OH 44870

(419) 626-6111

Hours: January–February, Saturday–Sunday Noon–5 P.M.; March–May and September–
December, Wednesday–Saturday 11 A.M.–5 P.M., Sunday Noon–5 P.M.; June–August,
Monday–Saturday 10 A.M.–5 P.M., Sunday Noon–5 P.M.

Cost: Adults $4; Seniors $3, Kids (4–14) $2

www.merrygoroundmuseum.org

Directions: Downtown on Rte. 6 (Washington St.), one block west of (Rte. 4)
Columbus Ave.

RAVENNA

A Ravenna man was sprayed with a clear liquid by a UFO on July 24, 1999. When he went to Robinson Memorial Hospital, the FBI showed up and reportedly confiscated his clothing.

SANDUSKY

Ten Sandusky cops were once busted for stealing Girl Scout Cookies instead of distributing them.

Two seven footers six feet under.

Seville
The Seville Giants

For a variety of ridiculous reasons, many men find it difficult to marry a woman who is taller than they are. So you can imagine how 7-foot, 8.5-inch Martin Van Buren Bates must have felt when he started dating

Anna Swan—she was almost three inches taller than him!

Bates had been born in Whitesburg, Kentucky, on November 9, 1845. The Kentucky River Giant (as he was later known) eventually tipped the scales at 478 pounds. Not one to let his size get in his way, Bates enlisted as a private in the Fifth Kentucky Infantry during the Civil War, then achieved the rank of captain after transferring to the cavalry—that poor, poor horse! After the war he signed on with a sideshow that eventually set sail for Europe.

Swan was born in New Annan, Nova Scotia, in 1848. Comparatively speaking, she was a svelt 413 pounds, and was billed as the Giantess of Nova Scotia. She spent her early years as a living attraction in P. T. Barnum's American Museum in New York, but after it burned to the ground in 1868, she embarked on her own tour. Swan met Bates in London where they performed sketches for Queen Victoria. They fell in love and were married at St. Martin's-in-the-Fields on June 17, 1871.

Upon returning to the United States they settled in Seville and purchased a farm in 1873. They had an 18-room mansion built that accommodated their height (it was torn down in 1948). They bought two Clydesdales to pull their oversize carriage, and they became active members in the Seville Baptist Church, which altered a row of pews to allow them to attend services in comfort.

On January 18, 1879, Anna gave birth to a 30-inch, 23.75-pound baby boy after a long, difficult labor. The baby died after only 11 hours, and was buried in Mound Hill Cemetery. Anna joined him a decade later on August 5, 1889. Her funeral was delayed because a Cleveland casket maker didn't believe the measurement he'd been wired, so he shipped a standard coffin. Bates remarried and lived another 20 years. When he died on January 14, 1919, he was buried beside Anna and Baby Bates. You can still visit their oversized plots.

Mound Hill Cemetery, E. Main St., Seville, OH 44273

No phone

Hours: Dawn–Dusk

Cost: Free

www.villageofseville.com/history.html

Directions: Two blocks east of Rte. 3 (Milton St.) on Main St.

The Seville Historical Society has some of the couple's clothing and personal artifacts, plus a full-size photo of the pair you can pose beside.

Seville Historical Society, 70 W. Main St., Seville, OH 44273

(330) 769-4056

Hours: First Sunday of the month, Noon–5 P.M.

Cost: Free

www.villageofseville.com/museum.html

Directions: Just east of Rte. 3 (Milton St.) on Main St.

The John Smart House in Medina also has Bates memorabilia, including the captain's boots and helmet.

John Smart House, Medina County Historical Society, 206 N. Elmwood, Medina, OH 44258

(330) 722-1341

E-mail: info@medinahistorical.com

Hours: March–December, Tuesday and Thursday 9:30 A.M.–5:30 P.M.

Cost: Free

www.medinahistorical.com

Directions: One block north of Rte. 57 (Liberty St.), one block west of Rte. 42 (Court St.).

STEUBENVILLE

Actress/porn star **Tracy Lords** was born Nora Louise Kuzma in Steubenville on May 7, 1968.

Dean Martin was born Dino Crocetti in Steubenville on June 17, 1917.

STRUTHERS

Struthers is the only major town in the United States without a cemetery.

Steubenville
Creegan Company

Anyone who's seen *Westworld* or *The Terminator* knows the danger robots pose to humans. But anyone who worries about robots based on a Hollywood movie is, well, a little nuts. A tour through the Creegan Company's factory will allay any fears you may have, because this much will be plainly obvious: robots are drop-dead *adorable!* Creegan's has been designing and manufacturing animated characters since 1959—characters such as Beary Bear, Strawberry Bunny, Plentiful Penguin, and the Gamuffins, and not one of them has ever attacked a human being . . . or at least not that anyone knows of.

In a remarkable display of corporate openness, Creegan's willingly shows tourists and customers how they turn a pile of circuits, motors, and eye patches into a swashbuckling robot pirate crew, or any one of a hundred other designs. The company even supplies custom-made animatrons to the likes of Disney World, Sea World, Hershey's Chocolate World, and several big-name casinos. It has recently manufactured talking, moving versions of Albert Einstein, King Tut, and Alexander Graham Bell. Creegan's is also pioneering Taxanimation, a copyrighted process of bringing dead critters—bobcats, raccoons, and squirrels—back to robotic life. All the furry fun and none of the mess—they're so cute!

510 Washington St., Steubenville, OH 43952

(740) 283-3708

E-mail: creegans@weir.net

Hours: Monday–Friday 10 A.M.–4 P.M., Saturday (Store only) 10 A.M.–2 P.M.

Cost: Free

www.creegans.com

Directions: Six blocks west of Water St. (Rte. 7) on Washington St. (Rte. 43).

WARREN

Actress **Catherine Bach**, who played Daisy Duke on *The Dukes of Hazzard*, was born Catherine Bachman in Warren on March 1, 1954.

To every cheese, a churn, a churn, a churn.

Sugarcreek
Cheese Museum

Sugarcreek calls itself "America's Switzerland," which means you're going to see plenty of cheese for sale in its flowerbox-covered shops and emporiums. Want to learn how the stuff is made? Then stop on by the Alpine Hills Historical Museum.

The museum contains more than just displays on the region's dairy industry; there are three floors filled with exhibits on Amish culture and local history, as well as demonstrations on quilting, tatting, and other crafts. But cheesemaking has been placed front and center with a re-created 1890 Cheese House. Push the button and hear how milk is transformed into this wonder food. Even if you're lactose intolerant, you'll enjoy learning about the cheesemaking process.

Alpine Hills Historical Museum, 106 W. Main St., PO Box 293, Sugarcreek, OH 44681
(330) 852-4113

Hours: April–June and October–November, Monday–Saturday 10 A.M.–4:30 P.M.;
July–September, Monday–Saturday 9 A.M.–4:30 P.M.

Cost: Free

www.sugarcreekohio.org

Directions: Just west of Broadway on Rte. 47 (Main St.).

Pool shark or pool weasel?
Photo by author, courtesy of Bed & Breakfast Barn

White Fawn Wildlife Display

When you're on vacation, why visit a natural history museum and then spend the night at a motel when, by staying at the Bed & Breakfast Barn, you can do both at the same time? Almost every square inch of this enormous and charming establishment is covered with stuffed North American critters. Don't be upset; none of them were killed just to decorate this place. They were all purchased at estate sales and moved here later.

What's most interesting about the collection, and perhaps a little disturbing, is the kind of taxidermy it's been able to acquire. The strangest mountings are downstairs in a basement collection called the White Fawn Wildlife Display. Sure, you expect to find an albino deer, given the museum's name, but what about those weasels playing pool? (I'm assuming that these weasels did not play pool in their natural environment.) They're just a few of the animals mounted by some creative hunter with a few too many dead animals on his hands.

Bed & Breakfast Barn, 560 Sugarcreek St., PO Box 454, Sugarcreek, OH 44681

(330) 852-2337

Hours: Daily 9 A.M.–7 P.M.

Cost: Adults and Kids $1; Free for guests at the Bed & Breakfast Barn

Directions: Head southeast of town on Main St., turn left on Sugarcreek Rd.

Twinsburg
Twins Festival

Any Willard Scott fan knows this already, but the town of Twinsburg holds a festival for identical twins every August. But what Scott never told you is that it's a little creepy. Most of the pairs wandering around town dress alike, which makes it difficult to figure out which is the Good Twin and which is the Evil Twin. Should a local convenience store ever be robbed during the festival (probably by an Evil Twin), it'll be that much more difficult for law enforcement officials to apprehend a suspect.

Regardless of this hazard, Twinsburg still loves its twins. The town was founded in 1827 by twins Moses and Aaron Wilcox. But not until 1976 did anyone think of organizing a festival in their honor. Today the event typically attracts 3,000+ pairs and a smattering of triplets, quads, and quints. The most popular event is the Double-Take Parade, but the festival also has a Most-Alike Contest and a Least-Alike Contest (in several age categories), and it's all capped off with a Twin Fireworks Display.

Glenn Chamberlin Park, Ravenna Rd., Twinsburg, OH 44087

Contact: Twins Days, PO Box 29, Twinsburg, OH 44087

(330) 425-3652

Hours: First full weekend in August

Cost: Free for twins

www.twinsdays.org

Directions: Head northwest from downtown on Ravenna Rd.; the park is on the left just before Holmes Dr.

Wellington
Spirit of '76 Museum

The image of three Revolutionary soldiers, two pounding drums and the third playing a fife, is well known to most Americans. Few, however, realize that the *Spirit of '76* was painted a century after the War of Independence was fought. Few people, that is, except the citizens of Wellington, Ohio. This is the hometown of Archibald M. Willard, the artist who painted the masterpiece in 1875.

Willard primarily worked as a wagon painter, but he dabbled in serious art. When his patriotic father died in 1875, he decided to honor him with a painting for the nation's upcoming centennial. His creation captured the spirit of the war from the American perspective, and has been reproduced so often it has become, next to the one of George Washington crossing the Delaware, the most recognized image of the war.

The original hangs at Abbot Hall in Marblehead, Massachusetts. Wellington honors its native son with a museum named for the painting, which contains other works from its hometown artist.

201 N. Main St., PO Box 76, Wellington, OH 44090

(440) 647-4576

Hours: April–October, Saturday–Sunday 2:30–5 P.M.

Cost: Free

www.vilageofwellington.com/arch.htm

Directions: One block north of Rte. 18 on Main St.

YOUNGSTOWN

There were no fewer than 87 bombings in Youngstown between 1951 and 1962, earning it the unwanted nickname Crimetown. Most were connected to rampant corruption in local government, which ignored gambling run by organized crime.

Colossal Cuckoo.
Photo by author, courtesy of Alpine-Alpa

Wilmot
World's Largest Cuckoo Clock

There are other cuckoo clocks out there that claim to be the world's largest, but the one here in Wilmot is an honest-to-gosh stand-alone structure that actually looks like a cuckoo clock, and that's gotta mean something. The *Guinness Book of World Records* has yet to bestow an official title, so I will: this is the biggest cuckoo I've ever seen, and believe me, I've seen a lot of cuckoos. The clock sits on the roof of this Swiss-themed restaurant/gift shop/cheese factory. Every hour, on the hour, a 13-inch bird comes out and announces the start of the show. A five-piece oompah band emerges from backstage and two Tyrolean cloggers dance in a circle. The restaurant's roof is lined with bleacher seating so that busloads of tourists can enjoy the show.

The clock would be reason enough to visit, but there's even more to be seen downstairs. A robotic Swiss milkmaid welcomes visitors from a balcony above the main entrance, and an animated band plays tunes for 25¢ from behind a large glass window in the central courtyard. The Black Forest Cuckoo Clock Shop displays more than 300 clocks, and they're all for sale; none are as big as the one upstairs, but they've got a few doozies. Diners at the restaurant sit beneath an alpine wonderland of snow-capped peaks, model trains, and twinkling stars. You've never felt so diplomatically neutral in your life.

Alpine-Alpa Cheese House, 1504 Rte. 62, Wilmot, OH 44689

(330) 359-5454

Hours: Daily 9 A.M.–8 P.M.

Cost: 25¢

www.alpine-alpa.com

Directions: Two and a half miles southwest of town on Rte. 62.

YOUNGSTOWN

You must have a license to keep a bear in Youngstown.

You may not, by law, insult the mayor of Youngstown.

Singer **Maureen McGovern** was born in Youngstown on July 27, 1949.

Don't mess with this Mary.

Windsor
Madonnazilla

In the past, Mary has been one of the more reserved figures of the Christian faith, but with another Madonna grabbing so many headlines, the original Madonna—the *virgin* one—has been given a makeover, at least on one farm in northeast Ohio. Her size is deceiving at first, for she stands a good quarter mile back from the parking lot at the Servants of Mary Center of Peace. But as you walk in her direction, and walk, and walk, and walk, she grows ever larger until she looms 50 feet over your head. It's Madonnazilla—aiiiiiiiiii!!!!!!!!!!

But this giant statue of the Virgin of Guadeloupe isn't the only over-size religious item on the site; there's a 15-decade rosary made of beach ball–sized beads ringing an artificial lake in front of her. If you visit in the evening, the rosary is illuminated so that you're not left saying your Hail Marys in the dark.

The Servants of Mary Center of Peace sits on an organic farm owned by Pat and Ed Heinz. It includes a fantastic religious gift shop. It's well worth a stop.

Servants of Mary Center of Peace, 6569 Ireland Rd., Windsor, OH 44099

(440) 272-5380

Hours: Grounds, daily 9–10 P.M.; Gift shop, Tuesday–Saturday 10 A.M.–5 P.M., Sunday Noon–5 P.M.

Cost: Free

Directions: Between Rte. 6 (GAR Hwy.) and Rte. 86 (Plank Rd.) on Rte. 542 (Ireland Rd.), west of Rte. 534.

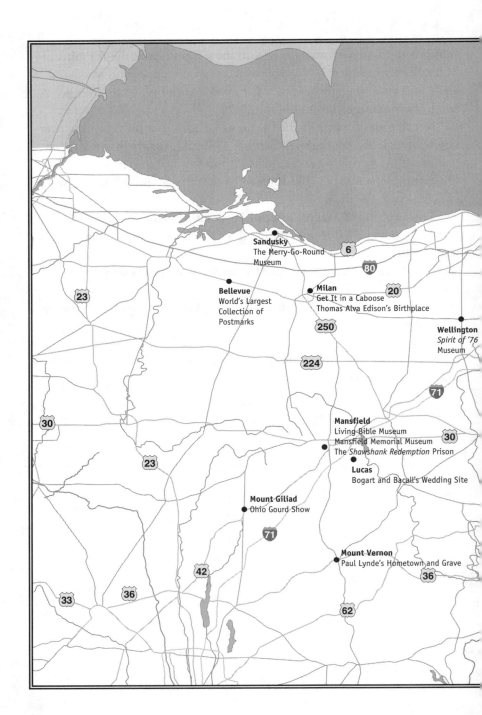

Sandusky
The Merry-Go-Round
Museum

Bellevue
World's Largest
Collection of
Postmarks

Milan
Get It in a Caboose
Thomas Alva Edison's Birthplace

Wellington
Spirit of '76
Museum

Mansfield
Living-Bible Museum
Mansfield Memorial Museum
The *Shawshank Redemption* Prison

Lucas
Bogart and Bacall's Wedding Site

Mount Giliad
Ohio Gourd Show

Mount Vernon
Paul Lynde's Hometown and Grave

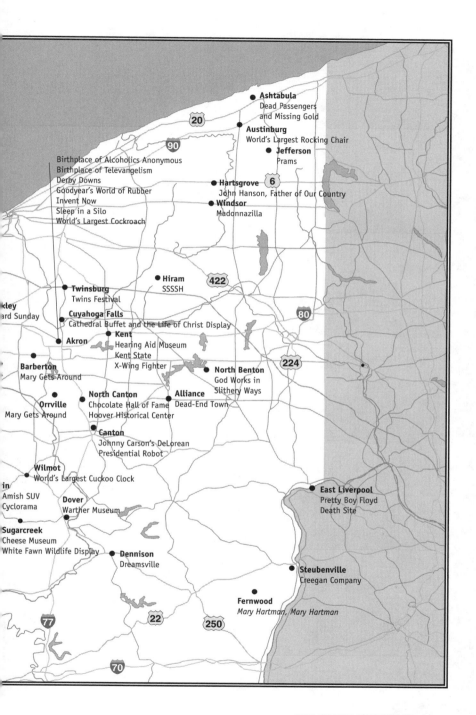

Ashtabula
Dead Passengers
and Missing Gold

Austinburg
World's Largest Rocking Chair

Jefferson
Prams

Birthplace of Alcoholics Anonymous
Birthplace of Televangelism
Derby Downs
Goodyear's World of Rubber
Invent Now
Sleep in a Silo
World's Largest Cockroach

Hartsgrove
John Hanson, Father of Our Country

Windsor
Madonnazilla

Hiram
SSSSH

Twinsburg
Twins Festival

kley
ard Sunday

Cuyahoga Falls
Cathedral Buffet and the Life of Christ Display

Kent
Hearing Aid Museum
Kent State
X-Wing Fighter

Akron

North Benton
God Works in
Slithery Ways

Barberton
Mary Gets Around

North Canton
Chocolate Hall of Fame
Hoover Historical Center

Alliance
Dead-End Town

Orrville
Mary Gets Around

Canton
Johnny Carson's DeLorean
Presidential Robot

Wilmot
World's Largest Cuckoo Clock

East Liverpool
Pretty Boy Floyd
Death Site

in
Amish SUV
Cyclorama

Dover
Warther Museum

Sugarcreek
Cheese Museum
White Fawn Wildlife Display

Dennison
Dreamsville

Steubenville
Creegan Company

Fernwood
Mary Hartman, Mary Hartman

3

CLEVELAND AREA

Cleveland has long been dismissed as the "Mistake on the Lake." And sure, the city's river did catch fire . . . more than once. But Americans have Cleveland to thank for the Christmas tree, Paul Newman, and the automated traffic signal. And don't those things more than make up for a little Lake Erie pollution? Don't they make up for a *lot* of Lake Erie pollution?

You know the old joke: "What's the difference between Cleveland and the *Titanic*?" Answer: "Cleveland has a better orchestra." Well, it's true! Not only that, it has a better natural history museum, a better polka museum, a better rock 'n' roll museum, a better space museum, and two better health museums. So if you're ever given a vacation choice between Cleveland and a bottom-bound ocean liner, go for Cleveland. And if you're looking for something to do while you're there, might I make a few suggestions?

And the answer is . . . Balto the Wonder Dog!
Photo by author, courtesy of Cleveland Museum of Natural History

Cleveland
Balto and Lucy

Long before Balto the Wonder Dog became the punch line to Johnny Carson's Karnak jokes, he was a true national hero. As the lead on an Alaskan dogsled team, he saved dozens, maybe hundreds, of lives during the 1925 diphtheria outbreak in Nome, Alaska. The only way for serum to be delivered to the remote town during a raging blizzard was by sled, and Balto led the final hand-off for the last 53 miles, even when his musher Gunnar Kaasen went temporarily blind en route.

With the residents of Nome saved, the dogs embarked on a coast-to-coast tour. When interest waned, they were stranded in a dumpy vaudeville house in California where Cleveland resident George Kimble came across them. Kimble encouraged the children of his hometown to raise the $2,000 needed to purchase the dogs and bring them to Ohio. In 1927 they were moved to their new home at the Cleveland Zoo. Balto lived out the remainder of his life as a local canine celebrity. After he died on

March 14, 1933, he was stuffed and put on display at the city's natural history museum. You can still see him there today, though he is occasionally placed in storage to keep his hide preserved.

Another of the museum's residents, Lucy, hasn't fared as well. But in fairness to her, she was 3.2 million years dead before Clevelander Donald Johanson uncovered her in 1974. At the time, Lucy's bones were the oldest and most complete fossil evidence of a human ancestor, *Australopithecus afarensis*. Though her petrified bones are in the possession of the National Museum of Addis Ababa, Ethiopia, a copy was made for Johanson to put on display in his hometown.

(If you're wondering how Lucy got her name, it turns out the dig crew was sitting around listening to the Beatles' "Lucy in the Sky with Diamonds" on the night they discovered her.)

Cleveland Museum of Natural History, 1 Wade Oval Dr., University Circle, Cleveland, OH 44106

(800) 317-9155 or (216) 231-4600

E-mail: info@cmnh.org

Hours: July–August, Monday and Friday–Saturday 10 A.M.–4:30 P.M., Tuesday–Thursday 10 A.M.–7 P.M., Sunday Noon–5 P.M.; September–June, Monday–Saturday 10 A.M.–p4:30 P.M., Sunday Noon–4:30 P.M.

Cost: Adults $6.50, Seniors $4.50, Teens (7–18) $4.50, Kids (3–6) $3.50

www.cmnh.org

Directions: Northeast of the intersection of Martin Luther King Dr. and Euclid Ave.

CLEVELAND

Author and poet **Langston Hughes** lived at 11217 Asbury Avenue in Cleveland as a teenager. He attended Central High School where he wrote for the school paper, *The Monthly*. When his family moved to Chicago, he stayed in Cleveland in a rented attic room (2266 E. 86th Street) until he graduated.

The Day-Glo Color Corporation was founded in Cleveland during the 1930s by Bob and Joe Switzer. They were the first company to popularize fluorescent pigments in paints, inks, and dyes.

Birthplace of the American Christmas Tree

When Reverend Heinrich Schwan placed a tree in the foyer of the Zion Evangelical Lutheran Church on Christmas Eve 1851, he thought he was giving his predominantly German congregation a treat by reminding them of their homeland's tradition of Tannenbaum. Instead, the tree drew jeers from Cleveland's largely anti-immigrant press. One local paper called it "a nonsensical, asinine, moronic absurdity," while another lashed out at "th[o]se Lutherans worshipping a tree . . . groveling before a shrub."

Though he had doubts, Schwan held firm, and the tree stayed. Year after year, the tradition got a larger foothold in the New World, eventually silencing most of the critics. Schwan's church moved to a new location (2062 E. 30th Street, (216) 861-2179) years ago, but a plaque marks the spot where the first tree was sacrificed for a new American tradition.

Lakeside and E. 6th St., Cleveland, OH 44114

No phone

Hours: Torn down

Cost: Free

www.lcms.org/cic/schwan.htm

Directions: One block west of E. 9 St., one block south of Rte. 2.

The Burning River

It's the fire everyone in Cleveland would just as soon forget, but nobody ever will. On June 22, 1969, an oil slick on the Cuyahoga River burst into flames. It only lasted 25 minutes, but the memory blazes on. Songwriter Randy Newman commemorated the event with his ballad, "Burn On, Big River, Burn On," a ditty you're not likely to hear played on many Cleveland stations.

Clevelanders are right in claiming that the magnitude of the story surrounding the fire far exceeded the actual blaze, but most also fail to mention that this wasn't the first time their polluted waterway had caught fire, not by a long shot. The river had been a waste trough for the city's refineries (along with every other industry) for years. The first Cuyahoga River fire ignited on August 29, 1868, at West 3rd Street, but since it didn't spread to the shore, nobody paid it much mind. Another river blaze started on shore at a grain elevator in August 1887, but soon spread across the water's surface on a trail of waste oil. Was anything done to correct the problem? Oh, please.

Then, on May 1, 1912, a tugboat ignited gasoline that was leaking into the river from a 100,000-gallon Standard Oil tanker docked near the Jefferson Avenue bridge. The three-hour fire killed five people, destroyed five tugboats, and torched three dry docks. As politically powerful as Standard Oil was, nothing was done to stop the petroleum spills from its tankers or plants. On October 29, 1922, another river fire almost consumed the Jefferson Avenue bridge, again, and on April 2, 1930, yet another inferno erupted at the river's Cincinnati slip. Still no cleanups.

Can you begin to see the pattern?

The Clark Avenue bridge suffered $100,000 in damage during a river fire on February 7, 1948. City officials started to take notice, but did little more than talk about what to do. Standard Oil's liquid waste was responsible for a third blaze near the Jefferson Avenue bridge on November 1, 1952. This time there was more than $1 million in damages, and the bridge was put out of commission for several months.

In a way, the 1969 fire was a blessing in disguise because, faced with the scorn of the nation, officials started cleaning up the mess. Their hands were forced by the 1972 Clean Water Act. At its dirtiest, the river was 50 percent acid and industrial waste. It was so polluted that even its sludge worms had died off. Today, the water is clean enough to swim in . . . though few people do. Old habits are hard to break.

Eggers Ave., Cleveland, OH 44109

No phone

Hours: Always visible

Cost: Free

www.cwru.edu/artsci/engl/marling/60s/pages/richoux

Directions: East of Independence Blvd. on Eggers Ave.; the fire took place at the railroad bridge just east of the eastern end of Eggers Ave.

CLEVELAND
You must purchase a hunting license to catch mice in Cleveland.

Where's the leg lamp?

A Christmas Story House

To many people, the holidays just wouldn't be the same without watching *A Christmas Story*. Released in 1983, it has already achieved cult classic status alongside *It's a Wonderful Life* and *Rudolph the Red-Nosed Reindeer*. The movie is based upon Jean Shepperd's fictionalized 1966 memoir, *In God We Trust: All Others Pay Cash*. It recalls Shepperd's childhood in Gary, Indiana, and his tireless efforts to lobby his parents, teachers, and an angry department-store Santa to bring him a Red Ryder Carbine Action Two-Hundred Shot Range Model Air Rifle, better known as a BB gun. You know, the kind that'll shoot your eye out.

The movie was not shot in Gary, however; the town looked a little *too* run down for a story set in the Midwest during the height of the Depression. Producers picked a working-class neighborhood south of downtown Cleveland for the exterior home shots. The Christmas parade was filmed on Cleveland's Public Square (Superior and Ontario Avenues).

The movie's little-seen sequel, *It Runs in the Family*, used this same home for its exteriors. The house has recently undergone significant modifications, including a very large picture window in front. All the better to display a lamp with an illuminated leg base covered in a fishnet stocking. Why? It's a *major award*.

3157 W. 11th St., Cleveland, OH 44109

Private phone

Hours: Always visible

Cost: Free

Directions: One block south of Clark Ave., three blocks east of 14th St., across the street from the Rowley Inn.

HOLLYWOOD ON LAKE ERIE

A Christmas Story isn't the only big-name movie to be shot on the shores of Lake Erie. Early scenes of *The Deer Hunter*, Oscar winner for Best Picture in 1978, were also filmed in Cleveland: the wedding at St. Theodosius Orthodox Christian Cathedral (733 Starkeweather Avenue, (216) 741-1310) and the reception at Lemko Hall (2335 W. 11th Street). St. Theodosius is a replica of the Czar's Cathedral, which still stands inside the Kremlin.

CLEVELAND

Ice cream vendors in Cleveland are required to use only soft chimes, and they may not shout.

The Collinwood School Fire

All the fire drills in the world couldn't have prepared the staff and children at Lakeview Elementary for what ultimately killed them: their own panic. It was Ash Wednesday, March 4, 1908, and it was like any other school day in Collinwood (a community that at the time was not part of incorporated Cleveland) where 350 students were shoehorned into a school designed for half that number.

Around 9:40 A.M., a fire broke out under the front stairwell, quickly blocking the exit onto 152nd Street (then called Collamer Avenue). The children who had practiced exiting by that route turned and ran to the only other exit, which was located at the rear of the building. They piled up against the rest of the classes who were descending from upper floors. Contrary to oft-repeated rumors, the kids were *not* trapped behind doors that opened inward, but were entangled in a writhing mass of young bodies at the bottom of the stairs. Local parents rushed to the scene but were unable to help.

In all, 172 students, two teachers, and one rescuer died that day. Nineteen unidentified and two known victims were laid to rest under a monument at Lake View Cemetery (see page 122), and a memorial garden was erected on the footprint of the school's charred foundation. The now-abandoned Collinwood Memorial School, which opened in 1910, sits on a lot adjacent to the garden.

400 E. 152nd St., Cleveland, OH 44110

No phone

Hours: Always visible

Cost: Free

Directions: Four blocks north of Rte. 2 on 152nd St.

CLEVELAND

Donald DeFreeze, leader of the Symbionese Liberation Army, was known to police and captor Patty Hearst as **Cinque**. After he was killed in a 1974 shootout in Compton, California, his body was returned to his hometown of Cleveland. Now Cinque is *seis* feet under at Highland Park Cemetery (21400 Chagrin Boulevard, (216) 348-7210).

CLEVELAND BURNS

The Collinwood fire is just the tip of Cleveland's burning iceberg; the city has seen plenty of fires over the years. Here are some of its most memorable conflagrations:

★ **The Cleveland Clinic Fire** On May 15, 1929, 125 people perished at the Cleveland Clinic (9300 E. Euclid Avenue) when fumes from burning nitrate X-ray film smothered patients and staff alike. The building is still used today, part of a larger medical complex.

★ **The Circus Fire** The Ringling Brothers and Barnum & Bailey Circus's menagerie tent burst into flames on August 4, 1942, killing 57 animals, including four lions, two giraffes, and a sacred Indian cow. The circus had erected its tents along Lakeside Avenue and E. 9th Street.

★ **The East Ohio Gas Company Blast** A liquid natural gas tank at Cleveland's East Ohio Gas Company (55th Street and St. Clair Avenue) exploded on October 21, 1944, killing 135 people at the plant and in the surrounding community.

★ **The Mysterious Exploding Sewer** A mile-long stretch of West 117th Street (between Lake Avenue and Berea Road) was destroyed on September 10, 1953, after a sanitary sewer running beneath the road exploded during rush hour. One commuter died and another 64 were injured. Investigators believed a flammable material had been dumped into the sewer, but they could not pinpoint its source.

★ **The Mayor Burns** During the opening ceremonies of a national metals convention in the mid-1970s, Cleveland Mayor Ralph Perk tried to cut the opening ribbon (made from metal) with a blowtorch. The flame ignited his hair while news cameras rolled.

CLEVELAND

Sixteen workers from the iron ore docks on Cleveland's Whiskey Island drowned in the Cuyahoga River after their overloaded commuter scow sank on July 16, 1896, near the Willow Street bridge.

By law, you may not sit on another person's lap to drive in Cleveland.

Death by Doctors

Yes, it is true, Charles Guiteau *did* shoot President James Garfield on July 2, 1881, but he probably didn't kill him. That job was left for the chief executive's incompetent doctors.

Guiteau was upset with Garfield because he had not been selected as the new ambassador to France, so he stalked the president for several days before choosing the perfect moment in a Washington, D.C., train station. He fired two shots; one nicked Garfield's right arm and the other entered his back. It did not, as doctors suspected, hit his spine. This should have been obvious to anyone probing the hole and, according to records, *everyone* seemed to want to stick a finger in the hole.

The first person to examine the wound was Dr. Willard Bliss, but he ended up jamming a new hole through the tissue with his unwashed finger. Other doctors, following Bliss's fresh but false trajectory, dug even deeper. The army surgeon general got as far as Garfield's rib cage with his grubby digit. A navy doctor punctured the president's liver with his bare finger. Sixteen different quacks systematically turned a three-inch wound into a twenty-inch gaping, gooey tunnel from Garfield's ribs to his groin. Alexander Graham Bell even joined the ghastly circus, using an experimental electronic device to try to locate the slug. The bed's springs kept setting off the sensor, giving surgeons far too many possibilities as to where they might operate. They operated anyway. *Three times.*

Garfield's temperature kept spiking due to one infection after another, while his blood was slowly poisoned by the lead slug nobody ever found (and easily could have been removed). Eventually Garfield's heart stopped on September 19, 1881. He was laid to rest in Cleveland's Lake View Cemetery.

And you thought *your* health-care plan sucked.

Lake View Cemetery, 12316 Euclid Ave., Cleveland, OH 44106

(216) 421-2665

E-mail: lakeview@buckeyeweb.com

Hours: Tomb, daily 9 A.M.–4 P.M.; Grounds, daily 7:30 A.M.–5:30 P.M.; Office, Monday–Friday 8:30 A.M.–5 P.M., Saturday 8:30 A.M.–12:30 P.M.

Cost: Free

www.lakeviewcemetery.com

Directions: On Rte. 20 (Euclid Ave.) at E. 123rd St.

ALSO PLANTED IN LAKE VIEW

President Garfield isn't the only big name in Lake View Cemetery. Everyone who's anyone in Cleveland—and dead, that is—is buried here. A detailed guide is available at the cemetery offices, but here's a shorthand list.

★ **Judge Edward Blythin** (1884–1958) presided over the first trial— the mistrial—of Dr. Sam Sheppard (see page 139).

★ **Alva Bradley** (1814–1885) was a Great Lakes shipbuilder, but he is best remembered as being the middle-namesake of Thomas Alva Edison. The Edisons and Bradleys were friends.

★ **Raymond John Chapman** (1891–1920), a shortstop for the Cleveland Indians, became the only major league player to die from injuries sustained during a baseball game after he was struck by a beanball thrown by Yankees' pitcher Carl Mays on August 16, 1920.

★ **Marcus Hanna** (1837–1904), known as the "President Maker," was a GOP leader who proved instrumental in getting James Garfield and William McKinley, both of whom were later assassinated, elected to the nation's highest office. Thanks for nothing, Marc.

★ **Cockburn Haskell** (1868–1922) invented the rubber-core wound golf ball in 1901, the same basic design used by manufacturers today.

★ **John Milton Hay** (1838–1929) served as Abraham Lincoln's personal secretary and later formed McKinley's Open Door policy toward China.

★ **Garrett Morgan, Sr.** (1877–1963) invented the gas mask in 1912 and the automatic traffic signal in 1914 (see page 136).

★ **Eliot Ness** (1903–1957), the "Untouchable" Chicago FBI agent, was cremated in 1957, but his ashes ended up in his daughter-in-law's garage. They were eventually scattered over this cemetery's Wade Lake on September 10, 1997, and a marker was placed on its eastern shore. Ness was Cleveland's Safety Director from 1935 to 1942 (see page 134).

★ **Gloria Hershey Pressman** (1923–1991) was one of the original Li'l Rascals, appearing under the stage name Mildred Jackson.

★ **John D. Rockefeller** (1839–1937), the world's first billionaire, founded the Standard Oil Company in 1870.

★ **Dr. James Salisbury** (1822–1905) invented the Salisbury steak, which he claimed had curative powers.

★ **Carl Stokes** (1927–1996), a two-term Cleveland mayor initially elected in 1967, was the first African American mayor of a major U.S. city.

★ **Rev. Heinrich (Henry) Christian Schwan** (1818–1905), considered the Father of the American Christmas Tree, erected the first one at the Zion Evangelical Lutheran Church on Christmas Eve 1851 (see page 116).

Dr. Dale had a skeleton in his closet.
Photo by author, courtesy of Dittrick Medical History Center

Dittrick Medical History Center

There's nothing like a trip to a medical history museum to make you appreciate modern medicine. Of course, it's a false sense of security because today's instruments will be tomorrow's artifacts; someday future tourists will look at a display case filled with HMO cards and gasp, "My God—how barbaric!"

No doubt the Dittrick Medical History Center will continue to document it all. Currently it has 75,000+ artifacts from stethoscopes to tongue depressors, obstetric forceps to bloodletting bowls, patent medicines to amputation kits, and all the best stuff is on display. Check out the iron lung made for an infant, and the 1935 craniotomy chair that allowed surgeons to operate on the skull while the patient was in a sitting position. See the 1875 office of Dr. John Dale; he had a skeleton in his closet—literally. Take a peek at an early eye chart where patients were asked to identify images less obvious than capital letters: an acorn, a watch, a crescent moon, a carriage, a silhouette, and what looks like a smiling crazy man. And learn the etymology of the names of surgical instruments like the ecraseur ("crusher"), used for destroying uterine polyps.

The bulk of the museum is on the third floor of the Allen Memorial Medical Library, but be sure to seek out the microscope collection in the Millikin Room on the second floor. It features more than 80 different models, one of the largest collections in the United States. The library also has 60,000+ books on anatomy, medicine, surgery, and science, some dating back as far as the 14th century. If you're a doctor, though, please use the updated texts.

Allen Memorial Medical Library, 11000 Euclid Ave., 3rd Floor, Cleveland, OH 44106

(216) 368-3648

Hours: Monday–Friday 10 A.M.–4:30 P.M.

Cost: Free

www.cwru.edu/artsci/dittrick/home.htm

Directions: At the corner of Adelbert and Euclid Aves., two blocks east of Martin Luther King Dr.

Drew Carey Town

Drew Carey was once asked to describe in five words what he was like growing up. He responded: "Weirdo, weirdo, underachiever, weirdo, weirdo." In other words, he was fairly typical. Carey, the third of Lewis and Beulah's three sons, was born at Deaconess Hospital (429 Pearl Road) on May 23, 1958. The family lived in the working-class neighborhood of Old Brooklyn, where Drew took up the accordion in the first grade. His 45-year-old father died of brain cancer when Drew was eight years old, a tragedy that shaped his life and comedy from that point on.

Carey eventually dumped the accordion and took up the trumpet, partly because it was lighter to carry, but more because it was less dorky. He also became obsessed with board games, which pushed him back into dork territory. He attended Mooney Junior High (3213 Montclair Avenue) where he showed up the first day wearing moon boots, looking like a "demented astronaut," and later Rhodes High School, where he played in the band, wrestled, and landed the lead in *The Pirates of Penzance*. After taking summer classes in 1975, he graduated a year early and headed off to Kent State.

At college, Carey developed and refined his partying skills, always slathered in Brut aftershave. He joined Delta Tau Delta (223 E. Main Street, Kent) where he lived a Blutoesque life; though he spent five years in college, he dropped out after his junior year having never declared a major. But it wasn't all beer and board games. Carey tried to kill himself at a frat party at the end of his freshman year; everyone seemed to be having a great time but him, so he went up to his room and downed a fistful of pills. When he had second thoughts, he asked his frat brothers to bring him to the emergency room to have his stomach pumped.

Carey headed for Vegas after dropping out, but he never forgot Cleveland. In fact, when his mother remarried in 1984, he bought his childhood home from her, a house he owns to this day (the address is confidential). When he's had enough of Hollywood, he plans to return to Cleveland for good where, presumably, he could be elected mayor any time he wants. Don't count on it, though. He'll probably just hang out with his friends at his favorite local bar, which would be OK by him.

John Ford Rhodes High School, 5100 Biddulph Rd., Cleveland, OH 44144

(216) 351-6285

Hours: Always visible, view from street

Cost: Free

www.jfrhodes.com

Directions: Two blocks west of Pearl Rd. (Rte. 3) at Fulton Rd.

Fun with Ick and Jane

Flying just isn't as entertaining as it used to be. But back in the 1970s, Hopkins International demonstrated just how interesting a trip through the airport could be.

On November 3, 1970, Jane Fonda was arrested here after she kicked a policeman and pushed a customs official in a mad rush to the airport bathroom. Police searched her and discovered a stash of Valium, Compazine, and Dexedrine. When she was booked, Fonda raised a defiant fist for her now-famous mug shot—power to the pill poppers! All charges against her were dropped when police learned that the drugs had all been prescribed for her.

Hopkins International was the scene of another odd event two years later on September 14, 1972. Authorities shut down the airport for 30 minutes because the runways were blanketed with millions of earthworms, which made it difficult for landing airplanes to brake properly. Flights resumed after crews swept the runway.

Cleveland Hopkins International Airport, 5300 Riverside Dr., Cleveland, OH
  44135
(216) 265-6030
Hours: Always visible
Cost: Free
www.clevelandairport.com
Directions: Southwest of the intersection of I-71 and I-480.

HealthSpace Cleveland

HealthSpace Cleveland (formerly the Health Museum of Cleveland) is currently undergoing a massive face-lift, but when it's finished, it should be remarkable. Here's hoping that in the name of "education" it doesn't jettison some of its goofier exhibits, such as Juno, the Transparent Talking Woman. A refugee from the 1939 New York World's Fair, Juno bares it all from the inside out, her organs illuminating one at a time as she tells visitors the story of how they all work together.

Knowing that children like to get close to the exhibits, the museum built oversize replicas of body parts for kids to crawl through. Their Giant Tooth is 384 times the size of a normal tooth, standing about 18 feet tall and weighing in at two tons—a mighty molar indeed! They've also got a Giant Brain, a Giant Eye, a Giant Hand, a Giant Ear, and a Giant Nose. (If you've ever wanted to pretend you were a Giant Booger, here's your chance.) They've also got models to explain the birds and bees, with marbles used to represent the sperm.

One of the museum's gigantic displays is actually life-size: it's a replica of the baby born to the Seville Giants, Anna Swan and Captain Martin Van Buren Bates (see page 98), on January 18, 1879. He weighed in at 23¾ pounds and was 30 inches long. Sadly, Baby Bates only lived for 11 hours. A plaster cast was made of his body before it was buried.

8911 Euclid Ave., Cleveland, OH 44106
(216) 231-5010
Hours: Monday–Friday 9 A.M.–5 P.M., Saturday 10 A.M.–5 P.M., Sunday Noon–5 P.M.
Cost: Adults $5, Kids $3.50
www.healthmuseum.org
Directions: Five blocks west of 105th St. on Rte. 20 (Euclid Ave.).

Not lost in space.
Courtesy of NASA Glenn Research Center

NASA Glenn Research Center

Good news: you don't have to go all the way to sunny Florida if you want to visit a NASA museum; there's one right here in Cleveland! Sure, the NASA Glenn Research Center doesn't have the launching pads and the full-size Space Shuttle mockup that the Kennedy Space Center has, but it does have a few artifacts from the American space program. For example, it's got the command module from *Skylab 3*, Jim Lovell's *Apollo 8* space suit, and a baseball tossed around in an early flight of the Space Shuttle *Columbia* that was later used for the first pitch in Game 5 of the 1995 World Series.

And there's more! A moon rock embedded in a Lucite pyramid. A mockup of NASA's Microgravity Laboratory. The facility's 1988 Emmy for Outstanding Achievement in Engineering Development. (The agency put up the Kuband satellites that have made Hollywood *piles* of money beaming *Baywatch* to every corner the globe, and they wanted to say thanks.) And out in front of the facility, you'll find a few early rockets that were mothballed by NASA years ago.

Lewis Field, 21000 Brookpark Rd., Cleveland, OH 44135

(216) 433-2000

Hours: Monday–Friday 9 A.M.–4 P.M., Saturday 10 A.M.–3 P.M., Sunday 1–5 P.M.

Cost: Free

www.grc.nasa.gov/Doc/visitgrc.htm

Directions: On the north side of Cleveland-Hopkins International Airport, west of Old Grayton Rd.

Rock and Roll Hall of Fame

Technically speaking, the Rock and Roll Hall of Fame is hardly a little-known tourist attraction. But because it is so chock-full of pop culture doodads, it merits inclusion in this oddball guide.

One interesting conclusion you're likely to draw after visiting the museum is that rock 'n' roll is as much about the costumes as the music. Though the hall is filled with endless guitars and drumsticks, it's the outfits you'll really recognize: Sid Vicious's boots and dog chain necklace (with lock), Ringo Starr's fuchsia *Sgt. Pepper's* jacket, Michael Jackson's 1992 sequined glove, Bruce Springsteen's *Born in the USA* jeans, David Byrne's oversized jacket, Madonna's 1990 pointy bustier, Mark Mothersbaugh's 1980 DEVO suit and hat, George Clinton's shoes, Elvis's Comeback Special jumpsuit, Freddie Mercury's 1985 long underwear outfit, Tina Turner's slinky *Private Dancer* dress, Elton John's 1974 feathered boa getup by Bob Mackie, Jimi Hendrix's purple vest and belt, the Temptations' blue suits with lamé lapels, and David Bowie's Ziggy Stardust jumpsuit. Compared to these aging masters' clothing, the teen idol costumes from New Kids on the Block, Britney Spears, Debbie Gibson, Hanson, Andy Gibb, David Cassidy, and 'N Sync in an adjoining room look downright . . . what's the word? . . . dumpy.

Better still, the museum has plenty of artifacts that you'd *never* expect: Jim Morrison's Boy Scout uniform and varsity swim letter; a life-size bust of Steven Tyler with his mouth gaping; the B-52s' towering wigs; Pete Seeger's junky banjo; a mangled piece of Otis Redding's death plane; a duffel bag of hotel keys collected by the Eagles' Timothy Schmit; Buddy Holly's high school diploma; Alice Cooper's guillotine and severed head; Elvis's army induction papers; ZZ Top's customized 1933 Ford "Eliminator" coupe; Phish's jumbo hot dog and fries props; Keith Moon's report card; and Janis Joplin's psychedelic Porsche 356C, rose eyeglasses, handmade God's eye, undipped LSD blotter sheet, and funeral invitation. My favorite, however, is a hand-scrawled note from Bruce Springsteen to his band: "OK Guys, Hands OFF All Food, except Cereal & Drinks. Sincerely, Boss." Who'd have thought the Boss was so bossy?

The question that often comes to mind is "Why is the Rock and Roll Hall of Fame in Cleveland?" The city hasn't exactly contributed a slew of prominent musicians. Yet it is here where the term *rock 'n' roll* was invented, popularized by disc jockey Alan Freed during his "Moondog Rock 'n' Roll Parties" on WJW radio in the early 1950s (based at the One Playhouse Square Building, 1375 Euclid Avenue). That wasn't the reason the museum was built here, however. Rather, Cleveland got it through a generous package of tax incentives and free land for the project's developers, beating out the likes of New York, Memphis, San Francisco, Chicago, and Philadelphia.

1 Key Plaza, East 9th Street Pier, Cleveland, OH 44114

(800) 493-ROLL or (216) 781-ROCK

Hours: September–May, Thursday–Tuesday 10 A.M.–5:30 P.M., Wednesday 10 A.M.–
  9 P.M.; June–August, Wednesday–Saturday 10 A.M.–9 P.M., Sunday–Tuesday
  10 A.M.–5:30 P.M.

Cost: Adults $12.95, Seniors (55+) $9.50, Kids (4–11) $9.50

www.rockhall.com

Directions: Just northwest of Rte. 2 at E. 9th St., north of downtown, at the lakefront.

SWINGING SWINGOS

From the late 1960s and into the '80s there was only one place for rock 'n' rollers to bunk when they came to Cleveland: Swingos Celebrity Inn. The motel was immortalized in a scene from the movie *Almost Famous*, one of the early stops on fictional band Stillwater's nationwide tour. Writer Cameron Crowe recalled its enormous lobby, which was often filled with groupies, "band aides," and fans hoping to catch a glimpse of their idols. It was here that Led Zeppelin tossed food from their suite's balcony, then blamed it all on Elton John. Elvis Presley took up 100 rooms on three floors when he bunked here. Bruce Springsteen, Pink Floyd, Kiss, Queen, and the Rolling Stones all visited, as did Frank Sinatra, Jerry Lewis, Al Gore, Duke Ellington, Bette Midler, Martin Luther King, Mel Torme . . . the list goes on and on. Today, Swingos is a Comfort Inn (1800 Euclid Avenue, (216) 861-0001).

BORN IN CLEVELAND

Drew Carey isn't the only famous Clevelander. Here are a few other stars to hail from this town:

Jim Backus	February 25, 1913
Halle Berry	August 14, 1968
Tracy Chapman	March 20, 1964
Wes Craven	August 2, 1939
Dorothy Dandridge	November 9, 1922
Ruby Dee	October 27, 1924
Phil Donahue	December 21, 1935
Joel Grey	April 11, 1932
Arsenio Hall	February 12, 1956
Margaret Hamilton	September 12, 1902
Hal Holbrook	February 17, 1925
Carol Kane	June 18, 1952

Science Can Be a Bummer

I'm not one to tell a museum how to run its business—wait a second, *yes I am*—but it seems a little odd that so many of this fantastic science museum's exhibits are wonderfully, horribly depressing. If you want to have a happy visit, stick to the upper two floors, because the ground floor is a real bummer.

It doesn't help that the first thing you find is a model of "The Sick Earth" lying on a hospital bed in intensive care. Beep . . . beep . . . beep . . . do you think it'll make it? Things don't look good. One exhibit asks accusingly, "How Much Oxygen Do You Use?" while another badgers, "Where Does Your Waste Water Go?" Yikes, so many questions! Slog through the Lake Erie Story; it's not as fun-filled as you might expect. Sure, you know about the pollution, but were you aware of the danger of fish-killing algae blooms? And how about deadly seiches? What's a seiche? A rare and massive lake wave created by certain weather conditions; it'll roll ashore and sweep you to your death when you least expect it!

Enjoy that trip to the beach.

Great Lakes Science Center, 601 Erieside Ave., Cleveland, OH 44114

(216) 694-2000

Hours: Daily 9:30 A.M.–5:30 P.M.

Cost: Adults $7.95, Seniors (65+) $6.95, Kids (3–17) $5.95

www.greatscience.com

Directions: Just northwest of Rte. 2 at E. 9th St., at the lakefront, just west of the Rock and Roll Hall of Fame.

MORE BORN IN CLEVELAND

Don King	August 20, 1931
James Lovell	March 24, 1924
Henry Mancini	April 16, 1924
Greg Morris	September 27, 1934
Paul Newman	January 26, 1925
Lawanda Page	October 19, 1920
George Stephanopolous	February 10, 1961
Debra Winger	May 17, 1955

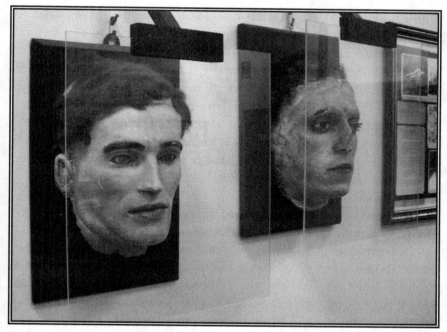

Anybody recognize these heads?
Photo by author, courtesy of Cleveland Police Historical Society

The Torso Killer

London had Jack the Ripper. Boston had the Strangler. And Cleveland had the Torso Killer. Between 1934 and 1938, no fewer than 13 unfortunate citizens fell prey to a serial killer with a unique calling card: he would decapitate his still-living victim, carve the body into manageable pieces, then dump the remains out in the open to be found by unsuspecting citizens.

This Depression-era murderer went unnoticed in the beginning. His first victim washed up on Euclid Beach on September 9, 1934. Police thought the headless woman might have died in a boating or swimming accident, but they couldn't establish her identity.

That was not the case for one of the two headless, emasculated corpses that were discovered on Jackass Hill in Kingsbury Run (E. 49th Street and Praha Avenue) on September 23, 1935. Both heads were found nearby, but it was the fingerprints of the younger body that led to his identification—he was Edward Andrassy, a petty criminal who hung with a rough crowd. He probably crossed the wrong hood, the police theorized, and maybe the other victim had, too.

Warning bells started to go off, however, when a picnic basket appeared in the alley behind the Hart Manufacturing Company (2315 E. 20th Street) on January 26, 1936. Inside were the right arm, lower torso, and thighs of a middle-age woman. Fingerprints identified the parts to be those of Florence Polillo, a part-time madam and rest-of-the-time prostitute who liked to drink. A lot. The remainder of her remains, minus the head, turned up 12 days later in a lot at 1419 Orange Avenue.

Police were baffled. The Torso Killer was choosing his victims from the gritty margins of society, drifters and troublemakers who weren't exactly missed when they disappeared; many of them lived in the Hooverville along Kingsbury Run. Most of the bodies were found in this wooded ravine along the Nickel Plate railroad tracks. Only Andrassy's and Polillo's bodies were ever positively identified; every subsequent victim was a John or Jane Doe. The Cleveland newspapers had a field day . . . and sold a lot of papers with each new body. The killer assisted their circulation departments by providing three more victims in 1936, three in 1937, and a final three in 1938.

Cleveland's Safety Director, Eliot Ness, didn't have as much luck tracking the killer as he had earlier with Al Capone in Chicago. The police profile pegged the killer as a butcher or doctor, judging from the skill with which the bodies had been dismembered. Nobody was ever definitively linked to the crimes, and only one suspect ever went before a grand jury. He died in police custody before going to trial.

The Cleveland Police Historical Society has an impressive exhibit on the Torso Killer case, including four death masks made from the few victims whose heads were still available. One of the masks, that of the 1936 "tattooed man," was placed on public display at the 1936–37 Great Lakes Exposition in hopes of finding a lead. Nobody came forward, though tens of thousands of fairgoers came to rubberneck.

The case is still officially open. Maybe you should stop by and take a good long look. Gawker.

Cleveland Police Historical Society and Library, Cleveland Justice Center, 1300 Ontario St., Cleveland, OH 44113

(216) 623-5055

E-mail: museum@stratos.net

Hours: Monday–Friday 10 A.M.–4 P.M.

Cost: Free

www.clevelandpolicemuseum.org

Directions: Downtown at the corner of St. Clair Ave. and Ontario St.

ANOTHER HEADLESS PROBLEM . . . AND A SOLUTION

On February 19, 1992, somebody walked into St. Catherine's Church (3443 E. 93rd Street) and made off with the parish namesake's skull. (Catherine had been canonized by the Pope after she was murdered by her father for giving away his money to the poor.) The relic of the third-century Roman teenager had been brought to Cleveland in 1925, where it lived a fairly uneventful afterlife—until it was lifted. The skull was found six days later in the parking lot of the St. Sava Serbian Orthodox Cathedral (6306 Broadview Road).

In the not-so-distant future, the rampant denogginizing of Cleveland's indigent and saintly populations could be corrected by a local research neurosurgeon, Robert J. White. This fellow has been pioneering research into head transplantation since the 1970s. Most of his work has been done on monkeys, one of which lived for 36 hours on a new body. It could see, smell, and hear. Will humans be next on the chopping block?

USS *Cod*

The USS *Cod* has the unique distinction of being the only intact, fully submersible U.S. submarine remaining from World War II. Translation? Don't bother visiting if you have a leg in a cast. There are several old subs across the country, but this is the only one where you get a sense of what it was like to live in a tin can with 90 other sailors for months at a time. Up ladders, down ladders, squeezing through bulkheads—it's all part of the claustrophobic tour.

The *Cod* had a distinguished record, sinking 10 enemy ships during World War II. It damaged five more vessels, and rescued a crew of Dutch sailors from their beached sub in the South China Sea during the Cold War. Still, the U.S. Navy isn't the sentimental type, and the *Cod* was decommissioned in 1954 after a flashier nuclear sub took its place. The *Cod* was towed to Cleveland's waterfront in 1959 and used for some time as a naval reserve trainer. When the *Cod* was stricken from the navy's inventory in 1971, a group of local veterans stepped in and rescued it from the scrap yard, which is why you can tour this last-of-its-kind vessel today.

Great Lakes Historical Society, 1089 E. 9th St., Cleveland, OH 44114

(216) 566-8770

E-mail: usscod@en.com

Hours: May–September, daily 10 A.M.–5 P.M.

Cost: Adults $6, Seniors $5, Kids $3

www.usscod.org

Directions: Just northwest of Rte. 2 at E. 9th St., at the lakefront, just east of the Rock and Roll Hall of Fame.

World's First Automated Traffic Signal

It was the first blow in the battle to oppress the American driver. The World's First Automated Traffic Signal was installed at the intersection of Euclid Avenue and 105th Street in Cleveland on August 5, 1914. The signal was built by Garrett Morgan, an African American inventor who had previously invented the gas mask and the zigzag stitch attachment for sewing machines.

You had to be literate to use Garrett's signal because it used words rather than colors. The cross-shaped device had *STOP* printed three times on its main face, and *GO* printed along its edge. The signal would rotate back and forth between 105th and Euclid on a regular basis, alternating the instructions that drivers on both streets received. Though he applied for a patent around the time the device was installed, Morgan didn't receive it until 1923. As soon as it arrived, he sold it to General Electric for $40,000.

Euclid Ave. and 105th St., Cleveland, OH 44106

No phone

Hours: Intersection always visible

Cost: Free

Directions: Two blocks west of East Blvd., one block south of Chester Ave. (Rte. 322).

Sign, sign, everywhere a sign.
Photo by author, courtesy of Western Reserve Historical Society

Though the intersection is still as busy as ever, Garrett's device was taken down years ago. You can find it at the Crawford Auto-Aviation Museum not far away.

Crawford Auto-Aviation Museum, Western Reserve Historical Society, 10825 East Blvd., University Circle, Cleveland, OH 44106

(216) 721-5722

Hours: Monday–Saturday 10 A.M.–5 P.M., Sunday Noon–5 P.M.

Cost: Adults $7.50, Seniors $6.50, Kids $5.50

www.wrhs.org/crawford/default.asp

Directions: Northeast of the intersection of Martin Luther King Dr. and Euclid Ave.

Source of some confusion.

World's Largest "FREE" Stamp

Sure it's big, but is it art? Sculptor Claes Oldenburg has a passion for turning small everyday objects into large uncommon sculptures. In 1982, the Standard Oil Company of Ohio (SOHIO) commissioned a piece for its Cleveland headquarters, and Oldenburg came up with a 28-foot-tall, 48-foot-long "FREE" stamp, titled (surprise!) *Free Stamp*, the kind an oversized office worker might use. But before the piece could be delivered, British Petroleum (BP) bought SOHIO, and with it a very large work of art.

In talks that must have sounded like Abbott and Costello's "Who's on First?" routine, BP negotiated with the city to donate the work for public display. Would you like a *Free Stamp*? Sure, what will it cost us? It's free. That's what you said—it says so right on the piece. Yes, "FREE." But what do we have to pay for it? Nothing; it's free. Will we have to pay to install it? Well, that's not free. But you said it was free. It is. Then what are we paying for? To get the free *Free Stamp* put up. So it's *not* free? Yes it is; it's a free *Free Stamp*. Stop saying that! What if we paid to have the free *Free Stamp* installed; would that be OK? Fine, we'll see if we have a park that's free. . . .

Willard Park, 800 E. Lakeside Ave., Cleveland, OH 44114

No phone

Hours: Always visible

Cost: Free

www.city.cleveland.oh.us/around_town/city.highlights/landmarks/freestamp.html

Directions: Between 6th and 9th St., just east of City Hall on the north side of
   Lakeside Ave.

Suburbs
Bay Village
The Real Fugitive

The Cleveland murder trial of Dr. Sam Sheppard was the 1950s Trial of the Century, and had many parallels to OJ Simpson's Trial of the Century 40 years later. Accused in the brutal murder of his wife, Sheppard was ill-served by the detectives and prosecutors investigating the case, was convicted by the press before he ever got to court, and was centerring at proceedings that looked more like a circus than a trial. But, unlike Simpson, he was innocent—and he was found guilty.

On the night of July 3 and the morning of July 4, 1954, somebody entered Sam and Marilyn Sheppard's lakeside home and attacked the pregnant Marilyn while she slept. Sam was sleeping on a couch downstairs, but he woke when he heard his wife screaming. He ran upstairs to the bedroom where he was knocked unconscious from behind. When Sheppard came to, he chased the man down to the beach where he was knocked out again, but not before getting a brief look at the "bushy-haired man."

Despite Sheppard's injuries, he became the police's prime suspect. When they learned four weeks later that the doctor was having an affair with a young lab technician, they arrested him and charged him with his wife's murder. Sheppard's trial received national attention, mostly because Judge Edward Blythin (who was running for reelection) freely issued press passes to national reporters, who in turn sensationalized case details, ensuring Sheppard would not receive a fair trial. Blythin even confided to columnist Dorothy Kilgallen that he thought "[Sheppard was] as guilty as hell, there is no question about it." That comment came back to bite the prosecution during arguments for a mistrial.

Sheppard was eventually convicted of second-degree murder and sentenced to life in prison. Sheppard's distraught mother committed suicide two weeks later, and his father died of a bleeding ulcer two weeks after her. His surviving family eventually hired F. Lee Bailey to appeal the case based upon unprecedented pretrial publicity. In 1966, the U.S. Supreme Court agreed with Bailey's argument that the trial had been tainted by "massive, pervasive, prejudicial publicity," called the proceedings "bedlam," and threw out the conviction.

Interestingly, back in 1959, police found Marilyn's wedding ring in the possession of window washer Richard Eberling. He had been arrested, and later convicted, of an unrelated theft. Eberling had worked with a maintenance crew at the Sheppard home prior to the murder, and police had found his blood at the crime scene. He claimed it was there because he cut himself washing a window a few days before the killing, though company records indicated that another employee had worked that day. Did police ever reveal this information to the defense in the retrial? C'mon. In 1984, Eberling was charged in the push-down-the-stairs death of Ethel May Durkin of nearby Lakewood, a crime he committed in order to get a $750,000 inheritance. In 1989 he went to jail for her murder. Curious, eh?

Bailey's vigorous defense in the 1966 retrial cleared Sheppard, but not in the court of public opinion. He abandoned any hope of reviving his medical practice, and ended up on the professional wrestling circuit, fighting under the ring name Killer Sheppard. He remarried, then divorced, and on April 6, 1970, died in Columbus at age 46, a poor, defeated alcoholic.

Hollywood capitalized on the well-known case as the basis for *The Fugitive*, starring David Janssen as Dr. Richard Kimble. A few of the details were changed—the bushy-haired man became a one-armed man, and Kimble escaped on his way to prison—but everyone who followed the 1963–67 TV series knew it was based upon the Sheppard case.

Sheppard Home, 28924 Lake Rd., Bay Village, OH 44140

Private phone

Hours: Private property; view from street

Cost: Free

www.samreesesheppard.org

Directions: One block west of Huntington Park on Rte. 6 (Lake Rd.).

Euclid
National Cleveland-Style Polka Hall of Fame

If you don't know who Frankie Yankovic is, what's the matter with you? Long before Alan Freed was flooding the airwaves with rock 'n' roll, polka reigned in Cleveland, and Yankovic was the Polka King. You'll see Yankovic's outfits and accordion here, as well as memorabilia from the museum's other inductees, such as Johnny Pecon, Walter Ostanek, Eddie Kenik, Johnny Vadnal, Lojze Slak, Joe Fedorchak, and others.

The hall of fame is run by volunteers from the American–Slovenian Polka Foundation. In addition to the exhibits, the place has a nice gift shop where you can find plenty of CDs, books, and polka outfits. If your traveling companion isn't a fan, earplugs are available at the drugstore down the street.

Shore Cultural Center, 291 E. 222nd St., Euclid, OH 44123

(866) 66-POLKA or (216) 261-FAME

Hours: Tuesdays–Fridays Noon–5 P.M., Saturdays 10 A.M.–3 P.M.

Cost: Free

www.clevelandstyle.com

Directions: South of Lake Shore Blvd. (Rte. 283) on 222nd St.

BEREA
Dogs and cats in Berea must, by law, wear taillights at night.

LAKEWOOD
Teri Garr was born in Lakewood on December 11, 1945.

Lyndhurst
Egg Shell Land

If you hadn't noticed already, Christmas home decoration has gotten out of hand. Stores encourage Americans to start stocking up on lights and plastic manger sets in mid-September, which hardly seems fair to the other holidays.

Well, don't worry about Easter, at least not in Lyndhurst. One dedicated family has been turning their front yard into an Easter eggstravaganza since 1957. They call their creation Egg Shell Land. Ron and Betty Manolio, along with the kids and a few helpers, arrange tens of thousands of plastic colored eggs into a variety of designs, from chicks emerging from their shells to Mickey Mouse, from Christian crosses to Chief Wahoo, the Cleveland Indians' mascot. The designs change from year to year. Egg Shell Land is only up for 10 days, so mark your calendars for the week after Palm Sunday.

1031 Linden Lane, Lyndhurst, OH 44124

Private phone

Hours: Palm Sunday–Tuesday after Easter

Cost: Free

Directions: Head east on Ridgebury Blvd. from Rte. 175 (Richmond Rd.), then north on Roland Rd., east on Ashwood Dr., then south on Linden Lane.

ROCKY RIVER

New York Yankees owner **George Steinbrenner** was born in Rocky River on July 4, 1930.

WILLOUGHBY

Comedian **Tim Conway** was born Thomas Daniel Conway in Willoughby on December 15, 1933.

WILLOWICK

More than 150 passengers and crew aboard the *G. P. Griffith* paddle-wheeler perished when it caught fire two miles offshore on June 17, 1850. The steamer tried to make it to land, but hit a sandbar 600 feet short of the shoreline. Most up the victims' bodies washed ashore near what is now 305th Street. A marker stands in Lakefront Lodge Park.

Macedonia
McUnionized

Part of working at an entry-level fast-food job is putting up with abuse from a bitter, loud-mouthed manager, right? Actually, no. Just ask Bryan Drapp. In April 1998, when his McDonald's boss, Jerry Guffey, blew up at 66-year-old worker Margaretha DeLollis for the unthinkable infraction of leaving a box of clean garbage bags next to the garbage cans, she burst into tears and ran out. Guffey told the burger-wrapping, 19-year-old Drapp to take her place. He refused, and walked out as well.

The next day, Drapp demanded that a list of employee grievances be addressed, but his manager refused. Drapp headed over to Wal-Mart, not to apply for another crummy job, but to pick up the supplies he needed to picket McDonald's. Soon, half of the restaurant's 40 workers were non-dues-paying members of Teamsters Local 416. The strike got Drapp on CNN, the *Tonight Show*, and Howard Stern. Management finally caved; employees were given a higher base pay, four days' notice on schedule changes, and one week's paid vacation after a year's service. Of course, the agreement only applied to the three franchises owned by Drapp's employer, Jed Greene. Still, it was the first time a McDonald's was McUnionized.

For Drapp, the victory was short-lived. Several months after returning to work he was fired for showing up at work with "Go Union" defiantly painted on his face. Kids these days. . . .

McDonald's, 6400 Macedonia Commons Blvd., Macedonia, OH 44056

(330) 467-9191

Hours: Monday–Saturday 6 A.M.–11 P.M., Sunday 7 A.M.–11 P.M.

Cost: Always visible; Meals $4–$6, Supersize +39¢

Directions: South of Aurora Rd. (Rte. 82), just west of I-271.

Willoughby Hills
Squire's Castle

Feargus B. Squire, a vice president at the Standard Oil Company (under president John D. Rockefeller), had grown tired of Cleveland. It was crowded and polluted—mostly by Standard Oil—so he built a castle out in the country where he could hunt, breathe, and relax.

His wife Rebecca wasn't so keen on the idea. She liked her Cleveland friends, and decided to stay in the couple's city home while the rest of the Squire family ran off to the woods. This war of wills went on for a few years until Rebecca realized her family would not give in and return, so she decided to give rural life a try.

But just like Lisa Douglas on *Green Acres*, Rebecca never quite adjusted. She found it difficult to fall asleep, so she roamed the house at night, ever worried that wild animals might break in and attack her children. One night she stumbled into her husband's trophy room and was spooked by the critter heads mounted on the walls. She ran out screaming, and on the way out "clotheslined" herself on a rope strung between two antlers near a wall. Her neck snapped like a twig.

Rebecca died instantly . . . but not entirely. Legend has it that you can still hear her wail at night in the ruins of the castle along Chagrin River Road. Sometimes her ghost is spotted wandering the grounds carrying the red lantern she toted on that fateful, clumsy night.

North Chagrin Reservation, Cleveland Metroparks, Strawberry Lane, Willoughby Hills, OH 44144

(440) 473-3370

Hours: Daylight hours

Cost: Free

Directions: Turn south on Rte. 91 (S.O.M Center Rd.) from Rte. 6 (Euclid-Chardon Rd.), east at the third left (Strawberry Lane).

4

THE SOUTHWEST

The folks of southwest Ohio are a clever bunch. Oh sure, there's the whole airplane thing, but did you also know that the banana split was invented here? That's right, four years after the Wright brothers' first powered flight at Kitty Hawk, North Carolina, the owner of Hazard's Drug Store in Wilmington made the region's next big scientific breakthrough. And when customers purchased their banana splits, how did the soda jerks ring them up? On a cash register, another local invention, which had been around since 1878. And today, if you go to the supermarket to buy the ingredients you need to make your own, how do the clerks check out your items? With a bar code scanner . . . another gift southwest Ohio has given the world.

But that's not all. When your teeth rot from all that sugar, who will repair your winning smile? A dentist, hopefully trained at a descendant of America's first dental school in Bainbridge, located in—you guessed it!—southwest Ohio. And if all those banana splits make you morbidly obese, and you have to consider career options on daytime talk shows, who do you have to thank? Phil Donahue. And *where* did he start? If you didn't know already, I bet you could make a pretty good guess.

Bainbridge
John Harris Dental Museum

The day Dr. John Harris showed his students how to yank out a rotten molar in 1825, dental education in America was born. Though his initial class was small, many of his early students went on to found other dental schools across America, including his brother who, in 1840, founded the world's first dental college in Baltimore, Maryland.

If going to a dentist today gives you the willies, you could probably pass on this place, though it will be painfully obvious that practices have improved (somewhat) since Harris's day. The museum's display cases are filled with gruesome contraptions used to drill, extract, and repair teeth, including a pair of forceps used to pull one of Abraham Lincoln's teeth.

This shrine to dentistry also boasts the World's Largest Collection of Wooden False Teeth. The strangest pair is a set of black ebony choppers purchased by a jealous husband who didn't want his wife to look attractive to other men. What a sweetie.

208 W. Main St., PO Box 424, Bainbridge, OH 45612

(740) 634-2246 or (740) 634-2228

Hours: April–May and September–October, Saturday–Sunday Noon–4:30 P.M.; June–
August, Tuesday–Sunday Noon–4 P.M.

Cost: Free

www.bainbridgedentalmuseum.com

Directions: On Rte. 50 (Main St.), two blocks west of Rte. 20.

Bradford
Wally's Filling Station

The first thing you should know about Wally's Filling Station is that it's not a filling station at all, so don't pull up on fumes hoping to fill your tank. Wally's *never was* a filling station; it was Goober and Gomer Pyle's imaginary business on *The Andy Griffith Show*. In the late 1980s, farmer Bob Scheib decided he wanted to re-create the sitcom's fictitious structure, right down to the oil cans and fan belts. So he built it in his cornfield. It took him three years.

You're welcome to visit and to buy modern sodas from its antique vending machine. Scheib also has four vintage police cars parked here, twice the number as were on the Mayberry police force. In mid-July each year the station hosts the Mayberry Squad Car Rendezvous, leaving fake small towns across the nation unable to respond to their low-grade emergencies.

10870 Sugar Grove–Circle Hill Rd., Bradford, OH 45308

Private phone

Hours: Daily 9 A.M.–5 P.M.

Cost: Free

Directions: East of Rte. 721 on Rte. 78 (Sugar Grove–Circle Hill Rd.).

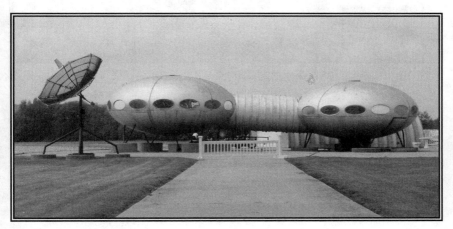

Take me to your architect.

Carlisle
My Favorite Martian House

Don't be alarmed, but a family of aliens—the outer space kind—have purchased a lot on the northwest side of Carlisle, and they look as if they plan on staying. Their home was built from two UFOs connected by a tubular hallway. Strangely, the neighbors don't seem to mind living next door to Martians, which is hopeful commentary on intergalactic relations. Now if we could all just get along with our fellow Earthlings.

OK, so Uncle Martin's family doesn't really live here . . . but look at it. Don't you think they could?

Central Ave. and Chamberlain Rd., Carlisle, OH 45005

Private phone

Hours: Always visible; view from the street

Cost: Free

Directions: At the northwest end of town along Rte. 123 (Central Ave./Carlisle Pike).

Mr. President, did you remember not to go before we take off?
Photo by author, courtesy of U.S. Air Force Museum

Dayton
Bockscar

"What's *Bockscar*?" you ask. Do you remember several years ago when the Smithsonian Institution chose to put the atom bomb–dropping *Enola Gay* on exhibit, and all the emotions that dredged up? Well, *Bockscar* is the plane that dropped the bomb on Nagasaki. Somehow it flew in under the sensitivity radar and is on display at the U.S. Air Force Museum in Dayton. Just behind it is a replica of Fat Man, the second atomic bomb ever used in warfare. A few folks have reported seeing the ghost of a small Japanese boy near the plane.

Yes, *Bockscar* might dredge up unpleasant memories for some visitors, but don't forget, this is a *military* museum. And what a museum it is! It's got more than 300 restored, near-mint-condition planes and artifacts stretching all the way back to the birth of aviation. The Early Years Gallery has the Wrights' 1916 wind tunnel, their anemometer, and a scrap of fabric from the first Flyer to soar over the beach at Kitty Hawk,

North Carolina. It's also got a British Sopwith Camel, Snoopy's plane of choice in a dogfight with the Red Baron.

The Air Power Gallery houses planes from World War II, Korea, and Vietnam, as well as non-airworthy items such as Glenn Miller's trombone. One of the gallery's bombers, the *Strawberry Bitch*, is said to be haunted by several of the B-24's crew who died onboard. The new Cold War Gallery brings visitors into the '50s and beyond. You might be surprised when you see a Soviet MiG-15 here, but you'll be no more surprised than the North Korean Air Force who lost it to a defecting pilot. He turned over the jet to the U.S. military in South Korea for a $100,000 reward. The Space Gallery contains a can opener and a "zero-G" razor used during the Apollo moon shots, along with the orbit module from *Apollo 15*.

Be sure to sign up for the shuttle bus ride over to the Presidential Aircraft and Research and Development/Flight Test Hangar. It's the only way you're going to see futuristic craft, such as the XB-70 Valkyrie, an enormous supersonic jet that looks like it belongs on the set of *Star Wars*. The hangar has most of the planes ever used as Air Force One: FDR's C-54 *Sacred Cow*, Truman's Douglas VC-118 *Independence*, Eisenhower's Lockheed VC-121E *Columbine III*, Kennedy's Boeing 707 (later used to transport his casket back from Dallas), and several smaller craft used for short presidential hops by Nixon, Ford, Carter, and Reagan. The *Independence* is connected to Ohio in another unique way: one of Truman's biggest congressional foes was Ohio's GOP Senator Robert Taft, and whenever the president flew over the state he would use the plane's lavatory, then ask the pilot to dump the holding tank from 35,000 feet.

Finally, in case you were wondering: Wright-Patterson AFB was obviously named, in part, after Dayton's famous Wright brothers. But who was this Patterson person? None other than Frank Patterson, a pioneer in military aviation who died during an unfortunate propeller–machine gun synchronization experiment in 1918.

U.S. Air Force Museum, 1100 Spaatz St., Wright-Patterson AFB, OH 45433

(937) 255-3286

Hours: Daily 9 A.M.–5 P.M.

Cost: Free

www.wpafb.af.mil/museum

Directions: Northeast of downtown off I-675, Exit 15, and follow the signs.

HANGAR 18

One of the most interesting things in Wright-Patterson AFB's collection is something you *don't* see: the dead alien bodies recovered from the flying saucer crash in Roswell, New Mexico, on July 4, 1953. Ufologists have long speculated that they were taken to this base's secret "Blue Room," commonly referred to as Hangar 18. (In actually, it's Hangar 13, which is Building 18.) Apparently everyone who participated in the transfer, from the doctors who performed the autopsies to the forklift operators who loaded their little green coffins onto the transport plane, were sworn to secrecy.

The story makes some procedural sense; if the Roswell crash were indeed true, it would have been investigated by Wright-Patterson's National Air Intelligence Center, known as T2, and its engineering office, known as T3. The base is also home to the Air Force's research institute on antigravity, and some have speculated that the Pentagon reverse-engineered the downed saucer to make the much-talked-about-but-supersecret Lenticular Reentry Vehicle.

Is any of this true? Rumors have swarmed around the base's role in the cleanup for years. Senator Barry Goldwater once asked General Curtis LeMay for a tour of the facility and LeMay ordered the senator "never to bring it up again." Hmmmmm . . . and what about the stories that the bureaucrats attending the Dayton Peace Talks on Bosnia were taken to Hangar 18 on a field trip? The truth must be told!!!

BORN IN DAYTON

Dayton is also the birthplace of several celebrities:

Erma Bombeck	February 21, 1927
Paul Lawrence Dunbar	June 27, 1872
Gerry Faust	May 21, 1935
Gordon Jump	April 1, 1927
Chad Lowe	January 15, 1968
Gary Sandy	December 25, 1945
Martin Sheen (Ramon Estevez)	August 3, 1940
Jonathan Winters	November 11, 1925
Orville Wright	August 19, 1871

Dead in Dayton

Dayton's two most famous former residents, Orville and Wilbur Wright, are still here, though they're a little under the weather. Actually, they're a little under the ground . . . at Woodland Cemetery. Wilbur died relatively young of typhoid fever on May 30, 1912. Orville lived to see the age of supersonic flight, but not by much; he passed away on January 30, 1948. They're buried at Woodland side by side, just as they were for most of their lives.

But the Wright brothers aren't the only well-known folks planted in this historic cemetery. Here are a few more you might recognize:

➡ **John H. Balsley** (1823–1895) invented the folding stepladder.

➡ **L. M. Berry** (1888–1980) was the founder of the Yellow Pages.

➡ **Erma Bombeck** (Fiste) (1927–1996), the humorist, is buried beneath a 14.5-ton boulder that was brought here from her Arizona home.

➡ **Paul Laurence Dunbar** (1872–1906), the famous African American poet, was born and died in Dayton.

➡ **Andrew Iddings** (1881–1974) invented the stereoscopic 3D camera.

➡ **Lorenzo Langstroth** (1811–1895) is often referred to as the Father of American Beekeeping; his marker is hive-shaped.

➡ **Madam Elizabeth Richter** (1840–1923) has a marker surrounded by her "fallen girls"; the statue on Richter's grave is believed to be the inspiration for Thomas Wolfe's *Look Homeward Angel*.

➡ **James Ritty** (1837–1918) invented the mechanical cash register in 1878, then sold the patent to John Patterson for $6,500; Patterson founded National Cash Register.

➡ **Valentine Winters** (1807–1890), founder of Winters Bank of Ohio, which later became Bank One, is the great-great-grandfather of actor Jonathan Winters.

Woodland Cemetery, 118 N. Woodland Ave., Dayton, OH 45409

(937) 228-3221

E-mail: info@woodlandcemetery.org

Hours: Grounds, winter, daily 8:30 A.M.–6 P.M.; summer, daily 8 A.M.–7 P.M.; Office,
   Monday–Friday 8 A.M.–4:30 P.M., Saturday 8 A.M.–Noon

Cost: Free

www.woodlandcemetery.org

Directions: Three blocks east of Main St. (Rte. 48), one block north of Stewart St.

Donahue Does Dayton

He probably didn't realize it at the time, but Phil Donahue revolution-
ized television on Monday, November 6, 1967. What had he come up
with? The first talk show with audience participation. The formula was
actually born out of domestic necessity; he had been hosting a daytime
radio call-in show called *Conversational Piece* on WHIO, as well as
anchoring the station's 11 P.M. TV news. The schedule seldom allowed
him to get home to see his family before midnight. When rival station
WLWD-TV offered him the opportunity to translate his radio show into
a television format, he jumped at the chance.

His first guest on that Monday morning was outspoken atheist
Madalyn Murray O'Hair. His Tuesday show was about what single men
want in a woman. (Remember, this was a time when some women still
cared about what men wanted.) Wednesday featured a Dayton obstetri-
cian who brought a graphic film of a baby's birth; on Thursday Phil visited with a local undertaker and reclined in a coffin; and on Friday the
discussion centered on a new anatomically correct Little Brother doll.

Though the topics were tame by today's standards, in 1960s Dayton they
were shockers. Donahue quickly developed a loyal daytime following. Writer
Erma Bombeck (who at one time lived across the street from Donahue in
nearby Centerville) explained his appeal: he was "every wife's replacement for
the husband that doesn't talk to her." Soon the show was being syndicated to
stations nationwide, and in 1973 he moved the show to Chicago.

WDTN-TV (formerly WLWD-TV), 4595 S. Dixie Dr., Dayton, OH 45439

(937) 293-2101

Hours: Always visible; view from street

Cost: Free

Directions: Three blocks northeast of Springboro Pike on Dixie Dr., the continuation of
  Central Ave. east of I-75.

DAYTON

The ghost of a young blonde girl in a blue sweater and Nike sneakers
has been spotted in Dayton's Woodland Cemetery (118 Woodland
Avenue) near a glowing tombstone.

I think I'm going to be ill. . . .

Greenville
The Wall of Gum

Have you every tried to eat a loose meat sandwich while chewing on a wad of gum? It ain't pretty. But you know what's even more disgusting? Pulling that gum out of your mouth and sticking it to a wall where everyone else has to look at it.

Strange as it sounds, that's exactly what the folks of Greenville have been doing for years at the Maid Rite Sandwich Shop: as customers pull up to the drive-through window they stick their wads of gum on the adjacent brick wall. And they're not the only culprits—dine-ins do it, too! Every square inch of the building's exterior is encrusted with used gum, including the window sills, the door frames, and the entire street-side facade! If there's a silver lining to this revolting local custom it's that nobody seems to be smacking away *inside* the restaurant, so the undersides of the tables are free from the masticated gunk.

This place's specialty, the loose meat sandwich, must be pretty darn good because this revolting collection doesn't seem to scare away any customers. Why they don't lose their lunches after leaving from lunch is still a mystery to me.

Maid Rite Sandwich Shop, 125 N. Broadway, Greenville, OH 45331

(937) 548-9340

Hours: Always visible; Restaurant open Monday–Thursday 10 A.M.–10 P.M., Friday–
   Saturday 10 A.M.–Midnight, Sunday 11 A.M.–9 P.M.

Cost: Free; Meals $4–$7

Directions: Two blocks northwest of the town square on Rte. 571 (Broadway).

Lebanon
That's What Law Clerks Are For

Clement Vallandingham was a no-good troublemaker; just ask Abraham Lincoln. This so-called Peace Democrat from Dayton was opposed to the Civil War, though he was not particularly offended by the violent institution of slavery. When he violated the president's General Order Number 38 by speaking to a rally of 20,000 Copperheads in 1863 (the law made anyone supporting the Confederacy a traitor), he was arrested and sent to prison. Because Vallandingham was running for Ohio governor at the time, the action of the federal authorities seemed a bit heavy-handed. Lincoln soon freed Vallandingham but shipped him off to the South.

Several years later in 1871, with his political career in ruins, Vallandingham was back in Ohio working as a lawyer and defending a murderer. While practicing the defense's closing arguments at the Golden Lamb Inn in Lebanon, he tried to demonstrate how the victim might have shot himself. The gun discharged, fatally wounding him. The argument must have been persuasive, because the jury later found his client not guilty.

Golden Lamb Inn, 27 S. Broadway, Lebanon, OH 45306

(513) 932-5065

E-mail: comments@goldenlamb.com

Hours: Monday–Friday 11 A.M.–3 P.M. and 5–9 P.M., Sunday Noon–3 P.M. and 4–8 P.M.

Cost: Meals $8–$20

www.goldenlamb.com

Directions: One block north of Rte. 123 (Main St.) on Rte. 48 (Broadway).

Peebles
Great Serpent Mound

About 3,200,000 years ago a meteorite slammed into southeast Ohio and left an enormous crater. Mother Nature did her best to cover up the mess. Then, about 3,197,000 years later (about 800 B.C.), the Hopewell Culture moved in and set up shop. They lived in the area for some time before building a snake-shaped effigy mound on the northeast shore of Brush Creek, sometime around 1100 A.D. The 20-foot-wide, 5-foot-high mound twists back and forth seven times over 1,335 feet, from the tip of its tail to its open-mouthed head. The serpent looks prepared to swallow a giant egg.

Or not.

Here's the problem: the Hopewells were a tidy bunch. Though they lived in the area for centuries, they left few tools, graves, artwork, or trash piles that might have given clues to their lives. They vanished as abruptly as they arrived, leaving only their earthen structures behind. This allows much room for interpretation as to who they were and what they were doing. And you'd better believe folks have come up with some wild theories.

Here's one: in 1066 A.D., Halley's comet passed close to the earth, and was extremely prominent in the night sky. Could the Great Serpent Mound actually be the Great Comet Mound? Or how about this one: did the Hopewells somehow know about the meteorite strike 3.2 million years earlier? Is the serpent instead a representation of a space rock burning through the atmosphere? Finally, with the image of a snake swallowing an egg so prominent in ancient Egyptian and European set-tlers, could it be that the Hopewells came from somewhere even farther away, across the ocean? Talk of Atlantis can't be far away. Climb to the top of the park's observation tower and draw your own conclusion. Or make up a new one.

Serpent Mound State Memorial, 3850 State Rte. 73, Peebles, OH 45660

(800) 752-2757 or (937) 587-2796

E-mail: serpent@bright.net

Hours: April–May and September–October, daily 10 A.M.–5 P.M.; June–August, daily
10 A.M.–8 P.M.

Cost: Free; Parking $6

www.ohiohistory.org/places/serpent

Directions: North on Rte. 41, then west on Rte. 73 at Locust Grove, ahead on the right.

Point Pleasant
Ulysses S. Grant's Mobile Birthplace

Early U.S. presidents were famous for being born in log cabins, but
Ulysses S. Grant was the first ever to be born in a mobile home. His
16-by-19.5-foot birthplace didn't start out that way, however.

Grant was born in Point Pleasant on April 27, 1822. When his family
moved to nearby Georgetown (219 E. Grant Street, (937) 378-4222) a
year later, they thought no more of their old homestead. But years later,
after Grant accepted Lee's surrender, the locals realized they had a collector's item on their hands. So in the late 1800s, the house was placed on a
barge and sent on a tour of the entire Mississippi River Valley, including
side trips up the Missouri and the Ohio. It was moved to the Ohio State
Fair in Columbus in the 1920s, where it stayed until 1936. A bit the worse
for wear, it was returned to Point Pleasant where it remains to this day.

But tomorrow . . . who knows?

Rte. 52, Point Pleasant, OH 45143

(513) 553-4911

Hours: April–October, Wednesday–Saturday 9:30 A.M.–5 P.M., Sunday Noon–5 P.M.

Cost: Adults $1, Seniors 75¢, Kids (6–12) 50¢

www.ohiohistory.org/places/grantbir

Directions: Along Rte. 52 at Rte. 232.

LEBANON
Actor **Howard Hesseman** was born in Lebanon on February 27, 1940.

Rest in peace—at last.

Sabina
Eugene the Mummy

Americans today find death an uncomfortable subject, but it wasn't so long ago that people weren't afraid to snag a dead body and bring it to a frat party, or prop it up at a bus stop as a practical joke. Well, at least a few Sabina residents had no problem doing that.

What am I talking about? Eugene the Mummy, Sabina's favorite dead guy! On June 9, 1929, the body of a middle-aged African American man was discovered in the ditch along Wilmington Pike (Route 3) east of town, near Borum Road. There didn't appear to be any foul play, so the coroner listed "natural causes" on his death certificate. Papers found on his body led authorities to a Cincinnati address: a vacant lot. Nobody in his old neighborhood seemed to remember him by his description.

Meanwhile, back in Sabina, the body was given a name—Eugene— the same name as the last person the police talked to in Cincinnati. Eugene's embalmed body waited at the Littleton Funeral Home (104 N. Jackson Street, (937) 584-2431). And waited. And waited. Then some- body came up with a unique idea: Eugene was given a new suit and propped up in a windowed brick shed on the east side of the funeral home. Maybe somebody passing through would hear about the town's mummy, stop by for a look, and recognize their long-lost uncle.

That was the plan. It was a weird plan, yes, but a plan nonetheless. Eugene was viewed by more than a million visitors over the next 30 years, but nobody said he looked familiar. Occasionally kids would take him out for a drive in the country, or up to Columbus for an OSU frat party.

Somehow Eugene always found his way back to Sabina. It was as if he belonged here. So, in 1963, the Littleton Funeral Home made it official: they buried him in a plot at the local cemetery under a simple, strange, and inaccurate—it lists the burial year as 1964—tombstone.

Sabina Cemetery, 330 N. College St., Sabina, OH 45169

No phone

Hours: Dawn–Dusk

Cost: Free

Directions: Three blocks north of Rte. 22 (Washington St.), one block east of Rte. 63 (Hulse St.).

IT COULD HAVE BEEN WORSE

Eugene the Mummy might have suffered a few indignities between his death and eventual burial, but it was nothing compared to another Ohio corpse. James "Slim" Davis, known among the Purple Gang as **Gold Tooth Jimmy**, was gunned down by law enforcement near Canton in the 1920s. When nobody claimed his body, the local undertaker sold Jimmy to a sideshow to recoup the embalming costs. Gold Tooth Jimmy saw more of the United States as a mummy than Davis ever did as a living, breathing human. Sideshow barker Captain Harvey Lee Boswell gave him top billing in his traveling Palace of Wonders from the 1960s to the 1990s.

Boswell eventually sold Jimmy to an unnamed collector with unique tastes. Jimmy's current whereabouts are unknown.

Springfield
Ben Hartman's Historical Rock Garden

Just because you're out of a job is no excuse not to keep busy. During the Great Depression, unemployed Ben Hartman was looking for something to do to pass the time, and ended up creating one of Ohio's greatest folk art environments: the Historical Rock Garden.

It started as the Non-Historical Fish Pond, a cement-lined divot designed to hold a few goldfish. Hartman found he enjoyed working with concrete, and with rocks from a nearby construction site he had an endless supply of raw material. Like a convict, Hartman broke the stones into manageable sizes using a hammer, but then he glued them back together in recognizable forms.

The result is an impressive collection of historic buildings and religious dioramas: *Independence Hall, Custer's Last Stand, Daniel in the Lions' Den* (complete with the bones of chowed-on Christians). There are also renderings of Lincoln's log cabin birthplace, a medieval castle, Noah's Ark, and salutes to John Brown, Joe Louis, and the Dionne Quintuplets.

Sadly, Hartman lived only seven years between the creation of his first sculpture and his untimely death in 1944. His family still owns the property, and has done a wonderful job of maintaining Ben's creation. Still, there has been some weather damage—better see this attraction while you can. Visitors are welcome to stroll through the property if there's somebody home, but if there isn't, please view it from the street.

1905 Russell Ave., Springfield, OH 45506

Private phone

Hours: Daylight hours

Cost: Free

Directions: Three blocks west of Yellow Springs St. on McCain Ave., at Russell Ave., on the southwest side of town.

WILBERFORCE
Boxer **Mike Tyson** was awarded a Ph.D. of Humane Letters from Central State University (www.centralstate.edu) in Wilberforce at the 1989 commencement ceremony.

The start of something big.

Troy
Birthplace of Bar Codes

When the cashier at Marsh Supermarket scanned a 10-pack of Wrigley's chewing gum at 8:01 A.M. on June 26, 1974, she started something BIG. No, it had nothing to do with the gum. It was the birth of the bar code! Yes, you take them for granted today, but there was a time when each and every food item had to be rung up by hand, when employees had to be familiar with the prices of the products on their shelves.

Well, no more. And sure, there have been tradeoffs for being able to check out at the supermarket in a reasonable amount of time. Originally there was the fear that you'd somehow go blind if the laser scanner hit your eye just right (you won't), but now folks worry that marketing firms are tracking their purchasing habits (they are), and that the government can take a look at, say, the books they're purchasing (it can, under the U.S. Patriot Act). So if you ever want to buy a book that says Attorney General John Ashcroft is a creepy zealot, be sure to pay in cash.

Oops . . . how did you pay for this book?

Marsh Supermarket, Sherwood Centre, 982 N. Market St., Troy, OH 45373

(937) 335-6750

Hours: Always open

Cost: Free; Groceries extra

www.marsh.net/mtc_chis.html

Directions: Four blocks northeast of Rte. 14 (Staunton Rd.).

Wilmington
Birthplace of the Banana Split

Things were pretty slow at Hazard's Drug Store in Wilmington during a January 1907 blizzard, so to pass the time the owner came up with a contest: which employee could make the best new ice cream dish?

Perhaps Ernest Hazard was declared the winner because he was the boss, but it's unlikely. His creation was by far the best: one scoop each of chocolate (topped with strawberry jam), vanilla (topped with chocolate syrup), and strawberry (topped with crushed pineapple), all covered in whipped cream and sprinkled with nuts, gently cradled between two halves of a banana sliced lengthwise. Oh, and don't forget the cherries on top.

Though the dessert was a hit, particularly with students at nearby Wilmington College, it didn't yet have a name. When Hazard asked his cousin Clifton for a suggestion, he immediately came up with "banana split." Clifton also suggested Ernest keep looking for a better name, but the one he came up with stuck.

Today Wilmington celebrates Hazard's invention with the Banana Split Festival each June. If you can't make it to the big event, Gibson's Goodies on the northwest side of town scoops up historic reproductions seven days a week.

Gibson's Goodies, 718 Ohio Ave., Wilmington, OH 45177

(937) 383-2373

Hours: Daily 11 A.M.–9 P.M.

Cost: Two scoops $2.89, Three scoops $3.50

www.bananasplitfestival.com

Directions: Two blocks west of Rte. 134 on Rte. 68, on the northwest side of town.

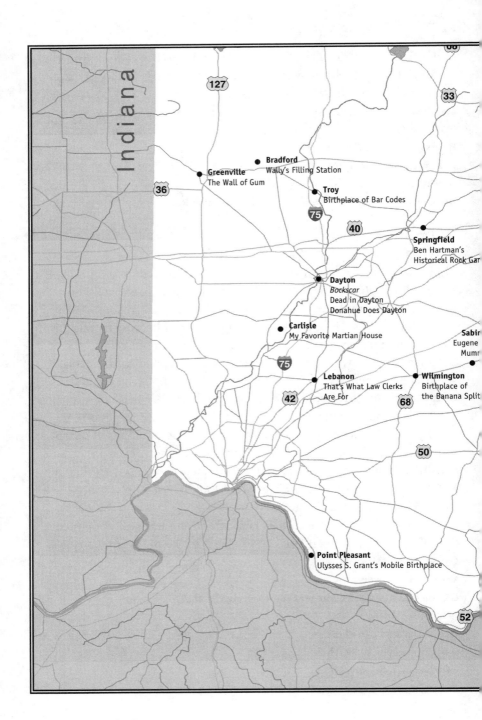

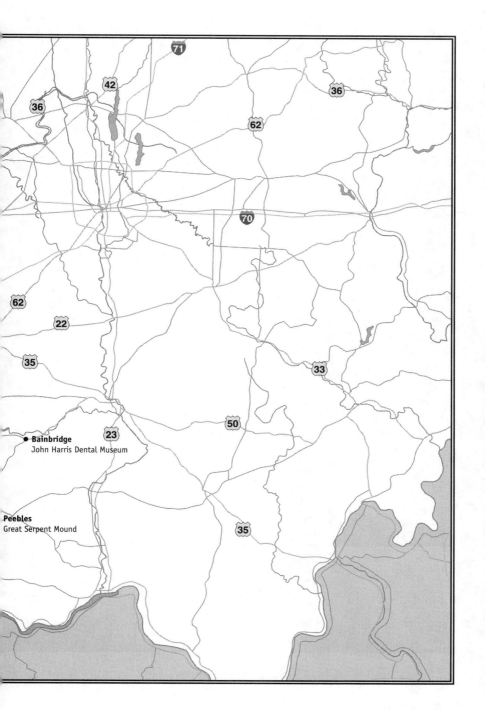

5

CiNCiNNaTi ARea

Cincinnati still takes it on the chin for its porcine history, and perhaps rightfully so. In the mid-1800s, the world's largest pig market was located in the city's Fountain Square. Visitors reported their observations to shocked folks back home: "If I determined upon a walk up Main Street, the chances were five hundred to one against my reaching the shady side without brushing by a snout fresh dripping from the kennel," Frances Trollope reported, while her son Anthony said the town reeked of "the odor of hogs going up to the Ohio heavens—of hogs in a state of transit from hoggish nature to clothes brushes, saddles, sausages, and lard." You just can't *buy* that type of publicity!

Figuring they might as well join in the fun, modern Cincinnati residents have embraced their piggy roots, sometimes calling themselves Porkipolitans. When the city was looking for art to place in Sawyer Point Park (Eggleston Avenue and Pete Rose Way), they chose sculptures that were reminiscent of the winged lions of Venice's Piazza San Marco, but Cincinnati's statues are of winged pigs.

Of course, this all might be part of a grand strategy to divert attention from other embarrassments, such as the city's popular ex-mayor, Jerry Springer. Or the fact that Iggy Pop invented stage diving here. Or that a prominent local hero almost talked the U.S. Congress into funding a voyage to the center of the earth. These stories should not be forgotten. These stories are what this chapter is all about.

Cincinnati
Busch Mountains

Who says kids these days don't have ambition? The Busch Brothers of Cincinnati have set their sights high: they want to break the record for the World's Largest Collection of Cans from a Single Brewery. They probably have already, but they're keeping at it until the editors at the *Guinness Book of World Records* take notice. (I bet they would if the Busch Brothers were collecting Guinness cans!)

It all started back in 1984 in a house just off the University of Cincinnati campus. The original Busch Brothers—not to be confused with the Bush brothers, also known to knock back a few brewskies in their college days—began collecting the empties from their frequent drinking get-togethers. They only saved the Busch cans, the brand most of them drank. In 1992 they moved their 2,400-can collection to its present location, the Busch Mountains home, and started decorating. With cans. *Everywhere.* The more beer they drank, the more walls they covered. The brothers guesstimate they knock back about 4,000 cans a year (the club has expanded), which puts them at about 40,000 empties lining every wall in this house and a few next door. The ceilings of the Busch Mountains house are papered with flattened Busch boxes.

Eight Busch Brothers have entered the house's elite Case Club over the years. The rules are simple: a nominee must consume 24 cans of beer in a single evening, all at the Busch Mountains house, without sleeping or vomiting. Seven of the Case Club members drank two dozen, but Rich Laske (that show-off!) drank 25 on April 23, 1994.

Future plans for expanding the Busch Brothers club to include a Liver Transplant chapter are in the works. The Busch Brothers just don't know it yet—they're too busy decorating.

2712 Jefferson Ave., Cincinnati, OH 45219

Private phone

E-mail: buschbros@buschmountains.com

Hours: Ask for an invitation by E-mail

Cost: Free, but donating a case of Busch would be a nice gesture

www.buschmountains.com

Directions: Three blocks north of McMillan St. on Jefferson Ave., on the east side of the UC campus.

Charlie Taft, First Son/Robot

Charlie Taft, born in 1897, was the third child of President William Howard Taft, but he was the only one of his offspring to be turned into a robot! This spunky animatron acts as your tour guide through his father's Cincinnati birthplace.

The 27th president, and later Supreme Court justice, was born in the first-floor front room of this home on September 15, 1857. A rotund child, Taft earned the nickname "Big Lub" from his friends, and went on to become our most massive chief executive at 332 pounds. Taft lived in this home until he went away to Yale in 1874.

He returned to Cincinnati in 1885 and a year later married Hellen "Nellie" Herron on June 19, 1886. The ceremony took place at her parents' home on Pike Street (since demolished), and the happy couple moved to 1763 East McMillan Street, a home they called The Quarry. This private home is not open to the public, nor are any other Taft sites around town, with the exception of this birthplace. Seems a bit skimpy for such a big, big man.

2038 Auburn Ave., Cincinnati, OH 45219

(513) 684-3262

Hours: Daily 8 A.M.–4 P.M.

Cost: Free

www.nps.gov/wiho/

Directions: Nine blocks north of Liberty St., six blocks west of I-71.

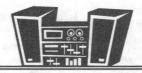

CINCINNATI

There is no WKRP in Cincinnati. There is, however, a WKRC (1906 Highland Avenue). Three of the 1970s sitcom's cast hailed from Ohio: **Howard Hesseman** (Lebanon), **Gordon Jump** (Dayton), and **Gary Sandy** (Dayton).

My hero!
Photo by author, courtesy of Cincinnati Fire Museum

Cincinnati Fire Museum

The Cincinnati Fire Department has come a long way from its early days. Back in 1808, somebody had to bang the big Fire Drum to summon volunteers to battle a blaze. But the department's methods and tools have improved. In 1816, Washington Company #1 purchased a newfangled Hunneman Pumper that could squirt water up to 133 feet. And in 1820, the city installed its first hydrant system; firefighters had to dig down to a buried wooden pipe and drill a hole to get the water. The holes were later patched with a cork plug, hence the little-understood nickname for a hydrant: a fireplug.

These are just a few of the things you'll learn at the Cincinnati Fire Museum. It still has the old Fire Drum, as well as an 1836 Hunneman Pumper, a classic engine known as "The Fox," an Atlas 400 Life Net, and a cab of a modern engine with working lights and siren. Next to the fire pole connecting the first floor to the basement, the bright and noisy cab is the biggest hit with schoolchildren who come here for safety training. The museum also operates a Safe Home to help kids identify and eliminate fire hazards, and how to survive a blaze by stopping, dropping, and rolling.

315 W. Court St., Cincinnati, OH 45202

(513) 621-5553

Hours: Tuesday–Friday 10 A.M.–4 P.M., Saturday–Sunday Noon–4 P.M.

Cost: Adults $5, Seniors $4, Kids $3

www.cincyfiremuseum.com

Directions: Two blocks north of 9th St., one block west of Central Pkwy.

CINCINNATI

Bloodlike acid fell on the Cincinnati home of Ed Mootz (440 Boal Street) on July 22, 1955, killing his peach trees. The liquid came from a red, pink, and green rolling cloud.

Author **Harriet Beecher Stowe** lived at her father's home in Cincinnati (2950 Gilbert Avenue, (513) 632-5320, www.ohiohistory.org/places/stowe) from 1832 to 1836. She moved away when she married.

Cincinnati Municipal Court Judge Leslie Gaines resigned from the bench in 1996 after seeing a vision of Jesus in a marble pillar inside the Hamilton County Courthouse (1000 Main Street).

Hunters: 5,000,000,000. Passenger pigeons: 0.

Photo by author, courtesy of Cincinnati Zoo

Goodbye Martha! Adios Inca!

Only the meteorite that wiped out the dinosaurs has a worse track record than humans when it comes to bumping off animal species. Dodo birds. Buffaloes. Unicorns. You name it, we've killed it. And it often took a lot of work; look at the passenger pigeon. Or, rather, look at the story of the passenger pigeon.

When you run the numbers, the systematic elimination of the passenger pigeon is shocking. In the 1860s there were between three and five *billion* in North America, but by 1914 hunters reduced that number to one. Not one billion. One bird. Her name was Martha. She lived at the Cincinnati Zoo, and she passed away on September 1, 1914.

To be fair, passenger pigeons were one of the most destructive species on the continent. Their flocks could be 320 *miles* long, and during their migration would eat every edible plant and bug in their path. So many would land on a single tree when they stopped to rest, the branches would often collapse. Witnesses claimed that the piles of poop beneath their temporary roosts were often more than a foot deep.

Of course, none of this was Martha's fault. When she passed away, her body was shipped off to the Smithsonian to be stuffed, which is where she is today. Members of the zoo's Langdon Club commissioned a bronze statue of Martha that now stands outside the Gorilla House. Its plaque also honors another bird, Inca, the last Carolina parakeet known to exist. Inca also lived at the Cincinnati Zoo; he died on February 21, 1918.

Cincinnati Zoo, 3400 Vine St., Cincinnati, OH 45220

(800) 94-HIPPO or (513) 281-4700

Hours: September–April, daily 9 A.M.–5 P.M.; May–August, Monday–Friday 9 A.M.–
6 P.M., Saturday–Sunday 9 A.M.–7 P.M.

Cost: Adults $11.50, Seniors $9, Kids (2–12) $6, Parking $6.50

www.cincinnatizoo.org

Directions: Three blocks north of Martin Luther King Dr., four blocks east of Clifton Ave.

MORE PIGEONS BITE THE DUST

Settlers often used passenger pigeons for target practice, so when the birds' numbers started to dwindle, people were looking around for something else to shoot. On September 7, 1880, Cincinnati inventor George Ligowsky received a patent for a cheap target that could be tossed in the air for a sportsman to blast at. He called it the clay pigeon. Then, in 1887, Clevelander Paul North developed a new design, called the Blue Rock, which closely resembled the clay pigeons used today. Too bad for Martha that Ligowsky and North weren't born a few generations earlier.

Jerry Springer Town

Though Cincinnatians today try to forget that Jerry Springer was once their mayor, there's no denying that while he was in office, he was one of the most popular leaders the town ever had. A pair of canceled checks *almost* put an end to all that.

Springer arrived in Cincinnati in 1969, fresh out of Northwestern Law School. He took a job with Frost & Jacobs, but quit before his first anniversary with the law firm; he wanted to run for the U.S. Congress. Springer defeated Democratic candidate Vernon Bible in the primary, but lost to GOP incumbent Donald Clancy in the general election. The Ohio governor appointed him head of the Ohio Youth Corps, a position he soon relinquished to run for the Cincinnati City Council.

It was 1971, and this time he won. Through a series of Springeresque stunts—posing as a vagrant to check out the Cincinnati Correction Institute, hijacking a city bus the day the city took over the service from a private firm, and so on—he kept the voters awake and amused, and became the most visible member of the nine-seat council. In 1973, he married teacher Margaret Velten and the couple moved out of his former bachelor pad at the Clifton Colony Apartments (714 Clifton Colony Drive) to a place in Western Hills.

Springer won his bid for reelection in 1974, garnering more votes than any other candidate. As was the practice at the time, the rest of the city council planned to name him mayor, which was a largely ceremonial post. Yet before they could swear the 30-year-old political phenom in, news leaked out of a vice squad sting at the Leisure Health Club, a thinly veiled massage parlor in neighboring Covington, Kentucky. It turned out that Springer had employed the services of prostitutes there on two occasions, and both times *paid with a personal check.* D'oh! On May 8, 1974, seven of the eight city council members who had been planning on crowning him mayor voted to kick him off the council.

Was it the end of his political career? Hardly. Shunned by the Democratic Party establishment, but with a sincere mea culpa under his belt, Springer ran as an independent for the city council in 1975, and won. In 1977, he was the top vote getter and was named mayor. He was only 33.

Springer resigned his post in 1981 to run for governor. When he came in last in the Democratic primary, he turned his talents to local

TV. He started as a commentator on WLWT-TV (1700 Young Street) in 1982, but was soon filling in on weekends as news anchor. The station made him an anchorman in 1984. His folksy style quickly moved the station's newscasts from a distant third to a strong first. In 1992, Springer left for Chicago to start a new talk show. Though he still toys with the idea of returning to Ohio to run for the U.S. Senate (as recently as 2003), he remains a resident of the Windy City.

Mayor's Office, Cincinnati City Hall, 801 Plum St., Room 150, Cincinnati, OH 45202

(513) 352-3250

Hours: Always visible

Cost: Free

www.ci.cincinati.oh.us/mayor/pages

Directions: Between 8th and 9th Sts., one block east of Central Ave.

BORN IN CINCINNATI

Though Jerry Springer was the mayor of Cincinnati, he was born in England. Not so for these Porkipolitans:

Theda Bara	July 20, 1890
Doris Day (Doris von Kappelhoff)	April 3, 1924
Charles Manson	November 11, 1934
Tyrone Power, Jr.	May 5, 1914
Roy Rogers (Leonard Slye)	November 5, 1912
Pete Rose	April 14, 1942
Steven Spielberg	December 18, 1947
Ted Turner	November 19, 1938

CINCINNATI

Actress **Judy Carne** was busted in November 1977 for heroin possession in Cincinnati. Though eventually cleared of the charges, she was fined $250 for jumping bail.

Winston Churchill once called Cincinnati "the most beautiful of America's Inland cities."

Rock 'n' Roll Rabble-Rousers

Cleveland may be home to the oh-so-stylish and oh-so-tame Rock and Roll Hall of Fame, but Cincinnati has been the site of some of rock's most notorious bad-boy and bad-girl moments.

During the middle of his set at the 1970 Cincinnati Pop Festival at Crosley Field, Iggy Pop jumped off the stage and into the crowd. Fans passed him around on top of their hands and returned him to the stage unharmed. Rock historians (some job!) now believe it to have been the birth of stage diving.

Crosley Field, Findlay St. and Western Ave., Cincinnati, OH 45214

No phone

Hours: Torn down in 1972

Cost: Free

www.foertmeyer.com/examples/crosley.html

Directions: Stood on the blocks bound by York St., Findlay St., Western Ave., and
   Bank St., just west of I-75.

Fans of The Who weren't as lucky as Iggy when it came to rowdy crowds. On December 3, 1979, thousands of anxious fans ignored their parents' warnings about pushing as they waited outside the gates at Cincinnati Riverfront Coliseum. Most had festival seating (general admission) tickets, which meant everyone had an interest in beating everyone else to the good seats down front. Concert organizers, for whatever dumb reason, didn't open the doors until almost show time.

When the doors finally opened, the crowd went bonkers. Eleven fans were trampled or crushed in the melee. Fearing a riot if the concert were canceled, The Who went on with the show. That night, many Cincinnati parents stayed up late to see if their kids were all right.

Firstar Center (former Cincinnati Riverfront Coliseum), 100 Broadway,
   Cincinnati, OH 45202

(513) 241-1818

Hours: Always visible

Cost: Free

Directions: Between Rte. 17 (Roebling Suspension Bridge) and Rte. 27 (Taylor
   Southgate Bridge), south of Pete Rose Way, next to Cinergy Field.

Nearby, at Riverfront Stadium, gun-lovin' nutcase Ted Nugent was arrested after he shot flaming arrows into the audience during his Damn Yankees concert in January 1993. He had to pay a $1,000 fine. Nugent wasn't the only rocker who was out of control that night; at the same show, Jesse James Dupree of Jackyl, the opening act, was cited for public indecency after he dropped his pants on stage.

Riverfront Stadium, 100 Broadway, Cincinnati, OH 45202

No phone

Hours: Torn down in 2002

Cost: Free

Directions: Between Rte. 17 (Roebling Suspension Bridge) and Rte. 27 (Taylor South-gate Bridge), south of Pete Rose Way, near where the new Cinergy Field stands today.

Two years after the Nugent show, on July 18, 1995, the lead singer of the Jesus Lizards, David Yow, exposed his penis onstage and mimed shoving a microphone up his rear end during a Lollapalooza concert at the Riverbend Music Center. Yow was carted away and eventually fined $327.

Courtney Love, champion of liberty, flashed her breasts after Yow was carted off. For some reason, she was not arrested. Why? She wasn't showing anything that everyone hadn't already seen . . . *plenty* of times.

Riverbend Music Center, 6295 Kellogg Ave., Cincinnati, OH 45228

(513) 232-6220

Hours: Always visible

Cost: Free

www.riverbend-music.com

Directions: At Sutton Ave., just north of the Ohio River and east of the I-275 bridge, southeast of downtown.

CINCINNATI

On April 26, 1838, the captain of the paddlewheeler *Moselle* was challenged by another ship to a race down the Ohio River. Moments after he pulled out of the Cincinnati wharf and ordered full speed ahead, the *Moselle*'s boiler exploded killing more than 200 passengers.

There's a three-alarm fire . . . on your tongue!
Courtesy of Jungle Jim's International Market

Suburbs
Fairfield
Jungle Jim's

Jim Bonaminio might be on to something. To many, a trip to the super-market is a chore, and if children are involved, it's a potential disaster. So, Bonaminio thought, why not make the grocery-buying experience more entertaining? The result is Jungle Jim's International Market, the coolest food store in the state of Ohio, and perhaps anywhere.

The aisles at Jungle Jim's twist and meander, and at every turn there's another giant stuffed robot waiting to spring to life. A lion with a pompadour and jumpsuit croons a few Elvis songs. The General Mills Big G Cereal Bowl Band serenades shoppers in the breakfast food aisle from the deck of the SS *Minnow*. A giant mushroom looms over the produce department, and a full-size 1952 fire engine marks the 1,000-variety hot sauce shelves.

But Jungle Jim's isn't just a refuge for robots. Want to take in a movie? Check out the *Jungle Jim Story* at Jungle Jim's International Market Theater. Looking for fresh fish? They don't come any fresher than the ones swimming around in the Fish Market Biopond; ask an employee to scoop one out for you. Wonder what your future holds? Ask The Brain, the wandering supermarket soothsayer.

Bonaminio has big plans for his marketplace megaplex, and though he's a goofball, he's not joking when he talks about the futuristic Food Adventure Tram—he's already purchased the monorail from King's Island! The tram will circle an Epcot-like food village that's being built just east of the present four-acre store.

Jungle Jim's International Market, 5440 Dixie Highway, Fairfield, OH 45014
(513) 674-6000
E-mail: contactus@junglejims.com
Hours: Daily 8 A.M.–10 P.M.
Cost: Free
www.junglejims.com
Directions: One block west of Holden Blvd. on Rte. 2 (Dixie Hwy.).

MASON
"The Beast" at Paramount King's Island Amusement Park in Mason is the World's Longest Wooden Roller Coaster. The ride has two lifts and takes four and a half minutes to traverse its 7,400 feet of track. (www.pki.com)

Yes, it all seems so clear!

Hamilton
The Hollow Earth

> To all the World: I declare the earth is hollow, and habitable within; containing a number of solid concentric spheres, one within the other, and that it is open at the poles 12 or 16 degrees. I pledge my life in support of this truth, and am ready to explore the hollow, if the world will support and aid me in my undertaking.

That pledge, made in 1818 (with an attached medical testament regarding his sanity), launched John Cleves Symmes on a fruitless odyssey to educate the human population about the caverns just beneath its feet. Of course, Symmes never saw the hollow inner world; he had only convinced himself that it *must* exist given the mathematical patterns of interlocking spheres he had observed in nature.

All right.

Symmes proposed an expedition to the unexplored regions of the North and South Poles where he expected to find entryways to the worlds below. Surprisingly, only a few people treated him as a nut, mostly because others with stronger scientific credentials had proposed similar theories over the years: Johannes Kepler, Edmund Halley, Leonard Euler, and Sir John Leslie.

So, through a relentless series of public lectures across the Midwest, Symmes was able to generate enough public enthusiasm to pressure the U.S. Congress into considering funding an expedition to the South Pole planned for 1822 and 1823. The Senate considered it, but they never approved the money (although 25 voted "Aye").

His efforts inspired another man, Jeremiah Reynolds, to take up the cause. Reynolds and Symmes traveled to the East Coast with a wooden model of the Earth (as they imagined it), packing lecture halls at 50¢ a head. The grueling tour almost killed the aging Symmes, who eventually asked to be returned to his farm in Hamilton. He died there in May 1829.

Reynolds pressed on alone, gaining the support of President John Quincy Adams. Before the funds came through, Andrew Jackson was elected to the nation's highest office and promptly threw Reynolds out of the White House, so to speak. Reynolds got a rich New York sucker named Dr. Watson to pay for a ship, the SS *Annawan*, to sail to Antarctica. No polar hole was ever found.

In the 1840s Symmes's son, Americus Vespucci Symmes, had a stone replica of his father's hollow earth model placed atop a monument to Symmes in Hamilton. Somewhat the worse for wear, it still stands in Ludlow Park.

Ludlow Park, Sycamore and 3rd Sts., Hamilton, OH 45011

No phone

Hours: Always visible

Cost: Free

Directions: Two blocks west of Rte. 127 (4th/5th Sts.), three blocks south of Rte. 128.

A Cincinnati eccentric in King Arthur's Court.
Photo by author, courtesy of Historic Loveland Castle

Loveland
Chateau LaRoche

In 1929, consummate bachelor Harry Andrews decided to build a castle to the memory of King Arthur, and create a society of strapping young lads to follow in his footsteps. So he formed the Knights of the Golden Trail from a group of Sunday school teens that he had been mentoring. Unfortunately, the Great Depression got in the way, and his cheap church-supplied labor dried up after many of the young men went off to work for the Civilian Conservation Corps.

That didn't stop Andrews. Chateau LaRoche moved onward and upward, a medieval-style castle with 30-inch-thick walls, several towers, and a two-cell dungeon. The walls were built from cement bricks Andrews molded using milk cartons, embellished with rocks that he pulled from the river. The job took more than 30 years. As the building took form, more and more visitors dropped by to visit. It soon became a tourist attraction.

The work invigorated Andrews, who lived to be 91. He might have lived even longer were it not for a tragic accident in 1981. While burning a pile of trash, the flames leapt out of control and Andrews tried to stomp them out. His polyester pants melted to his legs, and he later died from the burns.

Chateau LaRoche, now called Historic Loveland Castle, is still open to the public, and is a popular venue for weddings. In October, from 7 to 11 P.M., the castle offers Haunted Tours.

Historic Loveland Castle, 12025 Shore Dr., PO Box 135, Loveland, OH 45140

(513) 683-4686

Hours: April–September, daily 11 A.M.–5 P.M.; October–March, Saturday–Sunday 11 A.M.–5 P.M.

Cost: Adults $3, Kids (12 and under) $2; Haunted Tours, Adults $6, Kids $5

www.lovelandcastle.com

Directions: Six blocks west of Rich Rd. on Sycamore Rd., then south on Shore Rd.

Frogmen

At first they were thought to be trolls, four little men with froglike faces and lopsided chests standing along Loveland's Riverside Avenue, near the bridge. Three businessmen spotted them first in March 1955, and made a report to authorities. Police investigated—they even posted a guard at the bridge—but the frogmen never returned. . . .

Until 1972. On March 3 of that year, a police officer came across a four-foot, manlike frog creature climbing up and over the guardrail along the Little Miami River. It walked on its hind legs and ran off toward the river when the patrol car caught it in the headlights. Then, on March 17, it was spotted again in the same general area by another police officer, this time it was lying in the road. This cop wasn't taking any chances; he drew his sidearm. The frogman hopped up and ran for the underbrush, but not before the officer fired four shots at it. The bullets didn't seem to slow the creature down. No frogmen have been seen in Loveland since.

But you never know.

Riverside Ave., Loveland, OH 45140

No phone

Hours: Sometimes visible, best at night

Cost: Free

Directions: Riverside Ave. is the continuation of Kemper Rd. running on the north bank of the river.

North Bend
Button Up Your Overcoat

You mother always told you to button up your overcoat, and that even means *you*, William Henry Harrison, Mr. Bigshot President of the United States. And another thing, you shouldn't go on and on and on talking about yourself. Still, do you listen to your mother? No, of course not . . . Mr. Fancy Pants Commander-in-Chief.

Our nation's ninth president, William Henry Harrison, took office on March 4, 1841, and proceeded to give the longest inaugural speech before or since (1 hour and 40 minutes) . . . in a driving rainstorm . . . without a topcoat or hat. Result? Pneumonia. Harrison's administration lasted all of one month, most of which he spent hallucinating in bed with a high fever. On April 4 he expired. Harrison was interred in the family tomb atop Mt. Nebo, which overlooks Ohio, Indiana, and Kentucky, the three states where he spent the majority of his life.

In time, other family members ended up in this 24-vault mausoleum, but his son, John Scott Harrison, ran into a few problems. A week after he was buried in 1878, grave robbers from the Medical College of Ohio stole his fresh corpse. This was all in the name of science, mind you; they needed a cadaver to dissect for anatomy class. Authorities found Harrison hanging by his neck in a closet at the college's Cincinnati campus.

The scandal led to legislation legalizing the practice of donating one's own body to science, cutting out the grave-robbing middleman entirely. John Scott was returned to the North Bend tomb were he remains to this day, behind some *very* heavy iron gates.

Harrison Tomb, Cliff Rd., North Bend, OH 45052

(614) 297-2630

Hours: Dawn–Dusk

Cost: Free

www.ohiohistory.org/places/harrison

Directions: West off Rte. 50 on Brower Rd., then north on Cliff Rd.

6

THE SOUTHEAST

*L*et's face it, when driving around southeast Ohio it's sometimes difficult to tell that you're not in Kentucky. Call it the
hillbilly factor. Where else are you going to find a Moonshine
Festival? Or a free-roaming chicken that was named king of a
town? Or a home dedicated to the owner's favorite donkey?
Southeast Ohio has it all.

But the region has plenty of international panache to coun-
terbalance the backwoods vibe. You'll also find the birthplace
of the Liberator of Bulgaria here, as well as a castle-shaped
bed and breakfast with a medieval touch, a cemetery set
aside for all U.S. presidents, and the world's only example
of basket-shaped architecture, the Longaberger corporate
headquarters. Is cosmopolitan Cleveland this culturally
consecrated? I think not!

Ashville
World's First Traffic Light

Though Garrett Morgan invented the World's First Automated Traffic Signal (see page 136), Teddy Boor invented the World's First Traffic *Light*. This upside-down-teardrop-shaped device was installed at the intersection of Main and Long Streets in the 1920s. It had only one light on each of its four faces, which switched back and forth between green and red at regular intervals. It didn't have a yellow light, but it didn't need one; it had a black clock arm in the middle of each face. Each time it rotated into the vertical position, the light would change, thereby giving drivers an accurate sense of how much time was left before it turned green, or how much longer they could race through before it turned red.

Boor's contraption hung in downtown Ashville until 1982 when it was taken down for minor repairs. As soon as it was removed, the Ohio Department of Transportation sent the town a notice not to reinstall its nonstandard light, no matter how famous it was! It didn't matter that not a single accident was reported at that intersection during its 50+ years of service—it wasn't up to code, and rules were rules. Residents rehung it anyway, but in the local history museum, where today it regulates the flow of visitors in and around the display cases.

Main and Long Sts., Ashville, OH 43103

No phone

Hours: Intersection always visible; traffic light in museum

Cost: Free

Directions: Just east of the railroad tracks on the south end of town.

AVA

The U.S. Navy's first airship, the 700-foot-long USS *Shenandoah*, crashed near Ava on September 3, 1925. Captain Zachary Landsdowne flew the dirigible into a windstorm near Marietta and the craft broke in half. Landsdowne's gondola crashed to the ground, killing him and 13 others. Another 29 crew members were able to ride the slowly descending pieces to the ground. A monument can be found near the Caldwell Exit on I-77.

Forced into early retirement.
Photo by author, courtesy of Ohio's Small Town Museum

Most folks who stop by Ohio's Small Town Museum are looking for the traffic light, but there's so much more there to see. There's a display case on a local dwarf who appeared as a Munchkin in *The Wizard of Oz*, and another on Ashville puppeteer Vivian Michael, the first person to combine hand-moving rods with traditional hand-up-the-body puppets.

Another exhibit recounts Roy Rogers's short-lived career in the Ashville Canning Plant; he was fired for playing his guitar when he should have been working. And finally, you can read up on the activities of Chic-Chic, the smartest chicken in Ashville, and Buster, the town's most partisan pooch (see below).

Ohio's Small Town Museum, 34 Long St., Ashville, OH 43103

(740) 983-9864

Hours: Monday–Friday 1–3 P.M., Saturday 9 A.M.–Noon

Cost: Free

www.ashvilleohio.net/museum1.htm

Directions: One block north of the intersection of Main St. and Rte. 316 (Long St.).

WHY CHICKENS ARE SMARTER THAN DOGS

If ever there is any question as to which animal species is more intelligent than the next, there's some evidence on display at Ohio's Small Town Museum in Ashville. In a mental battle between chickens and dogs, the birds would probably win.

Consider **Chic-Chic**, the pet chicken of Mrs. A. B. Cooper. Every day Mrs. Cooper would give this clever clucker a dime, and he would carry it down to Clyde Brinkers's restaurant on Long Street and exchange it for a tin of cornmeal. When he was done with lunch, he would walk over to the bus stop and greet incoming travelers. Locals loved Chic-Chic, and coronated him "The King of Ashville," a title he held until his death in the 1950s. A couple of amateur taxidermists have since used other chickens to re-create Chic-Chic, dime in beak, for Ohio's Small Town Museum.

Now consider **Buster**, a mutt once owned by the aforementioned Clyde Brinkers. This dog would bark in approval every time Herbert Hoover's name was mentioned, but would growl every time he heard mention of Al Smith, Hoover's Democratic opponent in the 1928 presidential election. Brinkers indulged Buster to the point of letting the pooch pull the voting lever that November. A year later, the stock market crashed and Hoover ushered in the Great Depression, which is evidence enough that dogs should never be allowed to vote.

Bellaire
The House that Jackass Built

Jack was an ass. A jackass, actually. Still, his friend Jake Heatherington didn't seem to mind. In fact, he really appreciated that Jack was a jackass, because Jack lugged the coal Heatherington unearthed at his nearby mine. Jack was Jake's donkey.

As the mine grew and Harrington became rich, the industrialist never forgot his favorite pack animal. Because Jack worked so hard in those early days, his owner honored him with a portrait, carved in stone, that was used for the keystone. When the house was finished, Heatherington took Jack on a tour, even upstairs. The house became known as the House that Jack Built, and was a Bellaire landmark for years. (By the way, the house was named for the nursery rhyme, not the other way around.)

Long after Harrington and Jack were dead, their home was torn down to make way for a new addition to the 7 Inn (1601 Belmont Street). Jack's keystone was moved to the local library where you can still see it today.

Bellaire Public Library, 330 32nd St., Bellaire, OH 43906

(740) 676-9421

Hours: Monday–Friday, 9 A.M.–8 P.M., Saturday 9 A.M.–5 P.M., Sunday 1–5 P.M.

Cost: Free

www.geocities.com/Athens/Aegean/3088/Jack.html

Directions: Two blocks west of Rte. 7 at Belmont St.

Cambridge
The Living Word Outdoor Drama

You probably already know most of this story, but nothing compares to seeing it come to life in the great outdoors. *The Living Word Outdoor Drama* is Ohio's only outdoor passion play. It follows Jesus from the manger to the resurrection, with plenty of chariots, livestock, and Roman soldiers to keep things interesting. The play focuses on Jesus's final days after entering Jerusalem to a palm frond–waving crowd. There's the last supper, the trial, and the crucifixion. And for all you doubting Thomases, in this production you actually get to see Jesus ascend into heaven . . . on a wire.

If you plan on taking in the performance, be sure to arrive 45 minutes early and take the free tour of the set.

6010 College Hill Rd., PO Box 1481, Cambridge, OH 43725

(740) 439-2761

E-mail: livingword@speedy1.net

Hours: June–mid-July, Friday–Saturday 8 P.M.; mid-July–August, Thursday–Saturday 8 P.M.; September, Saturday 7 P.M.

Cost: Adults $12, Seniors (60+) $10, Kids (4–12) $6

www.visitguernseycounty.com/outdoor.html

Directions: Head northwest out of town on Rte. 209 (Bloomfield Rd.), turn left onto College Hill Rd.

OTHER OHIO OUTDOOR OFFERINGS

The thrill of outdoor theater revolves around all those scenes you just can't stage in a musty old theater: volleys of flaming arrows, stampedes of riders on horseback, burning log cabins, and casts of hundreds. If you like drama writ large, Ohio has a few more outdoor extravaganzas for you to appreciate under the stars (assuming it doesn't rain).

★ *Blue Jacket* (520 S. Stringtown Road, Xenia, (877) 465-BLUE, www.BlueJacketDrama.com) Watch as Daniel Boone and Simon Kenton battle Ohio's Shawnee Indians against the backdrop of the American Revolution. The Shawnee, under the command of Chief Black Fish, Blue Jacket (a white settler who was adopted by the Shawnee), and Caesar (an escaped slave), fight for their land and their way of life on the three-acre stage. Guess who wins.

★ *Tecumseh!* (5968 Marietta Road, Chillicothe, (866) 775-0700, www.tecumsehdrama.com) *Tecumseh!* follows the continuing struggle of the Shawnee people against the growing tide of American settlers. Watch in horror as settlers use flintlock rifles to mow down the Indians, one of whom plunges to his death off a 21-foot cliff. The play contains an authentic Native American score recorded by the London Symphony Orchestra, and is narrated by actor Graham Greene (on tape, of course).

★ *Trumpet in the Land* (PO Box 450, New Philadelphia, (330) 339-1132, www.trumpetintheland.com) Hardly an upper, this drama re-creates events leading up to the 1782 slaughter of 96 Mohican Indians during a Moravian church service in Gnadenhutten. The 300 Pennsylvania militiamen who committed the dirty deed mistakenly thought the Mohicans were British allies. Oops. . . .

Linus was right—there *is* a Great Pumpkin!

Circleville
The Great Pumpkin Watertower

Little did Circleville Mayor George Haswell know what he was starting when he erected a small pumpkin display outside his home on Main Street in 1903. Every year after that the display grew, and grew, and grew until Circleville was crowned (actually, crowned itself) the Pumpkin Capital of the World! Today the town hosts a four-day Pumpkin Festival that draws 300,000 visitors. Though the October event is free, the food is not: pumpkinburgers, pumpkin ice cream, whoopie pies, and the world's largest pumpkin pie (350 pounds and 5 feet in diameter) are among the festival favorites. And each year a Miss Pumpkin and Little Miss Pumpkin are crowned.

As befitting the town's station in vegetable lore, city crews have painted its watertower to resemble the World's Largest Pumpkin, though if you are the slightest bit color-blind it looks like the World's Largest Tomato. It's not. It's a pumpkin. And if you suggest otherwise, them is fightin' words in Pumpkintown!

Pumpkin Watertower, Walnut and Clinton Sts., Circleville, OH 43113

No phone

Hours: Always visible

Cost: Free

Directions: Three blocks east of Court St. (Rte. 188), eight blocks south of Main St.
  (Rte. 22).

Circleville Pumpkin Show, 216 N. Court St., Circleville, OH 43113

(740) 474-7000

E-mail: pumpkins@pumpkinshow.com

Hours: Starts the third Wednesday in October

Cost: Free

www.pumpkinshow.com

Directions: All over town.

Cumberland
The Wilds

If you've always dreamed of embarking on an African safari, but the trip was a little out of your price range, there's an alternative in southeast Ohio: The Wilds. Situated on 14 square miles of a reclaimed open-pit strip mine (donated by the American Electric Power company), this facility is as free-range as you're going to find in Ohio, unless one of the rhinos breaks through the perimeter fence. But not to worry; those fences are very secure. And what do you care if they get out—you're going *inside.*

Ironically, as a visitor to The Wilds, you will not be given the same freedom as the rest of the critters. You will, however, get the sensation that you're traveling through a Kenyan game preserve when you hop aboard your safari transport. The Wilds has more than 20 endangered species within its confines, and plenty of nonendangered animals to boot. Your tour will stop at the Overlook Café for a spectacular view of the surrounding hillside. Be sure to bring a pair of binoculars to get a good look. A pith helmet would also look sharp.

14000 International Rd., Cumberland, OH 43732

(866) 444-WILDS or (740) 638-5030

E-mail: communications@thewilds.org

Hours: May–September and October, Saturday–Sunday 10 A.M.–4 P.M.; June–August, Wednesday–Sunday, daily 10 A.M.–4 P.M.

Cost: Adults $12, Seniors (60+) $11, Kids (4–12) $7, Parking $2

www.thewilds.org

Directions: Between Rte. 284 (Big Muskie Dr.) and Rte. 340 (Cumberland Rd.) on International Rd.

DUNKINSVILLE

A four-foot-tall "devil monkey" was spotted by Debbie Cross of Dunkinsville on June 26, 1997. The hairy creature was strolling near her pond; it skipped away when it realized it had been spotted.

GALLIPOLIS

In 1946, Bob and Jewel Evans opened a truck stop restaurant in Gallipolis, serving home-cooked meals focused around a staple of the rural diet: sausage. It was the birth of Bob Evans Farm restaurants.

GALLIPOLIS AND THURMAN

Ohio's highest recorded temperature, 113°F, was reached twice, first in Thurman on July 4, 1897, and then in Gallipolis on July 21, 1934.

Behold, the Garage Basket!

Dresden
World's Largest Longaberger Basket

Students used to laugh at their friends when they took basket-weaving classes in college—but who's laughing now!!??! Not the 4,500 employees of the Longaberger Basket Company. They weave more than 8 million baskets each year. They also created this 23-foot tall, 11-foot-wide, 48-foot-long picnic tote in the center of town. It took 2,000 employees to weave it in 1980, and like all Longaberger baskets, its quality craftsmanship has withstood the test of time.

The key to Longaberger's success is Tupperware-like home marketing. Only one standard model is offered in stores (the Dresden Basket); otherwise you have to hold or attend a Basket Party. Longaberger baskets are nearly indestructible, and each weaver initials and dates every basket he or she makes as a testament to its quality.

Main & 5th Streets, Dresden, OH 43821

(740) 321-3447

Hours: Always visible

Cost: Free

www.longaberger.com

Directions: Four blocks east of Rte. 60 (Frazeysburg Rd.), four blocks north of Rte. 208/9th St.

Lancaster
Presidents' Cemetery

Ohio is sometimes called as the Modern Mother of Presidents because seven of the nation's former chief executives—Grant, Hayes, Garfield, Benjamin Harrison, McKinley, Taft, and Harding—are on its list of native sons. There are also six presidents laid to rest in Ohio—William Henry Harrison, Hayes, Garfield, McKinley, and Harding. Yet not one of them is buried in the Presidents' Cemetery, a graveyard southwest of Lancaster that was set aside for just that purpose.

The plots were deeded in 1817 by the land's then-owner, Nathaniel Wilson, to "James Monroe, President of the United States, and his successors in office forever." Yet here we are, almost 190 years later, and no one's accepted Wilson's offer. And don't expect a famous burial here any time soon; the graveyard has become rundown, and is more popular with beer-drinking teenagers than commanders-in-chief. Still, given recent elections, it's not impossible that one of Lancaster's wild kids will one day be elected to our highest office and return here to be planted.

But don't count on it.

Presidents' Cemetery, Stone Wall Cemetery Rd., Lancaster, OH 43130

No phone

Hours: Always visible

Cost: Free

Directions: Head southwest from town on Rte. 22 (Zanesville Rd.), turn south on Rte. 285 (Stone Wall Cemetery Rd.).

HARRISONVILLE

On October 26, 1901, all the men and boys of Harrisonville were ordered to meet on the town's main street. The community had been plagued by a mysterious stone-thrower for three days, and the mayor wanted to get to the bottom of it. The residents counted off, and all were there, yet during the proceedings, rocks continued to rain down.

New Lexington
The Liberator of Bulgaria

Never heard of Januarius Aloysius MacGahan? Well then, you're obviously not Bulgarian. MacGahan might have started life as an Ohio farmboy, but he died the Liberator of Bulgaria—not bad for a 34-year-old.

MacGahan's sense of adventure drew him to Europe where he landed a job as a reporter for the *London Daily News*. In 1872, the paper sent him to Bulgaria to report on the rebel forces fighting Turkish occupation. The atrocities he discovered persuaded him to side with the rebels: the Turks' elite Bashi-bazouk soldiers had been beheading Bulgarians right and left (but mostly off the top), including all 8,000 residents of the town of Batak. MacGahan's reports galvanized public opinion in London, and the prime minister let the Russian leadership know that he would not object if they wanted to drive the Turks out of Bulgaria. Nudge, nudge, hint, hint, say no more. . . .

The Russo-Turkish War of 1877 ended when the last of the Turks fled the country. MacGahan was hailed as a national hero and his June 12 birthday was declared a national holiday, a tradition that continues to this day.

The reporter didn't get to revel in the victory for long; he died of typhus in Constantinople in 1878. His body was returned to his Ohio birthplace where it was buried in the family plot. A statue of MacGahan was later erected across from the New Lexington courthouse, and a bust was placed over his grave.

New Lexington Cemetery, Swigart St., New Lexington, OH 43764

No phone

Hours: Dawn–Dusk

Cost: Free

www.netpluscom.cm/~cjrausch/

Directions: Head south on Swigart St. from State St., on the southwest side of town.

KNOCKEMSTIFF

The town of Knockemstiff received its name when two female settlers got in a fight over a man, and one threatened, "I'll knock you stiff!"

New Plymouth
Ravenwood Castle and Medieval Village

Why stay at a traditional bed and breakfast when you can sleep in a castle? There's plenty of room at Sue and Jim Maxwell's Ravenwood Castle in the Hocking Hills. It was built to resemble a 12th-century Norman fortress, but without the bone-chilling drafts off the moor or the invading armies. Each room has a medieval theme, from the King Arthur Suite to Queen Elizabeth's Room, from Rapunzel's Tower to the Duke's Dungeon. If you're on a budget, try the no-frills Gypsy Wagons. They might be more in your price range.

Ravenwood Castle has a Great Hall (as all castles should) where breakfast, lunch, and dinner are served. Rooms are not equipped with TVs or telephones; if Queen Elizabeth didn't have 'em, neither should you. And besides, you're on vacation—relax a little!

65666 Bethel Rd., New Plymouth, OH 45654

(800) 477-1541 or (740) 596-2606

Hours: Call for reservations

Cost: $45 (Gypsy Wagons, weekdays)–$225 (Silversmith's House, weekends)

www.ravenwoodcastle.com

Directions: You'll receive directions when you make your reservation.

LANCASTER

The 1827, the Lancaster County school board forbade any discussion of railroads in its classrooms, stating, "[I]f God had designed that His intelligent creatures should travel at the frightful rate of 15 miles an hour by steam, He would have foretold it through his Holy prophets. It is a device of Satan to lead immortal souls to Hell."

General William Tecumseh Sherman was born in Lancaster on February 8, 1820. His birthplace, built around 1814, is older than most buildings in Atlanta, and is now a museum (137 E. Main Street, (614) 687-5891).

New Straitsville
Fire Down Below!

The coal strike of 1884 was bad enough before the miners soaked a pile of old timbers in oil, placed them in a coal car, set them afire, and rolled the car into a Plummer Hill mine. In retrospect, it might not have been the strikers' best strategy. The burning timbers ignited a coal seam and launched an underground fire *that's still burning today.*

For the first few decades the blaze was an isolated nuisance. But it grew, spreading through abandoned mineshafts and cracks in the rock formations. By the 1930s it reached the surface, where flaming holes would open up without a moment's notice. The basement in the town's elementary school on Clark Street started to heat up, and the janitor realized the building was sitting on a coal vein. Locals were able to save the structure by blasting away the coal and replacing it with cement. (Kids later recalled that the dynamiting went on below their feet as they sat at their desks during classes.)

Roosevelt's WPA got involved in 1936. Though they spent $640,000 on the project, the fire raged on, and began attracting national attention. Local huckster Howard "Brick" Essex opened Under-Ground Fires, Inc., on Plummer Hill to capitalize on the tourist influx. William Hoy did the same over in abandoned Old Straitsville, but he called his attraction Subterranean Fires, Inc. Essex paid local children to fry eggs and percolate coffee over burning cracks. Not to be outdone, Hoy often dumped old tires and gasoline into the holes to keep the flames roaring. Each time a new hole burst open at the surface it was given a new name: Old Faithful, Devil's Garden, Hell's Oven, and so on.

Both tourist traps closed around 1940. Fearing it would make their town seem dangerous, undesirable, or both, town boosters began to downplay the fire. Believe it or not, the fire is still burning, though the evidence is not as apparent as it once was. Every so often a new hole opens in the Wayne National Forest to remind folks of the 1884 strike.

Plummer Hill, Rte. 595, New Straitsville, OH 43766

No phone

Hours: Always visible

Cost: Free

Directions: West of town along Rte. 595.

Straitsville Special

What's Straitsville Special? Spring Tonic. Rheumatis' Medicine. The Recipe. White Lightning. Hooch. You know—*Moonshine*. As southeastern Ohio coal mines began to close (or burn up), the locals turned a regional hobby into a booming interstate business. During Prohibition an estimated 175 illegal stills operated in the hollers and abandoned mineshafts around this small town, and the hooch generated a loyal following from coast to coast. Straitsville Special became moonshine's unofficial brand name in speakeasies everywhere. Very few local bootleggers were ever apprehended, but the owner of the New Straitsville Kroger went to prison for failing to accurately report the quantity of corn and sugar—moonshine's main ingredients—he was selling. He was selling it by the trainload.

New Straitsville has never forgotten its bootlegging roots, and celebrates each spring with a Moonshine Festival. Unfortunately, it is still against the law to operate a still in the United States, with one exception: here in town during its annual event. You're not allowed to taste the hooch once it's distilled, and ATF revenuers stand by to make sure nobody takes a nip. If you attend, you'll have to be satisfied with moonshine pies, moonshine burgers, and other nonalcoholic food items.

New Straitsville History Group, 200 W. Main St., New Straitsville, OH 43766

(740) 394-3133

Hours: Mid-May

Cost: Free

Directions: Along Rte. 216/93 (Main St.) in the center of town.

LOGAN

Each year the town of Logan hosts the International Washboard Festival (www.columbuswashboard.com/info.htm). The event honors the device more as a musical instrument than as a cleaning tool.

MARIETTA

Mound Cemetery in Marietta (5th and Scammel Streets) is located on land once gifted to France's **Queen Marie Antoinette**. The town is named in her honor.

Newark
Golf the Octagon

One of North America's most accurate astronomical observatories, the Octagon, is located on a private golf course on the southwest side of Newark. It is also the World's Largest Geometric Earthwork Structure. But as special as it is, this ancient earthen structure serves today as a course hazard at the Moundbuilders Country Club. Think about it—it's kind of like converting a Mayan pyramid into a giant water slide.

Archeologists believe the Octagon, a 14-foot-tall running mound that is 1,200 feet in diameter, was built around 1200 B.C. by the Hopewell Culture. Small mounds within the Octagon align with points on the rim to mark important mileposts in the celestial clock. It'll also tell you when it's tee-off time.

Octagon Earthworks, Moundbuilders Country Club, 99 Cooper Ave., Newark, OH 43055

(740) 344-1919

Hours: Daily Dawn–Dusk

Cost: Free

www.ohiohistory.org/places/newarkearthworks/octagon.cfm

Directions: Head west on Hopewell Dr. from Hebron Rd. (Rte. 79), and follow it around to the north.

MILLFIELD
A Millfield coal mine explosion on November 5, 1930, killed 82 miners. Most of the victims were suffocated by carbon monoxide gas.

MILLIGAN
The lowest temperature ever reached in the Buckeye State was –39°F, recorded at Milligan on February 10, 1899.

NELSONVILLE
Actress **Sarah Jessica Parker** was born in Nelsonville on March 25, 1965.

David Longaberger got what he asked for.
Photo by author, courtesy of Longaberger Basket Company

World's Largest Basket-Shaped Building

Some call it the World's Largest Basket, but let's be honest: Little Red Riding Hood would have to be the size of King Kong to use this thing. And since there is an actual *basket* basket in nearby Dresden (see page 192), let's just call it the World's Largest (and perhaps Only) Basket-Shaped Building.

This unique corporate headquarters for the Longaberger Basket Company was the brainchild of David Longaberger, who took over the company after his father John (who founded it in 1936) died in 1974. The building grew out of his frustration in dealing with inspirationally challenged architects; when they failed to present acceptable blueprints, Longaberger grabbed one of the company's most popular models, plopped it on the table, and demanded they come up with a design that matched it.

And so it came to be. The 160-times replica of a Medium Market Basket was completed in 1997. The basket-shaped building stands seven stories tall and has room for 500 employees. Its 75-foot-long handles rise up another three stories and are heated to keep ice from falling down onto the glass-roofed atrium. The design was officially finished when a gold-plated Longaberger tag was mounted on the side.

Luckily, David Longaberger lived to see his dream headquarters; he died in Newark two years later on March 17, 1999.

Longaberger Basket Company, 1500 E. Main St., Newark, OH 43055

(740) 321-3447

Hours: Always visible

Cost: Free; baskets extra

www.longaberger.com

Directions: On Rte. 16 east of town.

World's Largest Lettered Hedge

Beman Dawes, founder of the Pure Oil Company, must have felt he owed Mother Nature a favor for all his company's drilling. He decided to build an arboretum in 1929 near one of his mansions, and asked his famous friends to help him to landscape the place—folks like Orville and Wilbur Wright, Admiral Byrd, Wiley Post, Gene Tunney, Bobby Jones, General John J. Pershing, Red Grange, and 60-some others (mostly military brass) contributed trees to this endeavor. The tradition continues to this day with relatively recent additions from Jesse Owens and John Glenn.

The arboretum, for its part, decided to advertise its famous plants in a unique way: landscapers planted a 2,100-foot-long hedge. And it's not just any hedge, but one that spells out "Dawes Arboretum." It's rather difficult to read from ground level, but pilots can easily read it . . . for all the good it'll do them.

Dawes Arboretum, 7770 Jacksontown Rd. SE, Newark, OH 43506

(800) 44-DAWES or (470) 323-2355

Hours: Dawn–Dusk

Cost: Free

www.dawesarb.org

Directions: Three miles south of town on Rte. 13 (Jacksontown Rd.), north of Rte. 40.

Rushville
Listen to the Horse . . .

James Henry should have known better than to cross a psychic horse. Back in 1844, Henry was trying to decide which of his two girlfriends he wanted to marry. One night he fell asleep while riding in his buggy and his horse pulled the carriage to one of their homes. "A sign!" he thought, and proposed soon after to Mary, a woman whose maiden name has been lost to history.

Mary loved horses, and took a particular fancy to the one who brought her husband to her doorstep. The love affair was short-lived, for she died soon after the wedding and was buried in the Otterbein Cemetery. James was distraught, and visited Mary's grave every chance he got. James's family started to worry that he would never get over her. All that changed when his old flame showed up and offered a shoulder to cry on. James eventually married his romantic runner-up and tried to move on with his life.

Mary, on the other hand, was not moving on with her death. Soon, a bloody horseshoe appeared on her gravestone, an omen that was reported to James Henry. The two-timer dismissed the warning. A short time later he was found dead in his barn, kicked in the head by Mary's favorite steed. A bloody horseshoe print was neatly framed in the center of his face.

Locals were understandably freaked out. They replaced Mary Henry's tombstone when James was laid to rest beside her, and tried to forget the whole spooky story. But over time, a new horseshoe appeared on the second marker. It is still there today.

Otterbein Cemetery, Otterbein Rd., Rushville, OH 43150

No phone

Hours: Always visible

Cost: Free

Directions: Head northwest from town on Rte. 22, then south for a half mile on Otterbein Rd.

. . . OR *DON'T* LISTEN TO THE HORSE

In 1986, the Reverend Jim Brown of the First Church of the Nazarene in Ironton (2318 S. 4th Street, (740) 532-3413) made a startling discovery: when he played the theme song to *Mr. Ed* backward, he heard a message from the Devil! That's right, Brown warned, if you listen to "A horse is a horse, of course, of course" in reverse you can clearly hear "The source is Satan!" His congregation led the world's smallest boycott of the show, but to little effect. Of course, the fact that the TV series had been in reruns since 1966, and Mr. Ed had been dead since the 1970s, might have had something to do with their ineffectiveness.

Stockport
No Dancing on the Grave

Captain Isaac Newton Cook (1819–1906) must have known his wife wasn't his biggest fan, because he planned ahead. This Stockport resident designed a monument to be placed over his grave that was both elegant and functional. It tapered upward to a point, at a sharp angle, so steep that his wife would not be able to dance atop his grave.

Of course, none of this would have been necessary had he tried not to be such a bastard in life. Nobody knows whether his wife was disappointed that she couldn't celebrate her husband's demise with a graveyard jig, but, whatever the case, she was probably pleased that he croaked.

Old Brick Cemetery, Rte. 376, Stockport, OH 43787

(740) 962-5861

Hours: Always visible

Cost: Free

Directions: Off Rte. 376.

Take a left.

Zanesville
The Y-Bridge

If you ask for directions in Zanesville and somebody tells you to drive to the middle of the bridge on Route 40 and take a left, don't immediately assume he or she is trying to be a smartass. Your guide could be talking about Zanesville's historic Y-bridge, the only bridge in the world that, when you cross it, can lead you back to the same side you started from.

Zanesville is situated at the confluence of the Muskingum and the Licking Rivers. Rather than build three bridges connecting the three different sides of town, they built one with three branches that intersect in the middle. The town's first Y-bridge was constructed in 1814; the current structure is the town's fifth. It was built in 1984. Local police have a *Y* sewn into their uniforms to honor their unique roadway.

All that said, be sure you're on the correct bridge before you take that left.

Rte. 40, Zanesville, OH 43701

No phone

Hours: Always visible

Cost: Free

www.coz.org

Directions: The Y-Bridge connects Main St. (Rte. 40) to Linden Ave.

ANOTHER ALPHABET BRIDGE

Zanesville has its Y-bridge, but some Ohio towns have S-bridges. Why would engineers build a bridge in the shape of an *S*? One tale claimed that in 1830 an engineer on the National Road, John McCartney, bragged during a drunken stupor that he could build a bridge in any shape, so another bridgebuilder drew an *S* on a napkin. Rather than back down, McCartney went ahead and built his next bridge in the shape of an *S*. The story has been told so often that people have started to believe it, particularly people who hang out in saloons.

Another popular story claims the S-bridges were intended to halt runaway stagecoaches, but ask yourself: why would it be better to crash into a stone bridge than to run off the road somewhere else? And as for the rumor that engineers did it to avoid the trouble of cutting down trees, is building an intricate stone bridge around a tree any easier than chopping it down?

The real reason is structural. It was much easier (and cheaper) to build a stone arch at a right angle to the stream it crossed and bend the road at the approaches. To see how this works, check out the S-bridge in New Concord on Route 40W, 12 miles east of Zanesville.

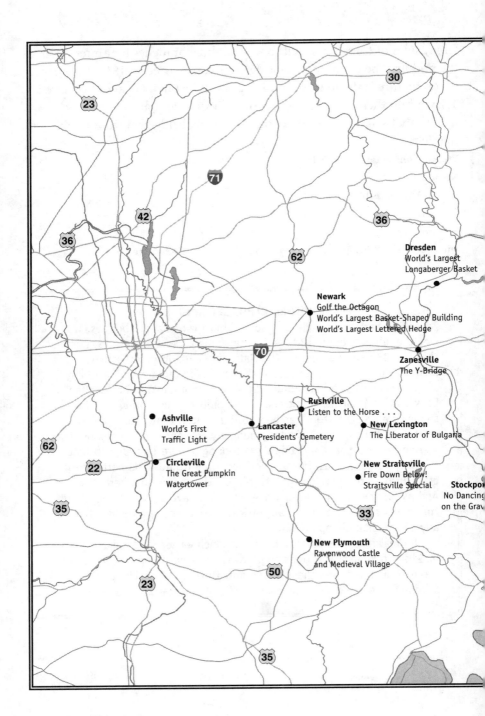

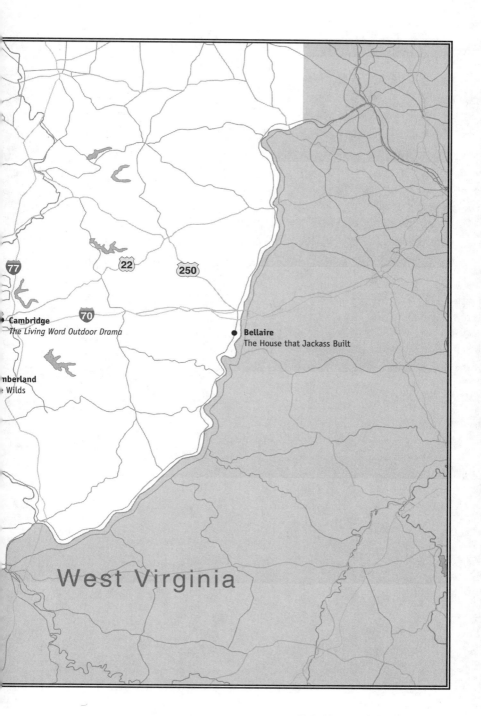

77

22 **250**

● **Cambridge**
The Living Word Outdoor Drama

70

● **Bellaire**
The House that Jackass Built

mberland
● Wilds

West Virginia

7

COLUMBUS Area

*N*ow that you've learned about Ohio's strangeness north and south, east and west, it's time to talk about the weirdos in the center. That's right, I'm talking about the Columbus area. The folks here are not odd because they live in the capitol city, as filled with politicos as it is (though the legislature should have to answer for that ugly statehouse), but because of something slightly more *genetic*.

I'm talking about mutants. There's the two-headed calf at the Ohio Historical Center. And the army of six-foot-tall ears of corn marching on Dublin. And the Impressionist painting that has come to life in a city park. And the Grade AAAAAAAAA eggs at a suburban mall. Weird stuff, things that shouldn't be but *are*.

Scared? Don't be. There are simple, logical, strange explanations for all of it, if you just read on.

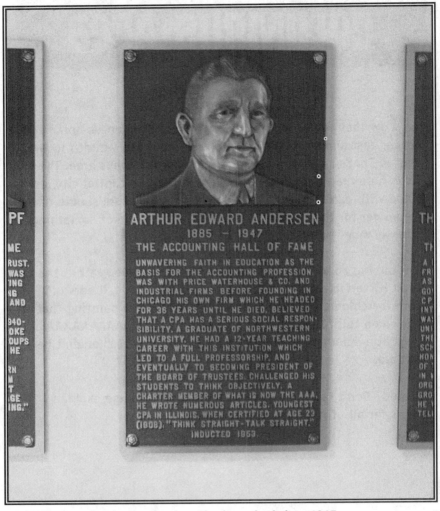

Don't blame me for the Enron mess—I've been dead since 1947.
Photo by author, courtesy of Accounting Hall of Fame

Columbus
Accounting Hall of Fame

If the Enron scandal taught the American public anything, it's that accountants aren't always the mild-mannered pencil pushers they're often portrayed as. Sometimes they can be a devious, destructive, sneaky bunch. But those aren't the type of accountants who make it into the

Accounting Hall of Fame. Good bookkeepers keep a single balanced ledger, not two, and their goal is to *account* for money taken in and spent, not *mask* it.

There have been accountants who understood their responsibilities, folks like Robert Trueblood, John Queenan, Ross Skinner, and Arthur Andersen (the man, not the firm). Never heard of them? Then stop on by the fourth floor of Fisher Hall and read their bronze plaques. Revel in the exactitude, the honor, and the basic arithmetic that is accounting.

Fisher College of Business, 2100 Neill Ave., 4th Floor, Columbus, OH 43210

(614) 292-9368

Hours: Monday–Friday 8 A.M.–5 P.M.

Cost: Free

http://fisher.osu.edu/acctmis/hall

Directions: One block south of Lane Ave., two blocks west of High St., on the OSU campus.

BORN IN COLUMBUS

Here are a few celebrities who were born in the capitol city:

Beverly D'Angelo	November 15, 1952
Jack Nicklaus	January 21, 1940
Tom Posten	October 17, 1927
Eddie Rickenbacker	October 8, 1890

COLUMBUS

Jeb Stuart Magruder, former Watergate operative and convicted felon, went on to become the head of the Columbus Commission on Values and Ethics.

World War I flying ace **Eddie Rickenbacker** was born in Columbus (1334 E. Livingston Avenue) in 1890, and is buried in Greenlawn Cemetery (1000 Greenlawn Avenue, (614) 444-1005).

John Denver? Farrrrr out!

Eyeglasses of the Stars

Apparently all you need to start a museum in this country is a funky idea, lots of stamps, and the nerve to ask a simple question. Optometrist Dr. Arol Augsburger did just that; he sent letters to celebrities asking that they submit their old eyeglasses to a museum being started at OSU's School of Optometry.

A surprising number of individuals responded: Phyllis Diller, Colonel Sanders, John Denver, Joan Collins, Gerald Ford, Orville Redenbacher, Jim Davis, Hal Linden, Sophia Loren, Shari Lewis, Miss Piggy, Ann Landers, Dean Martin, Larry King, Gerald Ford, Richard Petty, Red Skelton, Jack Nicklaus, Arthur Ashe, Paul Volker, Oleg Cassini, Mary Kay's Erma Thompson, Malcolm Forbes, Jack Hanna, Howard Metzenbaum, Stephen King, Dave Thomas, Jimmy Buffet, and Arte Johnson (who included a personal note saying, "I like glasses. They keep my eyebrows warm"). Yes, they do.

All those spectacles would be reason enough to visit, but the hallway museum also has a nice sampling of instruments and visual aids from the history of optometry, from early wooden glasses to monocles, and eye charts to modern frames.

Optometry Museum, Fry Hall, 338 W. 10th Ave., Columbus, OH 43210
(614) 292-2020
Hours: Monday–Friday 8 A.M.–5 P.M.
Cost: Free
http://optometry.osu.edu
Directions: Five blocks west of High St. on 10th Ave., on the OSU campus.

Flowers on the Grave

From the time Private Benjamin E. Allen died and was buried at Camp Chase, he was visited by his former fiancée, who would often bring flowers to place on his plot. Always dressed in gray, she continues to mourn at his tombstone. A sad story, yes, but what makes it downright *creepy* is that Allen was a Confederate soldier in the 50th Tennessee Regiment who died during the Civil War. Either his fiancée is 160-something years old or she's . . . a ghost!

Caretakers call her the Lady in Gray and don't seem to mind her occasional appearance. Then again, they're used to dealing with dead people, though rarely with ones who are still walking around. Although the Lady in Gray is spotted most often near her loved one's grave, she sometimes visits the cemetery's Tomb of the Unknown. Does she know his secret identity? If you see her, please ask.

Camp Chase Confederate Cemetery, 2900 Sullivant Ave., Columbus, OH 43223
No phone

Hours: Dawn–Dusk

Cost: Free

www.geocities.com/Pentagon/Quarters/5109

Directions: Two blocks west of S. Hauge Ave. on Sullivant Ave., west of downtown.

O. Henry's OHio pENitentiaRY

William Sydney Porter is often called the Father of the Modern American Short Story, though few people know him by that name. That's because he published under a pen name: O. Henry. He chose it because his old name had achieved a bit of a reputation—and it wasn't good. Accused of embezzling $5,000 from a Texas bank, he fled to Honduras, hoping things would cool down. When he returned to the United States to visit his ailing wife, police were waiting. After being found guilty of the crime, he was sentenced to five years in prison. Texas farmed out his incarceration to the Ohio Penitentiary. Porter served time from April 1898 to July 1901.

To pass the long hours locked in a cell, Porter wrote short fiction, works he published under his new assumed name. Some believe he chose his pen name in honor of a benevolent guard, Orrin Henry. That might be partly true, but more likely than not it is a shorthand contraction of Ohio Penitentiary, as in OHio pENitentiaRY. Porter never revealed where it came from, so your guess is as good as anyone's.

Spring St. and Neil Ave., Columbus, OH 43215

No phone

Hours: Torn down in 1997

Cost: Free

Directions: Six blocks west of High St., one block north of Long St. (Rte. 33).

The Santa Maria

Christopher Columbus might have sailed the ocean blue in 1492, but he sure as heck didn't navigate up the Mississippi, the Ohio, and the Scioto Rivers to anchor in what is now downtown Columbus. So how did the *Santa Maria* end up here?

The story goes something like this. In 1992, in honor of the quincentennial of Columbus's first voyage to the New World (which also just happened to be the capital city's bicentennial), the city of Columbus commissioned a replica of the explorer's flagship, the *Santa Maria*. It was built to be seaworthy; never mind that it would spend its entire nautical life hundreds of miles from any ocean. It was also outfitted with a complete scurvy-free crew.

The 98-foot-long sailing ship does little more than putt around in the Scioto River, one of those rare modern pleasure crafts that hasn't been outfitted with slot machines and blackjack tables. No matter what the crew says, you will be in no danger of sailing off the end of the earth, but you won't be able to sail out of Columbus, either.

Scioto River Dock, Battelle Riverfront Park, 770 Twin Rivers Dr., Columbus, OH 43216

Contact: 90 W. Broad St., 1st Floor, Columbus, OH 43215

(614) 645-0351

E-mail: info@santamaria.org

Hours: April–May and September–October, Wednesday–Friday 10 A.M.–3 P.M., Saturday–Sunday Noon–5 P.M.; June–August, Wednesday–Friday 10 A.M.–5 P.M., Saturday–Sunday Noon–6 P.M.

Cost: Adults $3, Seniors (60+) $2, Kids (5–17) $1.50

www.santamaria.org/index.php

Directions: Downtown, just north of the Broad St. bridge, at Marconi.

COLUMBUS

Three-hundred and twenty inmates perished in their locked cells at the Ohio State Penitentiary in Columbus during a fire on April 21, 1930. Fewer would have died had the warden, fearing a jailbreak, not prevented guards from unlocking their cells.

It is illegal to sell corn flakes on Sunday in Columbus.

Who took the top?

State Capitol

What a shame that in a state with so many stunning county courthouses, the Ohio State Capitol is so goofy looking. (Only Florida's high-rise office building capitol is uglier.) The first thing that pops into most folks' heads when they see it is, "Who took the top?"

It's a good question, but it doesn't have a good answer. The building design was open to competition, but in the end the Ohio legislature decided on a hybrid of two plans, one submitted by architect Alexander

Davis and the other from painter Thomas Cole. Honestly, it originally *did* include a dome. The cornerstone was laid on July 4, 1839, but because of cost overruns, an eight-year work stoppage, and a cholera outbreak, it took 22 years to complete. Actually, "complete" isn't quite the right word—how about "quit"? Workers had just finished the colonnade that would support the dome when the state legislature wrapped a tourniquet on the hemorrhaging budget. "Finish it off!" they demanded, and that's just what the workers did. The result is what looks like the World's Largest Hatbox. Good job, gang!

Broad and High Sts., Columbus, OH 43211

(888) OHIO-123 or (614) 728-2695

Hours: Always visible

Cost: Free

www.statehouse.state.oh.us/welcome/tourinfo.html

Directions: Downtown, just south of Rte. 40 (Broad St.), three blocks east of the river.

COLUMBUS

TV's *Family Ties* was set in Columbus.

Mildred "Axis Sally" Sisk is buried in St. Joseph Cemetery in Columbus.

A train derailment on May 17, 1998, spilled 20,000 gallons of liquid soap in Columbus.

Animal guru **Jack Hanna** is the director emeritus of the Columbus Zoo (9990 Riverside Drive, (614) 645-3550, www.colzoo.org).

A painting comes to life.
Photo by author, courtesy of Topiary Garden

A Sunday Afternoon with Kitty on the Island of la Grande Jatte

Here's the problem with paintings: as beautifully detailed as they can be, they only offer one perspective of a scene. Is anyone at *The Last Supper* wearing pants? With that long table in the way, you can only be sure about the apostles at either end. But what if you could step inside a piece of art, like Mary Poppins, to take a look around—wouldn't that be nice?

Now you can. Columbus artist James T. Mason has designed a topiary re-creation of Georges Seurat's 1887 masterpiece, *A Sunday Afternoon on the Island of la Grande Jatte.* Planted on a vacant lot created by the 1981 fire at the Ohio State School for the Deaf and Dumb, this living 3D painting contains 54 human figures, 8 boats (with clematis sails that bloom white in late summer), 3 dogs, a monkey, and a cat.

"What?" art experts gasp. "A cat?" That's right, if you inspect the original painting at the Chicago Art Institute, there's not a kitty to be found. And if you view the topiary garden from the park's knoll, the cat is blocked from view. But if you change your perspective by strolling through the park, the green kitty appears. *Ooo-la-la—c'est bizarre*!

Old Deaf School Park, E. Town St. and Washington Ave., Columbus, OH 43215

(614) 645-0197

E-mail: friends@topiarygarden.org

Hours: Daily 7 A.M.–11 P.M.; Gift shop, April–December, Monday–Friday 11 A.M.– 3 P.M., Saturday 11 A.M.–4 P.M., Sunday Noon–4 P.M.

Cost: Free

www.topiarygarden.org

Directions: Four blocks south of Rte. 40 (Broad St.), one block west of I-71.

Thurber House

"I suppose the high-water mark of my youth in Columbus, Ohio, was the night the bed fell on my father," James Thurber wrote, and he was probably right.

Though Thurber grew up in Columbus, he did not spend a lot of time in what is now the Thurber House. He only lived here with his parents for four years, from 1913 to 1917, while he attended Ohio State University. Shortly after graduation, he sold a story to the fledgling *New Yorker*, then was hired on as an editor by E. B. White. Once he left for New York, he never returned for any length of time until he died in 1961. He was buried in Greenlawn Cemetery (1000 Greenlawn Avenue, (614) 444-1005).

When you visit this home, be sure to ask your guide about the ghost that supposedly inhabits the building. Thurber heard it one night while arising from the tub, causing a chain of events that ended in his grandfather chasing off two Columbus policemen, believing they were advancing Confederate troops. The events were immortalized in his short story "The Night the Ghost Got In." There are several theories as to who this spook is. The first claims that the ghost is the unsettled spirit of a man who committed suicide in the house after learning about his wife's infidelity; the other says it is one of the seven patients who died in an 1868 fire at the Central Ohio Lunatic Asylum, which once stood on this site.

If you don't see the ghost on your visit, you will undoubtedly see Thurber's old typewriter (which he used while reporting for the

Columbus Dispatch), several first editions of his books, and mementos from the Thurber family.

77 Jefferson Ave., Columbus, OH 43215

(614) 464-1032

Hours: Daily Noon–4 P.M.

Cost: Adults $2, Seniors $1.50, Kids $1.50

www.thurberhouse.org/ThurberHouse.htm

Directions: Between Broad St. (Rte. 40/62) and Long St. (Rte. 3), just west of I-71, east of downtown.

Two-Headed Calf

This wonderful museum is filled with exhibits on everything Ohioan, from the early native cultures of the region to the state's industrial development, from the Cedar Bog Nature Preserve to the Civil War, and from fossilized trilobites to the lithographs of Currier and Ives.

Whatever.

The question on every schoolkid's lips is "Where's the two-headed calf?" This unique bovine was born in Darke County in 1910, but only lived for a short time. But it was given a second chance at life when its dead body was stuffed and placed in this museum's collection. You can find the mutated mooer in a glass case beneath the western staircase in the central atrium, next to the Egyptian mummy (another favorite with the little ones).

Ohio Historical Center, 1982 Velma Ave., Columbus, OH 43211

(800) OLD-OHIO or (614) 297-2300

Hours: Tuesday–Wednesday and Friday–Saturday 9 A.M.–5 P.M., Thursday 9 A.M.– 9 P.M., Sunday Noon–5 P.M.

Cost: Adults $6, Kids (6–12) $2, Parking $3

www.ohiohistory.org/places/ohc

Directions: Exit I-71 at 17th Ave., north of downtown, and head west two blocks to Velma Ave.; head north, following the signs.

World's First Wendy's

When Dave Thomas first opened the doors to a new fast-food chain, he was far from a novice. For years he had been Colonel Sanders's right-hand man, and he'd developed a professional network that he drew upon heavily to get him started. One friend he'd made, actor Danny

Thomas (no relation), was there when Wendy's Old Fashioned Hamburgers Restaurant grilled its first square burger on November 15, 1969. Danny Thomas saved his Frosty cup and spoon from the big event, and presented it to Dave Thomas years later.

You can still see that famous paper cup and spoon (behind security glass, of course) at the World's First Wendy's, a restaurant/museum in downtown Columbus. It's also got the original test griddle from Village Meats, as well as authentic foil wrap for those early square-patty burgers. The first restaurant, housed in an old auto showroom, was much smaller than the current venue, but feel free to sit in a four-table area with the original Tiffany-style lighting and plastic hippie beads if you want to take a trip down memory lane.

The restaurant is as educational as it is mouthwatering. You'll learn all about Dave's eight-year-old daughter, Melinda Lou Thomas, whose siblings couldn't pronounce her name; they ended up calling her Wendy, and she became the inspiration for the girl in the company logo. Melinda Lou looked nothing like Wendy, but Thomas gave her a makeover of pigtails and a gingham dress (also on display). Check out the sketches of the Wendy hairstyles and clothes that didn't make the final cut, including one girl with a bow so enormous that it rivaled the size of her head.

Clara Peller is prominently featured throughout the museum, as well she should be. When her 1984 "Where's the beef?" advertisement hit the airwaves, sales shot up 31 percent. What you *won't* find is any mention of why Thomas fired the old woman a year later: she unwisely made an advertisement for Prego spaghetti sauce, nullifying her exclusive contract. Adios, Clara!

Dave Thomas died on January 8, 2002, in Fort Lauderdale, Florida. His body was returned to Columbus and laid to rest in Union Cemetery (3349 Olentangy River Road, (614) 267-5471), where you can pay your respects if you'd like to make your Wendy's sojourn complete.

257 E. Broad St., Columbus, OH 43215

(614) 464-4656

Hours: Monday–Friday 10 A.M.–8 P.M., Saturday 10 A.M.–7 P.M., Sunday 11 A.M.–6 P.M.

Cost: Free

www.wendys.com

Directions: Six blocks east of High St. on Rte. 40 (Broad St.).

Ears to *Field of Corn!*

Dublin
Field of Corn

If you're the type who worries about genetic engineering, don't panic when you're driving though Dublin and you spot a field of megacorn, all lined up at attention in a neat military formation, as if waiting for marching orders. The ears aren't really corn; they're six-foot-tall replicas cast in concrete by Malcolm Cochran in 1994. The sculptor wanted to make a statement about urban sprawl and how it was gobbling up once valuable farmland. The irony is that by making a large installation of 109 ears, he gobbled up even more. Whether he intended to be ironic or stumbled into it is unclear. One thing is for sure: as public sculpture goes, *Field of Corn* makes for a very cool photo op.

Sam and Eulalia Frantz Park, 4995 Rings Rd., Dublin, OH 43017

No phone

Hours: Always visible

Cost: Free

www.dublinarts.org/onview/publicart.html#

Directions: On the southwest corner of Frantz and Ring Rds., north of Tuttle Rd.

Play all you want, kids.
Photo by author, courtesy of Mall at Tuttle Crossing

Play with Your Breakfast

Talk about mixed messages! Designers at the Mall at Tuttle Crossing in Dublin tried to come up with a clever theme for its kids' play space, and what did they choose? Gigantic breakfast food. A couple of oversize, sunny-side up eggs . . . a pair of mattress-size waffles . . . a few banana slices for chairs . . . and there you have it: every parent's nightmare. Yeah, the padded food is cute, but after a few dozen belly flops off the bacon strip into the cereal bowl just see if you can get the young 'uns to behave at the breakfast table.

Mall at Tuttle Crossing, 5043 Tuttle Crossing Blvd., Dublin, OH 43016

(614) 717-9300

Hours: Monday–Saturday 10 A.M.–9 P.M., Sunday Noon–6 P.M.

Cost: Free

www.shoptuttlecrossing.com

Directions: Just east of the Tuttle Rd. Exit from I-270.

Westerville
Anti-Saloon League Museum

As misguided as Prohibition looks in retrospect, around the turn of the century the notion of a constitutional amendment banning alcohol had plenty of supporters. The drive was spearheaded by the Women's Christian Temperance Union (in Evanston, Illinois) and the Anti-Saloon League (in Washington, D.C.). In 1909, the Anti-Saloon League was looking for a place to set up its printing operation, and the town of Westerville made a $10,000 bid for it. The League accepted the offer and the money and the American Issue Publishing Company was born.

The press printed books and pamphlets with titles such as *Beer the Traitor*, *Booze and a Boy*, *The Effect of Alcohol on the Sex Life*, *She Knows!*, and *A Whiff from Hell!*, all with the same basic message: drinking is *bad*. American Issue Publishing was no small-time operation; the company shipped more than 40 tons of literature each month.

The runaway temperance train couldn't be stopped. In 1918 the last state needed for ratification of the Eighteenth Amendment passed it, and congress empowered law enforcement with the Volstead Act of 1919. Yet it soon became obvious that a majority of Americans continued to drink—constitutional amendment be damned! Organized crime stepped in to fill the need and a whole new (and worse) set of social problems emerged. The noble experiment turned into the dismal failure and in 1934 Prohibition was repealed.

You can learn about the birth and all-but-death of the movement at the Westerville Public Library's Anti-Saloon League Museum. The

American Issue Publishing archives were donated to the library and constitute the nation's largest collection of dry-abilia.

Westerville Public Library, 126 S. State St., Westerville, OH 43081

(614) 882-7277 x160

Hours: Monday–Friday 9 A.M.–6 P.M., or by appointment

Cost: Free

www.wpl.lib.oh.us/AntiSaloon

Directions: Three blocks south of Main St. on Rte. 3 (State St.).

THE WHISKEY WARS

Westerville wasn't just a simple economic choice for the Anti-Saloon League's publishing efforts, it was the obvious *moral* choice. The town had been dry since 1858, and called itself the Dry Capital of the World. (Obviously they'd never heard of Tehran.) Temperance crusaders in Westerville demonstrated that they were willing to employ fairly extreme measures to cast out the Demon Rum, measures that today look a lot like terrorism. In 1875, Henry and Phyloxena Corbin's saloon at 36 W. Main Street was bombed, forcing the couple to flee town. (The building was repaired and still stands today.) The couple returned four years later, but their second saloon was soon leveled with 52 pounds of temperance gunpowder.

It should be acknowledged that Westerville's prudish nature didn't cross over into all elements of American society. As a matter of fact, during the Prohibition 1920s, the town's Kilgore Manufacturing Company was the nation's largest producer of children's toy guns and exploding caps. Gotta keep those kiddies armed!

REYNOLDSBURG

Alexander Livingston of Reynoldsburg is said to be the Father of the Modern Tomato. He developed the Paragon, Dwarf Aristocrat, Buckeye State, Golden Queen, Gold Ball, Royal Red, and Acme varieties. Each September the town hosts a Tomato Festival in his honor. Call (614) 866-2861 for information.

If you can't see your future in *this* crystal ball, you have no future.
Photo by author, courtesy of American Ceramics Society

World's Largest Crystal Ball

No, the World's Largest Crystal Ball is not a hand-me-down from the World's Most Nearsighted Gypsy. It's a 700-pound work of art intended to demonstrate the wonder of ceramics—in this case optical glass. It was created in 1987 by Christopher Ries of Schott Glass Technologies, and is a little smaller than the one at the witch's castle in *The Wizard of Oz*.

The colossal crystal ball sits on a pedestal in the front entrance at the American Ceramics Society. If you make an appointment, you can also visit the Ross C. Purdy Museum of Ceramics, located just off the lobby. The museum grew from Purdy's original ceramics collection (Purdy was the society's secretary from 1921 to 1946), and now contains more than 2,000 artifacts, from simple pottery to a tile from the Space Shuttle. If you catch the ceramics bug, the society has a library of more than 10,000 books on the subject. Who'da thunk?

Ross C. Purdy Museum of Ceramics, American Ceramics Society, 735 Ceramic Pl., Westerville, OH 43081

(614) 794-5890

Hours: Monday–Friday 9 A.M.–5 P.M., by appointment only

Cost: Free

www.acers.org/acers/museum.asp

Directions: One block north of I-270 on Cleveland Ave., east on Schrock Rd. two blocks to Ceramic Pl.

8

GUY TOUR

*O*hio is a guy-friendly state. It's the birthplace of pro football, ready-to-eat pasta in a can, and Woody Hayes. It's home to the World's Longest Bar, Arnold Schwarzenegger's tank, and the Pork Rind Heritage Festival. (Yeah, yeah, some women like this stuff, too—I'm talking about *averages*.)

And Ohio is not just friendly to human guys, but also to other male primates. A few years back, nursing mothers were brought to the Columbus Zoo to show two female gorillas how to breastfeed their babies. Unfortunately, a male named Oscar was the most interested. He became so entranced he blocked the females' view. Handlers had to coax him away with bananas.

So if you're a guy, or if you like guys, or if you enjoy laughing at guys being guys, gas up the Hummer for this Tour of Testosterone.

Here it is, if you give a damn.

Start Like a Guy

Ohio has given the world its fair share of guys. Guy guys. Guys who don't shy away from a little cholesterol. Guys who aren't afraid to scratch their privates on national TV in the bottom of the ninth in the final game of the World Series. Guys like **Clark Gable**.

Believe it or not, Ohio guy Clark Gable was listed as a girl on his birth certificate. He was born in Cadiz on February 1, 1901, and when doctors took a second look, the error was corrected. At the time his family lived on the second floor of a building on Charleston Street, but they soon moved to a new place on Lincoln Avenue. At the age of 20 he moved to Akron to work in a rubber factory, and didn't pay Cadiz much thought after that.

Cadiz didn't seem to give a damn about its famous native son, either; back in the 1960s they even tore down his birthplace! But in 1985 the town had a change of heart and hosted its first Clark Gable Birthday Celebration, which is now an annual event. They rebuilt his birthplace in 1998, and stocked it with MGM photos and Gable family heirlooms, like his childhood sled. The Clark Gable Foundation also owns the King of Hollywood's 1954 powder blue Cadillac, which it rolls out for special occasions. They've recently added a Clark Gable Bed & Breakfast next door.

Clark Gable Birthplace, 138 Charleston St., Cadiz, OH 43907

(740) 942-GWTW

Hours: October–April, Tuesday–Friday 10 A.M.–4 P.M.; May, Tuesday–Saturday 10 A.M.–4 P.M.; June–September, Tuesday–Saturday 10 A.M.–4 P.M., Sunday 1:30–4 P.M.; and by appointment

Cost: Adults $4.50, Seniors $4, Kids $3; B&B rooms, $80–$90/night

www.clarkgablefoundation.com

Directions: Three blocks east of Main St., one block north of Market St. (Rte. 250).

THE BIRTHPLACES OF GUYS

Clark Gable is just one of many guys born in Ohio. Here are a few more:

Jim Backus	February 25, 1913	Cleveland
Drew Carey	May 23, 1958	Cleveland
Larry Csonka	December 25, 1946	Stow
General George Armstrong Custer	December 3, 1839	New Rumley
Clarence Darrow	April 18, 1857	Kinsman
Phil Donahue	December 21, 1935	Cleveland
John Glenn	July 18, 1921	Cambridge
Woody Hayes	February 3, 1913	Clifton
Don King	August 20, 1931	Cleveland
Bobby Knight	October 25, 1940	Orrville
William Boyd Lawrence (Hopalong Cassidy)	June 5, 1895	Cambridge
James Lovell	March 24, 1924	Cleveland
Paul Lynde	June 13, 1926	Mount Vernon

Eat Like a Guy

Correct me if I'm wrong: the average guy's eating habits are, to say the least, atrocious. Fast food and food eaten fast—that's the way guys like it! Thankfully, Ohio folks like Henry Heimlich have made eating like a guy a little safer. This Cincinnati surgeon introduced his lifesaving maneuver in 1974, making it less risky to swallow without chewing, provided one of your buddies knows how to perform the procedure and isn't too involved in watching the game to give you a hand when you turn blue.

That said, what better place to start an Ohio tour of guy food than with the classic American hamburger? Believe it or not, there is considerable debate as to when and where the hamburger was invented, and by whom. Was it a squished meatball created by Charlie Nagreen at the 1885 Seymour-Outagamie County Fair in northeast Wisconsin? Or an 1895 ground beef concoction at Louie's Lunch in New Haven, Connecticut? Or did it first show up sometime in the 1880s at Frederic "Old Dave" Davis's lunch counter just off the town square in Athens, Texas?

The most compelling evidence, however, points to a sandwich introduced at the 1885 Erie County Fair in—drum roll, please—*Hamburg*, New York. Its inventors, Charles and Frank Menches, didn't much like the taste of a plain ground beef patty, so they added brown sugar . . . and *coffee* . . . and a "secret ingredient." The Menches family has kept that top-secret substance classified to this day so that the **Original Hamburger** you chomp into at their Akron or Uniontown restaurants is a true original.

The Mencheses also claim to have invented Gee-Whiz in 1893, the forerunner to Cracker Jack, and the ice cream cone in 1904. Did these guys have it in for the American waistline or what??!?

Menches Brothers Original Hamburgers, Canal Park, 300-R S. Main St., Akron, OH 44308
(330) 375-1717
Hours: Monday–Friday 11 A.M.–2 P.M.
Cost: Meals $8–$16
www.menchesbros.com
Directions: One block north of Exchange St., three blocks west of Broadway (Rte. 261).

Menches Brothers Original Hamburgers, Shops of Green, 3700 Massillon Rd., Suite 130, Uniontown, OH 44685
(330) 896-2288
Directions: One block south of I-77 on Rte. 241 (Massillon Rd.).

A slider lover's Camelot.

Burger fans will no doubt want to visit another fast-food shrine, of sorts, in Columbus: the Porcelain Steel Building Company, home of **White Castle Systems**, Inc. This is not where the hamburgers—or sliders, as they're known—originate, but the castles themselves. The factory has been churning out the classic franchise stores since 1934. Though you cannot tour the facility, you can admire its glimmering, white-paneled tower from the nearby street.

White Castle Systems, Inc., 555 W. Gooddale Blvd., Columbus, OH 43215

(614) 228-5781

Hours: Always visible, view from street

Cost: Free

Directions: Just east of the Olentangy River and Rte. 315 on Gooddale Blvd., just west of I-670.

There was a time when I thought a plate of Spaghetti-Os was fine dining. I happened to be six years old at the time. But not every guy has kicked the pasta-in-a-can habit. Those guys can thank Cleveland's Hector Boiardi, better known by his phonetic trade name, Chef Boyardee.

Boiardi was born in Italy in 1897, and immigrated to New York in 1914, where he worked for some time in the kitchen at the Ritz Carlton. From the Big Apple he moved to Cleveland where he landed a job as chef at the Hotel Winton (1012 Prospect Avenue, now Carter Manor). After developing a loyal gastronomic following, mostly for his spaghetti sauce, he opened his own restaurant, Il Giardino d'Italia, in 1924. The establishment had seating on the main level, while the second floor was dedicated to what quickly became a booming takeout business.

Takeouts became so successful Boiardi began factory production of the **First Pre-Packaged Meal** in 1928: a bundle of dry spaghetti, a packet of grated Parmesan cheese, and a milk bottle filled with spaghetti sauce. The meal sold for 60¢ and fed a family of four. Boiardi changed the company's name to Chef Boyardee in 1936 after a focus group of truck drivers suggested it would be easier for consumers to sound out.

Boiardi sold his company for $6 million shortly after the end of World War II, yet his face remains on cans of Beefaroni and Spaghetti and Meatballs to this day. Chef Boyardee is now part of ConAgra Foods.

Il Giardino d'Italia, E. 9th St. and Woodland Ave., Cleveland, OH 44115

No phone

Hours: No longer there

Cost: Free

www.chefboyardee.com

Directions: Located roughly at the interchange of I-90 and I-77, south of downtown.

If you're not the type of guy to eat right out of a can but don't want to be thought of as a connoisseur of haute cuisine, perhaps you should try a **Fried Bologna Sandwich**. Though this culinary delight can be found in many Ohio establishments, the G&R Tavern and Grille in Waldo claims to be its home. The bologna here is not sliced school cafeteria–thin; it's a half-inch thick. It is grilled until it obtains a blackened crust, and is then topped with Monterey Jack cheese.

How good is it? The proof is in the poundage; this establishment serves up a half-ton of bologna *each week*.

G&R Tavern and Grille, 103 N. Marion Rd., Waldo, OH 43356

(740) 726-9685

Hours: Monday–Thursday and Saturday 8 A.M.–Midnight, Friday 8 A.M.–1:30 P.M.

Cost: Sandwich $3.15

Directions: Exit Rte. 23 at Waldo heading west, turn south on Marion St., and two blocks south to Main St.

MORE BIRTHPLACES OF GUYS		
Charles Manson	November 11, 1934	Cincinnati
Dean Martin		
(Dino Paul Crocetti)	June 17, 1917	Steubenville
Greg Morris	September 27, 1934	Cleveland
Thurmon Munson	June 7, 1947	Akron
Paul Newman	January 26, 1925	Cleveland
Jack Nicklaus	January 21, 1940	Columbus
Ed O'Neill	April 12, 1946	Youngstown
Luke Perry	October 11, 1966	Mansfield
Arnold Palmer	September 10, 1929	Youngstown
Ara Parseghian	May 10, 1923	Akron
Johnny Paycheck	May 31, 1941	Greenfield
Norman Vincent		
Peale	May 31, 1898	Bowersville
Tyrone Power, Jr.	May 5, 1914	Cincinnati
Eddie Rickenbacker	October 8, 1890	Columbus
Roy Rogers		
(Leonard Frank Slye)	November 5, 1912	Cincinnati
Pete Rose	April 14, 1942	Cincinnati

How are your arteries holding out? OK? Well, then head on over to Harrod's **Pork Rind Heritage Festival**, held each June and sponsored by the Rudolph Foods Company, the world's largest producer of pork rind snacks. Rudolph Foods, with its headquarters in the area, produces more than 2 million pounds of pig products each week—what's not to celebrate?

The company's Web site is filled with useful information about its often-misunderstood snack. For example, did you know that pork rinds contain roughly the same number of calories as peanuts (per serving), but they're higher in protein *and* lower in fat? And no carbs! Take that, Peanut Heritage Festival, wherever you are! And if you ever wondered if pork rinds are *really* from the skin of hogs, the answer is yes: Regular Rinds are made from skin off the belly and back of the hog, Washpots & Tender Cracklin's come from the skin between the shoulder and head, and Hard Cracklin's come from the rump. Mmmm-mmmmm!

All Over Town, Harrod, OH 45850

No phone

E-mail: info@rudolphfoods.com

Hours: Early June

Cost: Free; Food extra

www.rudolphfoods.com/pork_rind_heritage_festival.htm

Directions: All over town.

Another porcine food celebration, the **Bratwurst Festival**, is hosted by the town of Bucyrus each August. More than 27 tons of brats are consumed during the three-day event, and not all of that is during the Brat Eating Contest. There is also a Bratwurst Parade and ceremonial crowning of the annual Bratwurst Queen and Junior Princess. And in case you're wondering, *no*, they do not earn their titles by choking down the most brats.

Contact: 301 S. Sandusky Ave., Bucyrus, OH 44820

(419) 562-BRAT

Hours: Mid-August

Cost: Free; Food extra

www.bratwurstfestival.org

Directions: All over town.

If there's a Bratwurst Festival, could a **Sauerkraut Festival** be far behind? Since 1970 the town of Waynesville has hosted an annual celebration honoring fermented cabbage on the second full weekend in October. More than 11,000 pounds of sauerkraut are consumed during the three-day event, and not all of it in its traditional form. You can also indulge in sauerkraut ice cream, sauerkraut donuts, sauerkraut brownies, and sauerkraut pizza.

Contact: Waynesville Area Chamber of Commerce, PO Box 281, Waynesville, OH 45068

(513) 897-8855

E-mail: waynesville@aol.com

Hours: On the second full weekend in October

Cost: Free

www.waynesvilleohio.com/Sauerkraut.htm

Directions: Events take place along Old Main St., one block northwest of Rte. 142 (New Main St.).

Pretzels earned an unwarranted bad rap after attacking George W. Bush, but they're really not as dangerous as the president made them appear. Guys have been eating these snacks for a long time without ill effects, as Germantown residents can attest. They've hosted an annual **Pretzel Festival** since 1980. The event is held on the fourth weekend in September each year. Come and enjoy these tasty, twisty treats, but please, chew them thoroughly before swallowing.

Contact: Germantown Pretzel Festival, PO Box 42, Germantown, OH 45327

(937) 859-8331

E-mail: pretzelfest@donet.com

Hours: Fourth weekend in September

Cost: Free

www.mvcc.net/germantown/gtour.htm

Directions: In Veterans Memorial Park.

One way to avoid being attacked by rogue snacks is to wash them down with plenty of fluids, and what better place to do this than the **World's Longest Bar**? The main counter at the Beer Barrel Saloon is 405 feet, 10 inches long. It has 160 barstools, 56 taps, and is staffed with 20 bartenders when the joint is at capacity.

The Beer Barrel Saloon was built in 1989 on the ashes of Put-in-Bay's historic Colonial dance hall, which burned to the ground a year earlier. To get an idea just how long its bar is, take a look at the Perry Monument (see page 34) as your ferry chugs over from the mainland. Now imagine: the World's Longest Bar is more than five stories longer than the Perry Monument is tall.

Beer Barrel Saloon, 324 Delaware Ave., PO Box 398, Put-in-Bay, OH 43456

(419) 285-BEER

E-mail: beerbarrel@beerbarrelpib.com

Hours: Daily 11 A.M.–12:30 A.M.

Cost: Free; Booze extra

www.beerbarrelpib.com

Directions: East of Catawba Ave., one block south of the ferry docks.

Act Like a Guy

If you want to be a guy, you've got to act like a guy. You don't sip cocktails, you chug beers. You don't pee sitting down, you stand up. And you don't get your hair styled at a salon, you get it cut at a barber shop.

That's where Edwin Jeffers comes in handy. If you've forgotten how hair cutting used to be done, stop on by his barber shop in Canal Winchester for a trim *and* an education. Jeffers operates a shop on the ground floor, but upstairs is a fantastic **Barber Museum** that traces not only the profession's contribution to hair care, but to health care as well. That's right, many early barbers were also surgeons; in fact, the red and white barber pole is a throwback to the days when barbers would hang their bloody surgical rags out to dry.

The Barber Museum has antique razors (more than 600) and shaving mugs (about 450), but they're not half as interesting as the bloodletting bowls and dental pliers. Jeffers has also restored 14 chairs and more than 50 barber poles to their original glory.

2½ S. High St., Canal Winchester, OH 43110

(614) 833-9931

E-mail: barbermuseum@earthlink.net

Hours: By appointment only

Cost: Free

www.edjeffersbarbermuseum.com

Directions: Just south of Waterloo St. (Rte. 18) on High St.

One of the most common ways for a guy to leave his mark on the world is to leave a genetic mark, and to that end, the Guy Tour takes us to the **Select Sires Bull Hall of Fame**. There are currently only 12 inductees, but boy have they earned their props; one honoree, Mars, sired more than 96,000 offspring! He didn't do it all himself, but had a hand (or two) from the folks at Select Sires, the nation's largest artificial insemination operation.

The Hall of Fame isn't much more than a bunch of plaques, so if it leaves you wanting more, arrange a tour of the facilities to watch a "collection" first hand. In a weird, cow-porn display, a common bull is made to mount a female cow while the semen-producing bulls watch. This is supposed to get them ready for collection. Unless you want to answer a bunch of interesting questions, better leave the kids at home.

Inductees who have given their last drop (and dropped dead) are buried around the complex under granite headstones, just like people.

11740 Rte. 42N, PO Box 143, Plain City, OH 43064

(614) 873-4683

E-mail: info-line@selectsires.com

Hours: Daily 8 A.M.–4:30 P.M. by appointment

Cost: Free

www.selectsires.com

Directions: Northeast of town on Rte. 23.

MORE BIRTHPLACES OF GUYS		
Martin Sheen	August 3, 1940	Dayton
Jimmy "The Greek" Snyder	September 9, 1919	Steubenville
Steven Spielberg	December 18, 1947	Cincinnati
Ted Turner	November 19, 1938	Cincinnati
Jonathan Winters	November 11, 1925	Dayton

Guys love guns, that's true, but far too many guys use them for criminal behavior—nothin' to be proud of! Trapshooters, on the other hand, are by and large a polite, law-abiding bunch. And who can fault anyone for blowing a clay pigeon out of the air before it drops clay doo-doo on someone? These sportsmen and -women are honored at the **Trapshooting Hall of Fame** in Vandalia, home of the annual Grand American Trapshooting Tournament since 1924.

The biggest star of this guy-friendly museum isn't a guy at all, but Annie Oakley. She was born just up the road near Greenville. Her favorite trapshooting trick was to disintegrate six glass balls that had been tossed into the air at the same time, using three double-barrel shotguns—and she did it all while lying on her back and firing over her head. One of the few target balls Oakley ever missed is on display here.

You won't see anything like that trick reenacted at this place, but you will see plenty of clay pigeons, launching machines, composer John Philip Sousa's collection of trapshooting stuff, and guns, guns, and more guns.

601 W. National Rd., Vandalia, OH 45377

(937) 898-4638

E-mail: hof@shootata.com

Hours: Monday–Friday 9 A.M.–4 P.M.

Cost: Free

www.traphof.org

Directions: West of I-75 on Rte. 40 (National Rd.).

One distinct advantage of being a guy is being able to pee while standing up. Big deal? Apparently it is to the folks of Salem—they've honored one of the town's urinals with a plaque. Of course, it isn't just any porcelain fixture that receives a historic marker; this just happens to be a **urinal used by President John F. Kennedy**!

Now sure, JFK unzipped his fly in a lot of places (and not always to do number one), but he only did it once in Salem . . . that historians are aware of. He was attending a game at Reilly Stadium, and he went to the locker room to relieve himself. Somebody thoughtfully took notice of which fixture he used, and now, that famous piece of plumbing is marked for generations to come.

Reilly Stadium, 491 Reilly Ave., Salem, OH 44460

(330) 332-8946

Hours: Always visible

Cost: Free

Directions: Two blocks south of Rte. 14 (State St.), one block east of Rte. 9
   (Lincoln Ave.).

Drive Like a Guy

In 1908, the Cincinnati mayor claimed that women were not suited for automobile driving. And while time has proven his sexist theory wrong, the idea that jackasses are not suited for public office has yet to become widely accepted, despite all the evidence on file to back it up.

The mayor's observation might have grown out of a guy's traditional insecurity, and let's face it, the Model Ts of the era didn't cut it as phallic projections. Those days are long gone, and now there are places like the **Welsh Jaguar Classic Car Museum** to celebrate automotive excess.

The museum is housed alongside a Jaguar (pronounced "jag-wahr," not "jag-wire") dealership, repair shop, and the Jaggin' Around Restaurant & Pub. They've got dozens of models on display, all in mint condition and ready to tear up the road. They've also got an impressive Jaguar-themed gift shop; if you've got a Jaguar need, Welsh's can fill it. The only thing they can't offer you is a plan as to how you might be able to afford one of these babies in the first place.

223 N. 5th St., PO Box 4130, Steubenville, OH 43952

(800) 875-JAGS or (740) 282-8649

E-mail: contact@welshent.com

Hours: Monday–Friday 9 A.M.–5 P.M., Saturday 9 A.M.–1 P.M.

Cost: Free

www.welshent.com/museum.htm

Directions: Five blocks west of Rte. 2 (Water St.) on Rte. 43 (Washington St.).

Now if you're the kind of guy who prefers bulk over style in his driving machine, come on by Motts Military Museum where you can check out **Arnold Schwarzenegger's tank.** Long before he was elected governor of California, Ah-nuld was cruising around Austria in the Korean War–vintage M-47 tank as part of that country's army. Years later, after making millions from guy flicks, he purchased the old vehicle and brought it to America. He eventually donated it to Motts when he bought something a little larger—a Hummer.

Motts Military Museum has so much more to see than this old rust bucket. It's got artifacts for all of this nation's conflicts, from a salt-glazed ring jug from the Revolutionary War to a Huey helicopter from Vietnam. It's got an "extra" French Legion of Honor medal from Eddie Rickenbacker, one of General MacArthur's corncob pipes, and a Civil War sword found in an old chicken coop. It's even got the *Apollo 13* lunar module logbook from the U.S.–Martian conflict of 1971. Never heard of that war? Now you can read all about it.

Motts Military Museum, 5075 S. Hamilton Rd., Groveport, OH 43125

(614) 836-1500

E-mail: info@mottsmilitarymuseum.org

Hours: Tuesday–Saturday 9 A.M.–5 P.M., Sunday 1–5 P.M.

Cost: Adults $5, Seniors $4, Kids $3

www.mottsmilitarymuseum.org

Directions: Head south on Rte. 317, then left onto Hamilton Rd.

Fight Like a Guy

Sometimes a guy's gotta do what a guy's gotta do, and for a few hotheads what a guy's gotta do seems to be all about fighting. *You lookin' at my gal? Wanna take it outside?* It's a caveman thing, and not very becoming.

Ohio has been the scene of plenty of fistfights and worse, some of which were instigated by, or finished by, celebrities. A drunken **Woody Harrelson** was arrested after he was found dancing along the center line of a Columbus street on October 10, 1982. As the paddy wagon pulled away from the curb, carting the actor off to jail, the door popped opened and Harrelson jumped out. Police apprehended him a second time, but not before Harrelson punched one of the cops. The actor was given a $390 fine for misdemeanor assault and resisting arrest.

Police didn't have to get involved in a brawl at the Toledo Sports Arena a quarter-century earlier: **Elvis Presley** didn't start the fight, but he finished it. And the King *didn't* get a fine.

It all started when an unemployed steelworker found a picture of Elvis in his wife's wallet. While there was no evidence that Presley even knew the woman, it was clear to her husband that she had become infatuated with the hip-gyrater. So the guy bought a ticket to the King's November 22, 1956, concert to settle an imaginary score.

Finding his prey backstage, the steelworker threw a punch, but missed. Elvis counterpunched, decking the guy. No doubt the brawler's wife was even *less* impressed with her he-man husband after that pathetic display.

Toledo Sports Arena, 1 Main St., Toledo, OH 43605

(419) 698-4545

Hours: Always visible

Cost: Free

www.toledosportsarena.com

Directions: On the south side of the Maumee River, at the intersection of Main and
   Front Sts., just west of I-288.

You probably would have guessed this anyway, but singer **Johnny Paycheck** (famous for his 1978 country-western megahit "Take This Job and Shove It") had an attitude problem. This wasn't anything new—years earlier he had served three years at the Chillicothe Correctional Institute for shooting a man at the North High Saloon in Hillsboro. The bar was torn down years ago to make way for a city office building, but you can still see the prison where Paycheck served on the north side of Chillicothe. If you can think of a better way to spend your vacation than looking at a prison that held this loudmouth, why don't you just take this suggestion and . . . well . . . you know.

Chillicothe Correctional Institute, 15802 State Rd. 104N, PO Box 5500, Chillicothe,
   OH 45601

(740) 774-7080

Hours: Always visible

Cost: Free

www.drc.state.oh.us/Public/CCI.htm

Directions: North of town on High St. (Rte. 104).

Elvis Costello made an even bigger mistake (career-wise) than Paycheck when he badmouthed Ray Charles and James Brown in front of Stephen Stills and Bonnie Bramlett (of Stills's band) on March 16, 1979, in the Columbus Holiday Inn lounge. The word he used to describe both icons started with an *n* and is not the type of word anyone should use no matter how many drinks one's had, and if the reports of the incident are accurate, they'd all had *plenty*. Bramlett stuck her good-ol' American fist in the Brit's big mouth, then left him to explain his racist comments to the press for the next decade or so. Ironically, Costello had earlier signed up for a British tour call Rock Against Racism. Musician, heal thyself!

Holiday Inn, 175 E. Town St., Columbus, OH 43215

(800) 367-7870 or (614) 221-3281

E-mail: glclm@lodgian.com

Hours: Check-in 3 P.M., Check-out Noon

Cost: Free; Rooms $70–$200/night

www.ichotelsgroup.com/h/d/hi/hd/cmhet

Directions: Three blocks east of the State Capitol building.

Die Like a Guy

One of Ohio's strangest deaths was that of Stella Walsh. She had competed in the 1932 Olympics on behalf of Poland, her home country, and won the gold medal in the 100-meter dash after she broke the 12-second mark. Walsh lived in Cleveland until 1950, when she was murdered during a robbery. During her autopsy, the coroner made a discovery: Walsh had always been a man. Surprise!

As far as anyone knows, the following guys had no similar postmortem revelations. They're not going anywhere if you'd like to visit and pay your respects.

➡ **John H. Balsley** (1823–1895), a carpenter, was the inventor of the folding stepladder (Woodland Cemetery, 118 Woodland Avenue, Dayton, (937) 228-3221).

➡ **Ermal C. "Eddie" Fraze** (1913–1989) invented the beer can pull-tab (Miami Valley Memory Gardens, 1639 E. Lytle-Five Points Road, Dayton, (937) 885-7779).

➡ **Cockburn Haskell** (1868–1922) created the rubber-core wound golf ball, essentially the same design used for today's modern golf balls (Lake View Cemetery, 12316 Euclid Avenue, Cleveland, (216) 421-2665).

➡ **Wayne "Woody" Hayes** (1913–1987), renowned OSU football coach, was fired after slugging a Clemsen player during the 1978 Gator Bowl (Union Cemetery, 3349 Olentangy River Road, Columbus, (614) 267-5471).

➡ **Joseph Hooker** (1815–1879), commander of the Army of the Potomac during the Civil War, is perhaps best known for his efforts to corral Washington, D.C.'s prostitutes into a single, manageable red-light district; the women were later called hookers (Spring Grove Cemetery, 4521 Spring Grove Avenue, Cincinnati, (513) 681-7526).

➡ **Steve Nagy** (1913–1966) was named Bowler of the Year in both 1952 and 1955 (Highland Park Cemetery, 21400 Chagrin Boulevard, Cleveland, (216) 348-7210).

➡ **Eliot Ness** (1903–1957) was cremated after dying in 1957, but his ashes were not scattered over this cemetery's lake until 1997. (Lake View Cemetery, 12316 Euclid Avenue, Cleveland, (216) 421-2665).

➡ **Charlie Henry Rich** (1856–1929) dealt what has become known as the dead man's hand—two pair, aces and eights—to Wild Bill Hickok in Deadwood, South Dakota, shortly before Wild Bill was shot in the back (Evergreen Cemetery, Route 126, Miamisville).

➡ **Eddie Rickenbacker** (1890–1973), the World War I "Ace of Aces" and onetime owner of the Indianapolis Motor Speedway, died at the ripe old age of 82 (Greenlawn Cemetery, 1000 Greenlawn Avenue, Columbus, (614) 444-1005).

➡ **Dr. James Salisbury** (1823–1905) invented a meat dish he claimed had certain curative properties; he named it the Salisbury Steak (Lake View Cemetery, 12316 Euclid Avenue, Cleveland, (216) 421-2665).

➡ **Jimmy "The Greek" Snyder** (1918–1996), professional oddsmaker, was rightfully fired from his gig as a CBS sports commentator in 1988 after theorizing on Martin Luther King's birthday that blacks were better athletes because of slave owner's breeding techniques (Union Cemetery, 1720 Sunset Boulevard, Steubenville, (740) 283-3384).

And now for a dissenting opinion . . .

Akron
"Ain't I a Woman?"

OK, so not everyone buys into all this guy crap.

One of the most passionate spokespersons for abolition was also a groundbreaker for women's suffrage: Sojourner Truth. In 1851, at the National Woman Suffrage Convention in Akron, she delivered her famous "Ain't I a Woman?" speech, much to the surprise of the delegates. The roster had her following a long list of speakers, many of them men, who were saying that women could not possibly advance without the help of men. Truth laid into them all:

> That man over there says that women have to be helped into carriages and lifted over ditches and to have the best places everywhere. Nobody ever helped me into carriages or over mud puddles or gave me any best place. And ain't I a woman?

> Look at me! Look at my arm! I have plowed and planted and gathered into barns and no man could head me—and ain't I a woman? I could work as much and eat as much as a man, when I could get it, and bear the lash as well—and ain't I a woman?

> I have borne 13 children and seen most of them sold off into slavery, and when I cried out with a mother's grief, none but Jesus heard me—and ain't I a woman?

> . . . If the first woman God ever made was strong enough to turn the world upside down all alone, these women together ought to be able to turn it back, and get it right side up again! And now they is asking to do it. The men better let them.

She made her point, and earned a place in feminist history as well. Today a stone monument marks the spot where she delivered the speech. The building on the site today bears her name.

Sojourner Truth Building, 37 N. High St., Akron, OH 44308

No phone

Hours: Always visible

Cost: Free

Directions: Between Perkins and Market Sts., just north of downtown.

EPiLOGUe

*I*n 1820, Daniel Drake ("The Ben Franklin of the West") opened the Western Museum of Cincinnati to show off his collection of minerals, fossils, and stuffed animals. However, the 25¢ admission was a little steep. Attendance was low, and the museum was in danger of closing its doors. But then Joseph Dorfeuille was hired on as curator. Dorfeuille had a stronger sense than Drake of what the public *really* wanted to see. He started all his museum tours by offering visitors a whiff of laughing gas . . . you know, to get them in the mood. He added human skeletons to the collection—and they moved!—as well as a diorama of Mr. Cowan, a local ne'er-do-well who had hacked up his wife and two children with an ax; and the pickled head, heart, and right hand of murderer Mathias Hoover. Best of all, he built The Infernal Regions, a chamber of horrors depicting Hell in all its grisly glory. The King of Terrors, a mechanized, pitchfork-wielding Devil, welcomed patrons through a haze of billowing smoke. Viewers were treated to images of both the hot *and* cold versions of Hell, where sinners fried for eternity or were entombed in ice—take your pick. These tortured wax souls were protected from grabby patrons by a screen of chicken wire, electrified, for good measure.

All that fun for a quarter??!? Sadly, the museum closed in 1867.

Well, you might have been born a century too late for the Western Museum of Cincinnati, but not for the Kahiki Supper Club. Built on the east side of Columbus in 1960 and 1961, Kahiki was a Polynesian wonderland in an A-frame structure that was decorated to look like a South Pacific war canoe. It had palm trees and grass huts and live tropical birds, all surrounding a 30-foot-tall tiki-head fireplace with glowing red eyes and a fiery mouth. If you ordered the Mystery Drink it was delivered by a scantily clad Mystery Girl as the bartender whanged a mighty gong. Fake lightning flashed at regular intervals, though no rain ever dampened your table. And though the International Restaurant and Hospitality Rating Bureau selected it for a Millennium Award as one of the Top 100 Restaurants *of the Century* (italics mine), the Kahiki Supper Club closed its doors for good in 2000 so that the company could devote more energy to its frozen entrée product line. Oh, my (tiki) god . . . the horror . . . the horror!

It gets worse. The land was sold to Walgreens, which bulldozed the restaurant and replaced it with yet another drugstore, the warm glow of ceremonial torches replaced by the unflattering buzz of fluorescent lighting. Those corporate bastards!

If the message isn't obvious, it should be: roadside attractions—even the best of them—don't last forever. The *Titanic* Memorial Museum in Sidney? Sunk. The Ghost Town amusement park south of Findlay? Today it's a ghost town . . . a *real* ghost town. And the zeppelin-shaped diner at Bob's Motel in Rootstown? There's more of the *Hindenburg* still left on this planet.

Also gone: the cigarette-smoking chimp that puffed through several packs a day at his home on the Loveland bike trail. OK, so he probably shouldn't have been smoking in the first place, but what about Andy D-Day, a four-eyed, two-nosed, four-horned bull owned by Brooksville farmer W. A. Rasor? For two bits, tourists along Route 40 could hand feed him saltine crackers, which as far as I know do not cause cancer. Still, Andy died several decades ago and his body was stuffed and sold. And it disappeared. Forever.

What's next to go? The Hollow Earth Monument? The Genoa Privy? Egg Shell Land? There's no way of knowing. And if you're not careful you could someday find yourself with your grandchild on your lap pleading, "Gramps (or Grandma), tell me about the Great Wall of Gum! Please, oh please!!" and all you'll be able to say is, "Well, I *read* about it." How sad.

Gas up. Get going.

ACKNOWLEDGMENTS

*T*his book would not have been possible without the assistance, patience, and good humor of many individuals. My thanks go out to the following people for allowing me to interview them about their roadside attractions: Mari Artzner-Wolf (McKinley Museum and National Memorial), Tami Brown (Crawford Auto-Aviation Museum), Donna Collins (Allen County Museum), Ron and Betty Manolio (Egg Shell Land), Nick Pahys, Jr. (Hartsgrove Presidential Museum), Bob Scheib (Wally's Filling Station), Kelli Stegman (Jungle Jim's), "Steve" (Dr. Bob's Home), Laura Travis (Dittrick Medical History Center), and Mac Worthington (Art in the Woods).

For research assistance, I am indebted to the librarians in the Ohio communities of Akron, Ashtabula, Bellaire, Bellefontaine, Bellevue, Cadiz, Canton, Carlisle, Chillicothe, Cincinnati, Cleveland, Clyde, Columbus, Dayton, Dennison, Dover, Fremont, Greenville, Hamilton, Lima, Lorain, Loveland, Mansfield, Marion, Milan, Mount Vernon, New Lexington, Oberlin, Piqua, Reynoldsburg, Sabina, Seville, Springfield, Toledo, Vandalia, Wellington, Westerville, and Xenia. Thanks also to the Visitors Bureaus and/or Chambers of Commerce in Akron, Ashville, Berlin, Bowling Green, Canton, Cincinnati, Circleville, Cleveland, Columbus, Dayton, Dover, Dresden, Dublin, East Liverpool, Findlay, Kent, Lancaster, Mansfield, Marblehead, Marietta, Marion, Mount Gilead, New Straitsville, Newark, Port Clinton, Put-in-Bay, Sandusky, Steubenville, Sugarcreek, Troy, Twinsburg, Youngstown, and Zanesville.

Thank you, Nick Pahys, Jr., for enthusiastically posing outside your fabulous museum. I extend my appreciation as well to President William McKinley (the robot) for his dignified pose.

To my Ohio and Ohio-born friends, Maureen Bachmann, Jenny and John Birmingham, Mary Kay Carson, and Lisa Rosenthal, I hope I did right by the Buckeye state, and if not, that at least you got a few laughs.

Many thanks (as always) to everyone at Chicago Review Press for supporting the Oddball travel series, particularly its champion from the get-go, Cynthia Sherry; this book's editor, Allison Felus; and Gerilee Hundt, Goddess of Production. To everyone at WBEZ, Chicago Public Radio, thanks for the continued support of Cool Spots, especially Gianofer Fields.

And lastly, to Jim Frost: thanky, thanky, thanky.

ReCOMMeNDeD SOURCES

If you'd like to learn more about the places and individuals in this book, the following are excellent sources.

General Ohio Guides

Free Ohio Fun by Frank R. Satullo (Self-published, 2001)

Life in the Slow Lane by Jeff and Nadean Disabato Traylor (Monroeville, OH: Backroad Chronicles, 1995)

Ohio Off the Beaten Path, Eighth Edition by George and Carol Zimmerman (Guilford, CT: Globe Pequot Press, 2001)

Treasures of Northeast Ohio by Joseph C. Quinlan (Cleveland, OH: Global Editorial, 1999)

Ohio (History)

A Treasury of Ohio Tales by Webb Garrison (Nashville, TN: Rutledge Hill Press, 1993)

Ghosts by Randy McNutt (Wilmington, OH: Orange Frazer Press, 1996)

Heroes of Ohio by Rick Sowash (Bowling Green, OH: Gabriel's Horn Publishing Company, 1998)

Ohio (Trivia)

Awesome Almanac: Ohio by Jean Blashfield (Walworth, WI: B&B Publishing, 1995)

Critters, Flitters & Spitters by Rick Sowash (Bowling Green, OH: Rick Sowash Publishing Company, 2003)

Ohio (Ghosts)

Ghost Stories of Ohio by Edrick Thay (Edmonton, Alberta: Ghost House Books, 2001)

Ghost Hunter's Guide to Ohio by Chris Woodyard (Dayton, OH: Kestrel Publications, 2000)

Haunted Ohio by Chris Woodyard (Dayton, OH: Kestrel Publications, 2000)

1. The Northwest
America's First Concrete Streets
"Oldest Concrete Streets in the United States," by Luke M. Snell and Billie G. Snell. (*Concrete International*, March 2002)

Heal!
A History of the Basilica and National Shrine of Our Lady of Consolation by Brother Jeffrey (Carey, OH: Basilica and National Shrine of Our Lady of Consolation, 1993)

Winesburg, Ohio
Winesburg, Ohio by Sherwood Anderson (New York: Modern Library, 1999)

Remember the Maine
The Fate of the Maine by John Edward Weems (College Station, TX: Texas A&M University Press, 1992)

The Spanish-American War and President McKinley by Lewis L. Gould (Lawrence, KS: University Press of Kansas, 1982)

Rutherford B. Hayes
Fraud of the Century: Rutherford B. Hayes, Samuel Tilden, and the Stolen Election of 1876 by Roy Morris, Jr. (New York: Simon & Schuster, 2003)

Rutherford B. Hayes: Warrior and President by Ari Hoogenboom (Lawrence, KS: University Press of Kansas, 1995)

Airstream
Airstream: History of the Land Yacht by Bryan Burkhart and David Hunt (San Francisco: Chronicle Books, 2000)

John Dillinger
Dillinger, the Untold Story by G. Russell Girarden and William J. Helmer (Bloomington, IN: University of Indiana Press, 1994)

Dillinger: A Short and Violent Life by Robert Cromie and Joseph Pinkston (Evanston, IL: Chicago Historical Bookworks, 1990) .

The Dillinger Days by John Tollard (Cambridge, MA: DaCapo Press, 1995)

Warren G. Harding
Growing Up with Warren G. Harding by Jack Warwick (Marion, OH: Self-published, 1938)

Presidential Sex by Wesley O. Hagood (New York: Citadel Press, 1995)

The Strange Deaths of President Harding by Robert H. Ferrell (Columbia, MO: University of Missouri Press, 1996)

Warren G. Harding by John W. Dean (New York: Times Books, 2004)

Admiral Perry

Oliver Hazard Perry and the Battle of Lake Erie by Gerard Altoff (Put-in-Bay, OH: The Perry Group, 1999)

Neil Armstrong

First on the Moon by Neil Armstrong, Michael Collins, and Edwin Aldrin (New York: William S. Konecky Associates, 2002)

Neil Armstrong Air and Space Museum by John Zwez, Erin Bartlett, and Bonie Wurst (Columbus, OH: Ohio Historical Society, 2000)

2. The Northeast

Alcoholics Anonymous

Not God: A History of Alcoholics Anonymous by Ernest Kurtz (Center City, MN: Hazelden Information Education, 1998)

Origins of Alcoholics Anonymous by John F. Seiberling (Akron, OH: Dr. Bob's Home, 1972)

Rex Humbard

Miracles in My Life by Rex Humbard (Old Tappan, NJ: Spire Books, 1972)

Derby Downs

Champions, Cheaters, and Childhood Dreams: Memories of the All-American Soap Box Derby by Melanie Payne (Akron, OH: University of Akron Press, 2003)

Charles Goodyear and Vulcanized Rubber

"Prophet of Rubber" in *Raw Deal* by Ken Smith (New York: Blast Books, 1998)

Ashtabula Train Disaster

Hidden Treasure by Bill Yenne (New York: Avon, 1997)

William McKinley

Murdering McKinley: The Making of Theodore Roosevelt's America by Eric Rauchway (New York: Hill & Wang, 2003)

Warther Museum

Warther Carvings by the Warther Family (Dover, OH: Self-published, 1990)

Pretty Boy Floyd
Pretty Boy by Michael Wallis (New York: St. Martin's Press, 1992)

John Hanson, Father of Our Country
What Every American Should Know by Nick Pahys, Jr. (Hartsgrove, OH: Pahys Limited, 2001)

Kent State
The Killings at Kent State by I. F. Stone (New York: New York Review Book, 1971)

Thomas Edison
Edison: A Biography by Matthew Josephson (New York: John Wiley & Sons, 1992)
Edison: Inventing the Century by Neil Baldwin (Chicago: University of Chicago Press, 2001)
Edison: A Life of Invention by Paul Israel (New York: John Wiley & Sons, 2000)

Paul Lynde
"Funny Man," by Betty Garrett. (*Ohio Magazine*, December 1978)

The Seville Giants
Very Special People by Frederick Drimmer (New York: Citadel Press, 1976)

3. Cleveland Area
Cleveland Crime, Death, and Disaster (General)
The Corpse in the Cellar by John Stark Bellamy II (Cleveland, OH: Gray & Company, 1999)
The Killer in the Attic by John Stark Bellamy II (Cleveland, OH: Gray & Company, 2002)
The Maniac in the Bushes by John Stark Bellamy II (Cleveland, OH: Gray & Company, 1997)
They Died Crawling by John Stark Bellamy II (Cleveland, OH: Gray & Company, 1995)

Balto the Wonder Dog
The Cruelest Miles: The Heroic Story of Dogs and Men in a Race Against an Epidemic by Gay and Laney Salisbury (New York: W. W. Norton and Company, 2003)

James Garfield
Dark Horse: The Surprising Election and Political Murder of President James A.

Garfield by Kenneth D. Ackerman (New York: Carroll & Graf, 2003)

Garfield: A Biography by Allen Peskin (Kent, OH: Kent State University Press, 1998)

Lake View Cemetery

Lake View Historical Trail by Lake View Cemetery (Cleveland, OH: Lake View Cemetery, 1988)

Drew Carey

Dirty Jokes and Beer by Drew Carey (New York: Hyperion, 1997)

Home Brewed by Kathleen Tracy (New York: Boulevard Books, 1997)

The Torso Killer

In the Wake of the Butcher by James Jessen Badal (Kent, OH: Kent State University Press, 2001)

Torso: A True Crime Graphic Novel by Brian Michael Bendis and Marc Andreyke (New York: Image, 2000)

Torso: The Story of Eliot Ness and the Search for a Psychopathic Killer by Steven Nickel (Winston-Salem, NC: John F. Blair, 1989)

The Real Fugitive

Mockery of Justice by Cynthia L. Cooper and Sam Reese Sheppard (New York: Onyx, 1997)

The Wrong Man by James Neff (New York: Random House, 2001)

4. The Southwest

U.S. Air Force Museum

The United States Air Force Museum Official Guide (Lawrenceburg, IN: The Creative Company, 2000)

Hangar 18

MJ-12 and the Riddle of Hangar 18: The New Evidence by Timothy Green Beckley and Sean Casteel (Self-published, 2003)

Donahue

Donahue: My Own Story by Phil Donahue (New York: Simon and Schuster, 1979)

Great Serpent Mound

Serpent Mound by Robert C. Glotzhober and Bradley T. Leper (Columbus, OH: Ohio Historical Society, 1994)

Ulysses S. Grant

Grant by Jean Edward Smith (New York: Simon and Schuster, 2001)

Ulysses S. Grant: Triumph Over Adversity, 1822–1865 by Brooks D. Simpson (New York: Houghton Mifflin, 2000)

5. Cincinnati Area

President William Howard Taft

The Life & Times of William Howard Taft by Henry F. Pringle and Katherine E. Speirs (New York: American Political Biography Press, 1998)

William Howard Taft and the First Motoring Presidency, 1909–1913 by Michael L. Bromley (New York: McFarland & Co., 2003)

Passenger Pigeons

The Silent Sky: The Incredible Extinction of the Passenger Pigeon by Allan Eckert (LaVergne, TN: Lightning Source, 2000)

A Gap in Nature: Discovering the World's Extinct Animals by Tim Flannery and Peter Schouten (New York: Atlantic Monthly Press, 2001)

Jerry Springer

Jerry Springer by Ailen Joyce (New York: Zebra Books, 1998)

The Hollow Earth

Banvard's Folly by Paul Collins (New York: Picador USA, 2001)

Chateau LaRoche

Chateau LaRoche by Harry Andrews (Loveland, OH: Self-published, 1975)

President William Henry Harrison

Old Tippecanoe: William Henry Harrison and His Times by Freeman Cleaves and Katherine E. Speirs (New York: American Political Biography Press, 1990)

6. The Southeast

Longaberger Baskets

Longaberger: An American Success Story by Dave Longaberger (New York: Harper-Business, 2001)

The Longaberger Story: And How We Did It by Dave Longaberger and Steve Williford (New York: Lincoln-Bradley Publishing Group, 1991)

The Liberator of Bulgaria

Januarius MacGahan: The Life and Campaigns of an American War Correspondent by Dale L. Walker (Columbus, OH: Ohio University Press, 1998)

Mine Fires and Moonshine

Our Journey Continues: The History of New Straitsville, Ohio, Volume Two, 1925–1950 by Chris Bogzevitz and John Winnenberg (Logan, OH: Fine Print, 1996)

7. Columbus Area

James Thurber

James Thurber: His Life and Times by Harrison Kinney (New York: Henry Holt & Company, 1997)

My Life and Hard Times by James Thurber (New York: Perennial, 1999)

Wendy's and Dave Thomas

Dave's Way: A New Approach for Old-Fashioned Success by Dave Thomas (New York: Berkely Publishing Group, 1992)

Anti-Saloon League

Organized for Prohibition: A New History of the Anti-Saloon League by K. Austin Kerr (New Haven, CT: Yale University Press, 1985)

8. The Guy Tour

Annie Oakley

Annie Oakley: Legendary Sharpshooter by Jean Flynn (Berkeley Heights, NJ: Enslow Publishers, 1998)

INDEX BY CITY NAME

Stockport

No Dancing on the Grave (Old Brick Cemetery), 202

Sugarcreek

Cheese Museum (Alpine Hills Historical Museum), 102

White Fawn Wildlife Display (Bed & Breakfast Barn), 103

Toledo

Big Boy Brouhaha, 37

Elvis Presley Fight Site, 240

Tony Packo's and the Bun Museum, 36

Troy

Birthplace of Bar Codes (Marsh Supermarket), 160

Twinsburg

Twins Festival, 104

Uniontown

Menches Brothers Original Hamburgers, 230

Vandalia

Trapshooting Hall of Fame, 238

Waldo

Fried Bologna Sandwich (G&R Tavern and Grille), 233

Wapokoneta

Neil Armstrong Air and Space Museum, 39

Waynesville

Sauerkraut Festival, 235

Wellington

Spirit of '76 Museum, 105

West Liberty

Ohio Caverns, 40

Westerville

Anti-Saloon League Museum (Westerville Public Library), 222

Whiskey Wars, The, 223

World's Largest Crystal Ball (Ross C. Purdy Museum Ceramics), 224

Willoughby Hills

Squire's Castle, 143

Wilmington

Birthplace of the Banana Split (Gibson's Goodies), 161

Wilmot

World's Largest Cuckoo Clock (Alpine-Alpa Cheese House), 106

Windsor

Madonnazilla (Servants of Mary Center of Peace), 108

Xenia

Blue Jacket, 188

Zanesville

Y-Bridge, The, 202

INDEX BY Site Name